Voices in Bali

MUSIC / CULTURE

A series from Wesleyan University Press

Edited by George Lipsitz, Susan McClary, and Robert Walser

Published titles

My Music by Susan D. Crafts, Daniel Cavicchi, Charles Keil, and the Music
in Daily Life Project

Running with the Devil: Power, Gender, and Madness in Heavy Metal Music
by Robert Walser

Subcultural Sounds: Micromusics of the West by Mark Slobin

Upside Your Head! Rhythm and Blues on Central Avenue by Johnny Otis

Dissonant Identities: The Rock'n'Roll Scene in Austin, Texas by Barry Shank

Black Noise: Rap Music and Black Culture in Contemporary America
by Tricia Rose

Club Cultures: Music, Media and Distinction by Sarah Thornton

Music, Society, Education by Christopher Small

Listening to Salsa: Gender, Latin Popular Music, and Puerto Rican Cultures
by Frances R. Aparicio

Any Sound You Can Imagine: Making Music/Consuming Technology
by Paul Theberge

Voices in Bali: Energies and Perceptions in Vocal Music and Dance Theater
by Edward Herbst

A Thousand Honey Creeks Later:
My Life in Music from Basie to Motown—and Beyond
by Preston Love

EDWARD HERBST

❀

Voices in Bali

ENERGIES AND PERCEPTIONS
IN VOCAL MUSIC AND
DANCE THEATER

Foreword by Judith Becker
Afterword by René T. A. Lysloff

❀

WESLEYAN UNIVERSITY PRESS
Published by University Press of New England
Hanover and London

WESLEYAN UNIVERSITY PRESS
Published by University Press of New England, Hanover, NH 03755
© 1997 by Edward Herbst
Printed in the United States of America   5 4 3 2 1
CIP data appear at the end of the book

Unless otherwise noted, photographs are by the author

*This work is dedicated
to my father,
who showed me what both singing
and
being human are about.*

Contents

❀

Foreword by Judith Becker   ix
Acknowledgments   xiii
Introduction   xvii
A note on language and orthography   xxiii
A note on musical notation   xxv

Désa kala patra: *place-time-context*   *1*
Aji nusup *'lessons in penetration'*:
the désa kala patra *of experience*   *5*
Vocal qualities   *25*
Tembang   *38*
Masolah: *the* désa kala patra *of spirit*   *57*
Panasar   *71*
Désa kala patra *within performance*   *87*
Perkembangan: *spontaneity and*
the flower of désa kala patra   *97*
Kala   *103*
Désa kala patra *of the arts in contemporary Bali*   *111*
Intrinsic aesthetics: désa kala patra *within performance,*
continued   *121*
Bali—no longer—unplugged: electronic technology,
amplification, and the marginalization of presence   *134*

*Further penetration: "branching out of Bali"
into other interpretive modes*   142
Penetrating what, where, and how   145
Afterword by René T. A. Lysloff   163

Notes to Companion Compact Disc   171
Glossary   179
Bibliography   185
Index   191

Foreword

❋

The title of this book, *Voices in Bali: Energies and Perceptions in Vocal Music and Dance Theater*, should prepare the reader for the polyphony of the text itself. Not one voice, or energy, or perception is present here, but several: the voices, energies, and perceptions of Balinese teachers, of several of Herbst's former American mentors, and of the author himself are woven in and out of the text, disappearing and reappearing again within a new context. The gnosis of this text lies in its closeness to experience, what it is like to study with a Balinese teacher of performance. Particularities, the minutiae of learning a phrase of song, what tones are bent or stretched or stressed—these speak to larger issues of the way a total performance is ultimately put together. By following along the way from lesson to performance, witnessing its process, the reader gains deeper insight into Balinese performance and the way one learns to be a performer. As Herbst says, "The learning process is, in many ways, the music." He also shows how the learning process is intrinsic to the dance, the drama, the total event. By remaining close to the particularities of what happens in the interaction between student and teacher, avoiding generalities, the author also gives the reader the freedom to draw his or her own conclusions. This text is noncoercive, more poetical than didactic. While the role of the author is always in the foreground, the book never crosses over the delicate, invisible line between commendable self-reflexivity and annoying self-indulgence. Knowing the situation of the author at every point in the text helps the reader to see, to hear, and to feel what he perceives.

A fundamental concept of Balinese theatrical pedagogy is a set of terms that Herbst translates as "place," "time," and "context" (*désa, kala, patra*), three modes of attunement to which every singer/actor/dancer must attend. *Désa, kala, patra* form the unifying theme of the book. Starting with the body of the singer and "the movement of sound through the body," extending to the social context of the performance, to the audience seen and unseen, to attunement with the forces of the cosmos, these three terms become a catalyst for metaphoric extension, embodying all aspects of the art and science of performance. To attune oneself and one's dramatic character to a particular story presented before a particular audience necessarily involves reshaping, rearranging, and recreating (i.e., improvising) within a highly stylized performance tradition. Drawing from a fund of past performances, which are the prior texts of any present performance, the singer/actor/dancer creates a unique characterization that will never happen again in quite the same way. All Balinese performances thus take place "in the presence of the past" and simultaneously predicate a future that is neither fixed nor predetermined.

A more personal and mysterious attunement must also take place between an actor and his mask. The mask carries its own past, which must be integrated into the physical, spiritual, and intellectual present of its wearer. One of the senses of *kala* is this bridging of different times and different realms. Herbst associates the word with *kalangén*, a kind of aesthetic rapture in which one loses the strong sense of "I-ness." Whether associated with trance or not, whether in rehearsal, before an audience, at a lesson, in private, or playing only for the deities, the surpassing joy of performance pervades Balinese arts.

Herbst states throughout the book that structure is "a place for something to happen." He is most interested in how structure is generated and what happens through it, rather than in structure itself. Briefly, he sees stylization and structure as resonating with the intuitions of the audience, allowing them to construct individidual interpretations, permitting lapses of attention, even integrating the state between wakefulness and sleep into the process of experiencing a performance, the "what" that is happening.

Superficially, the terms *désa* 'place', *kala* 'time', and *patra* 'context' resemble the Sufi terms *saman* 'time', *makan* 'place', and *akhwan* 'company', which describe the constraints surrounding a ceremony of listening to sacred music. But while the Sufi terms are intended to control the situation of a performance to prevent its abuse or exploitation, the Balinese terms are more a guide to performance, a way for the actor/singer/dancer to think about the singing of a phrase, about the merging with one's mask, or about the reaching out to an audience. The English translations of both sets of terms might lead one to suspect some connection between them. But the Balinese use of the terms is so distinctive, so particular, and so unlike the Sufi that it points up the difficulty of translation itself. Herbst is sensitive to the limitations of translation and does not attempt to give a clear exposition of the meanings of these terms; he does not "unpack" them for us. Rather, by presenting many instances and contexts in which they are used or in which they are implied, the reader begins to get a feel for their semantic range and emotive power. Like his Balinese teachers, Herbst prefers to leave room for us to find our own interpretations.

By changing the usual typography of the printed page, a technique borrowed from Cage, the author signals to the reader that this is not a text of expository prose. Margins indicate changes of voice and register, anecdotes as well as quotes set with wide margins on each side. Empty spaces are inserted at points where a pause is useful. As readers, we are implicitly requested not to rush through the book for the information it imparts but to try to approach this text as a Balinese student approaches the study of singing/dancing/acting: as a journey. ("The learning process is, in many ways, the music.")

Issues of transcription—whether to do them, and if so, how to do them—continue to agitate ethnomusicologists. And for good reason. Our readers need to be able to imagine the music we are describing. I believe that every method yet invented by scholars, Western and Indonesian, has been applied, at some time or another, to describe the music of the Balinese and Javanese *gamelan* ensembles. Herbst has devised yet another strategy, incorporating new technologies not available before. His aim is to enable his readers to "be able to hum a tune" and thereby gain an "immediate musical impression" while simultaneously reminding the reader of the approximate nature of his or her rendition. He uses varying spaces between the lines on which he positions his notes and only uses lines that indicate the tones of a particular scale, not all possible Balinese scales. He has thus removed one level of abstraction and brought the transcription closer to a particular performance. By transferring his handwritten transcriptions to the computer program *Finale*, he was able to play back what he had written. While ignoring the Western pitch values built into *Finale*, he was able to adjust rhythmic values by simultaneously playing the *Finale* version and his field recording, a procedure he calls "exhilarating." The adjective suggests just one thing. His ear transcriptions were very accurate indeed. Following the "humming" heuristic, I found myself able to gain an "immediate musical impression," as the author had hoped. His transcriptions are also uncluttered and visually pleasing.

Toward the end of the book, as we leave the world of Balinese lessons and turn to issues of modernization in Balinese performance, the author's writing and presentation change to a more familiar, expository, academic style. It is almost as if the presentational style were cued by the subject matter itself. No prior knowledge about Balinese performance is needed to follow these later essays. Elsewhere, some background in Balinese or Javanese performance is helpful, as Herbst offers little assistance to the uninitiated. He has opted rather for depth, subtlety, and nuance, not bald information.

Although this book is not a musicological treatise, it yet contains some strictly musicological information. In his presentation of the ways in which singers inflect phrases, notes, modes, and tunings to adjust to conditions of *désa*, *kala*, and *patra*, we come to see that Balinese modes and tunings are much more complex than the texts we have read would lead us to believe. As has been pointed out for Javanese *rebab* and vocal modes (Hatch 1980; Walton 1987) the tunings and modes found on the keyed *gambelan* instruments do not totally define Balinese modalities. (Herbst uses the Balinese transliteration *gambelan* rather than the more familiar romanized Javanese term *gamelan*.) No purely structuralist description can hope to encompass the myriad individual shapings of tune and mode to *désa*, *kala*, and *patra*.

Writing in the style of a personal journey is a risky endeavor for an author who is not already well known to his readers. We, as readers, are asked to trust an author about whom we know little. It requires an act of faith and trust on our part, a favor we do not grant lightly, especially to fellow academics. The more than twenty years of study this book represents, including several extended trips to Bali, would not of itself guarantee our trust. It is rather the sense one gets that the fluid presentation and the unorthodox, noncompulsory style of delivery reflect something fundamental about the author himself. In combination with finely tuned descriptions, detailed analysis, and engaging stories, we come to accept the author, the book, and the message.

February 1997   Judith Becker
University of Michigan

Acknowledgments

❀

The sources that inspire and inform this work are numerous, but a few are especially relevant. At Bennington College, as an Inter-Divisional major in Music and Anthropology from 1969 until 1973, I was continually inspired, challenged, and confounded by musicians Gunnar Schonbeck and Frank Baker, anthropologists Lucien Hanks, Jane Richardson Hanks, and Peter J. Wilson, and Buddhist poet Claude Fredericks. I did my M.A. at Wesleyan from 1976 to 1978, and studies leading to my doctorate in ethnomusicology from 1978 to 1979 and 1981 to 1982. At Wesleyan, Jon K. Barlow was my advisor and faithful guide, always seeking truth in music and the discussion of music. Sumarsam and Jeremy Zwelling helped shape these writings with probing questions and reflections. In later stages of writing, I have been fortunate to receive critiques and encouragement from Madé Bandem, Clifford Geertz, Mark Slobin, David P. McAllester, June Nash, Judith Becker, James R. Cowdery, René T.A. Lysloff, Judith McCulloh, Jon B. Higgins, and an anonymous reader. At the press, Eileen McWilliam, Suzanna Tamminen, Mary Crittendon, Katherine Kimball, Carol Sheehan, and series editor Susan McClary provided valuable support and perseverance. The flexible staff grew out of Frank Denyer's concept (1977). I am deeply indebted to composer José Evangelista, whose instruction in the use of the *Finale* music notation computer program enabled me to better represent aspects of Balinese vocal music on the printed page. But even more so, these transcriptions result from our rigorous collaborative process, listening to the original audio recordings together, and reconciling each of our musical perceptions with the conventions of notation as well as with my aural and kinesthetic memory derived from the learning process. Although I bear full responsibility for any shortcomings the reader may find in these notations, the level of accuracy would have been impossible without his insight into rhythmic nuance. Music copyist Michel Léonard joined in on a few of these transcription sessions, and added his perspective on how to relate phrasing and lyrics in the most communicative manner possible. My original analog field recordings from 1980 and 1972 were restored and remastered for the CD at the Bregman Electro-Acoustic Music Studio at Dartmouth College, by audio engineer Kevin Parks.

I was first in Bali from January through December 1972, researching in collaboration with Beth Skinner, and sponsored by Bennington College, Lembaga Ilmu Pengetahuan Indonesia (Indonesian Institute of Sciences) and Konservatori Karawitan Indonesia Bali (KOKAR). I was principally studying and performing *gendér wayang* with Madé Gerindem in Teges, and *gambelan* making and acoustics in Tihingan, Klungkung, with *Pandé* Sebeng and others. For six months, we lived in the village of Peliatan and I studied the relationship between dance and instrumental music. The following six months we lived in the village of Batuan, in the home of Nyoman Kakul, with whom Beth Skinner was studying *baris* dance and *topéng* mask dance theater. For four of those months, I resided several days each week in the mountain village of Tihingan.

Our second stay in Bali was from January 1980 through April 1981, sponsored by a Fulbright-Hays fellowship, *Departemen Pendidikan dan Kebudayaan* (the Indonesian Government Department of Education and Culture), and in Bali, *Akademi Seni Tari Indonesia*, now named *Sekolah Tinggi Seni Indonesia* (Indonesian College of the Arts). My main study involved vocalization and the creative process in relation to instrumental music, dance, and theater. Residing in Bedaulu, I continued to perform as a member of Madé Gerindem's *gendér wayang* ensemble for occasional *wayang* performances and ceremonies. Beth Skinner's work involved mask dance, *topéng* and *jauk*, studying mainly with *Pandé* Madé Kenyir of Singapadu.

The third trip was for three months in 1992, on an Asian Cultural Council grant facilitated by its director, Ralph Samuelson. The purpose of this visit was to review and reflect with Balinese colleagues on my writings, analyses, and interpretations, while taking in the great contextual changes occurring in contemporary Bali. Since some of the ideas I present are not often explicitly addressed in Balinese musical/performance discourse, I felt it necessary to re-evaluate their veracity and relevance. This continuation of a dialogic process begun in 1972 also allowed certain old ideas to spin off in new, unexpected directions.

Amongst friends, colleagues, teachers, and family in Bali, I am particularly indebted to Nyoman Kakul, Madé Gerindem, *Pandé* Madé Kenyir, Madé Netra, Madé Bandem, Ni Nyoman Candri, Madé Pasek Tempo,

Madé Sija, Ketut Rinda, Wayan Rindi, Ketut Kantor, Madé Ruju, Wayan Diya, Nyoman Rangkus, Déwa Putu Dani, Wayan Tangguh, Madé Regug, Ketut Madra, Wayan Nartha, Nyoman Rajeg, Nyoman Rembang, Anak Agung Gedé Mandera, I.G.B.N. Pandji, Nyoman Tusan, *Pandé* Sebeng Tihingan, *Pandé* Madé Gableran, Nyoman Sumandhi, Anak Agung Rai Cebaang, Poedijono, Michael Crawford, Nyoman Catra, Wayan Dibia, Ketut Kodi, Wayan Lantir, Wayan Sura, Ida Bagus Baskara, Nyoman Cerita, and in Java, Sardono Kusumo, Sal Murgiyanto, and Endo Suanda.

Joel Leipzig was my inspiration to learn trombone at age ten, and now he is my invaluable computer guru. Peter Herbst has been a lifelong musical colleague. I am indebted to my mother for decades of indulgence and often wise advice. My children, Nico and Gabi, have kept me ever aware of the intrinsic rewards of dance and musical activity, in Bali and at home. More than anyone else, my artistic collaborator and research colleague Beth Skinner has had an active role in the growth of my ideas and music, through our shared creative process.

E.H.

Introduction

❀

The key concepts constantly echoed amongst my Balinese artist friends are *perkembangan* 'creative flowering', *kesenangan* 'pleasure', *menjiwai* 'transmitting spirit', *masolah* 'characterization', *pengalaman* 'experience', *nusup* 'penetration', *désa kala patra* 'place-time-context', and *bayu sabda idep* 'energy-voice-thought (perception).'[1]

In Balinese aesthetics, the prevailing creative process involves ways in which spirit enters into form. My own interest has been as a musician, to experience musical phenomena from within, setting my compass with these indigenous (or at least what my Balinese colleagues consider to be intrinsically Balinese) concepts of performance theory.

Balinese people generally use the word "world" with a qualifier, to specify whether they are speaking of *buana agung* 'macrocosmos', or 'greater world', *buana alit* 'microcosmos' or 'smaller world', or *dunia kita*, literally 'our world', but often meant to suggest 'the contemporary world community'. I apply this multiple usage to the practice of "world music," a process of reflecting inward, outward, and around.

I try to differentiate my own intellectual concerns, intellectual concerns of people I know in Bali, my intuitive sense, and intuitive sense as expressed by people in Bali. A few of my own "intellectual" concerns going into this study have been how stylization affects form and perception; dramatic characterization as manifested musically, choreographically, and

---

1. *Perkembangan*, in the Indonesian language, denotes "development," and nowadays refers to anything—a building project or commercial growth, for instance. However, in the realm of art and religion, the word takes on the more poetic and mystical meaning of the root word, *kembang* 'flower', with more subtle and varied connotations. The words *kesenangan* and *pengalaman* are Indonesian but are commonly used in Balinese discussion. *Menjiwai* and *désa kala patra* are found in both languages, whereas *masolah* and *nusup* are Balinese words and concepts. *Bayu sabda idep* is a *Kawi* 'Old Javanese' phrase and a common theme in Balinese philosophical and aesthetic discussion.

spiritually; subtle acoustic phenomena as kinesthetic artistic properties; and performance as an integral collective aspect of community life.

To sample a few evident contemporary Indonesian intellectual questions: does sacredness lie in properties, activities, or contexts? How can we apply the generally accepted conceptions of *pélog* and *sléndro* tuning systems to Balinese vocal music? How can artistic change and innovation progress, reflecting exposure to the rest of the world and contemporary influences, within indigenous parameters. Sardono Kusumo (1978) has further extended this question into issues of the environment.

My own intuitive musical directions related to this study have to do with vocalization as it relates to focused consciousness states and the imagination. This has shed light on the nature of breathing, timbre, flow of vibrations throughout the body for vocal expression, sound as density and shape, and the character of sound in space. These personal musical interests relate directly to my experiential and analytical work in Indonesia, and elsewhere.

My questions have been how to use sound stylistically, how forms are generated from—and lead to—other than human realities, and how consciousness states are expressed formally. Forms are generated from a pool of resources that covers the entire living and ever-changing culture, and crossbreeding is always occurring; so to understand the references and points of departure used in the evolution of forms, one needs a broad base. One can penetrate the generative process in a culture as contexts shift and adaptations occur.

Perhaps the best way to get into the various intuitive processes of Balinese artists is through the actual learning process. The manner in which music is taught reveals some of the deepest levels of the creative process, and it is through that unfolding of musical reality that a teacher imparts what he or she can of the subtle and intuitive information necessary for musical knowledge and fluency. One way to gain some understanding of a Balinese artist's intuitive sense (as opposed to one's own sense) is to undergo a degree of training following traditional methods within the indigenous cultural context. Although the distinction between anyone's personal and cultural intuition is quite ambiguous, it seems a fruitful path for the intercultural artist to pursue. In any case, within any musical performance style exist various intrinsic teaching methods. The learning process is, in many ways, the music.

I have attempted to avoid applying artificial systematization to these writings, but rather to bring information to the reader's attention in gradually shifting contexts of discussion. I feel this attention to specific little details, each in their living context, rather than overall generalizations, reflects the revelatory process in Balinese aesthetics and learning. I have also avoided systematization that would suggest standardization where a great variety of practices, views, and terminology exists.

Many of my mentors and friends passed away before this book could be completed; Nyoman Kakul, Ketut Rinda, Madé Pasek Tempo, Madé Gerindem, *Pandé* Madé Kenyir, *Pandé* Sebeng, Déwa Putu Dani, Wayan Rindi, Ketut Madra, and others. This fact further highlights the issue of writing, as I do, in the present tense. Johannes Fabian (1983) critiques the practice of writing in the "ethnographic present," which can misrepresent and mythologize a living, dynamic subject, creating a false transcendence over historical time and place. Anthony Seeger (1987) considers this view, and then, referring to his own ethnographic work, answers, "By using the present tense . . . I mean to emphasize the particularity of the events, not their normativity . . . [T]he use of the present is meant to convey the unfolding of the events." Charles Keil (1979) rejects objectified and packaged "ethnographic presents" and envisions an alternative in "intersubjectivity" and the use of "diary . . . the best possible record of what happens at the point of perception." My own writing aims for the immediacy and inward-outward focus found in many "present tense" poetic and narrative genres, avoiding the pitfalls of the "ethnological present" mode of description by contextualizing my Balinese colleagues and myself within a dialogic process, a continual exchange, and a multiplicity of perceptions and divergent opinions. Another way has been by having the writing suggest an aspect of Balinese literary tradition that J. Stephen Lansing (1983) refers to as "sounding the texts," a performative process that keeps texts and their meanings alive, vital, and relevant: "Sounding the texts dispels the illusions of ordinary consciousness and brings to light the underlying structures that bind man and nature, past and present, inner and outer." I have attempted to reflect this to some degree in the text itself, by weaving into descriptive and analytical discussion accounts of my perceptions or those of my Balinese colleagues, as well as hermeneutic and poetic means of evoking a sense of the aesthetic and spiritual dimensions coming into play. A very different sense of "sounding this text" has been to orally present these ideas and musical forms in diverse contexts over several years, bouncing them off of Balinese, Javanese, and American colleagues and listening for what resonates in the intended environs. I identify some of the chapters of this book in terms of the contexts in which they were written, as they are intended to offer multiple viewpoints rather than one singular argument or one straight line of thought.

The writings of John Cage have profoundly influenced the style of writing and format of presentation in this work. I have always found his writing style, mixing theory, anecdote, context, philosophy, and humor, to be a truly musical mode of discourse. I believe his example to be very instructive in the evolution of a musical anthropology.

In writing this book I have refrained from including very many references to other scholarly works within the text, as I feel they would take the reader out of the "present moment" and obstruct the phrasing and resonance of the narrative or discussion. As part of the point of this particular book, I have intended to keep as much focus as possible on first-hand knowledge—what I have experienced or heard about in Bali, or speculated about with ideas growing out of my experience in Bali—and I have tried to avoid focusing on what other scholars have written concerning their experiences, or what they have theorized about concerning what they have read, or how their ideas relate to my own. This difficult choice was made in favor of aesthetic flow over an invasive scholarly apparatus. The bibliography lists many of the written sources that relate to the themes at hand.

To prepare those readers who might be disoriented by my somewhat unconventional style of writing in this book, let me sum up my theoretical intentions. In seeking ways of approaching a "musical other" without objectifying it, I base much of my method upon indigenous performance theory. My hypothesis suggests that, by challenging some standard relationships between subject and object, we can better approach "what" is really happening in a given artistic world. I argue against a limited, positivist conception of musical materials, in favor of inner processes and ideational contexts. The subjective/objective dialogue throughout, and the style of writing, are intended to address particular issues in intercultural studies, stressing internal relationships and variations rather than formalized classifications. Bringing together the Balinese concept of *désa kala patra* 'place-time-context' with John Cage's concepts of structure, method, and form returns us to the critical issue of what scholars and intercultural artists are doing, and "what" is their "object" of study. I suggest that what we generally think of as our object of study is actually "where" it is happening (within the musical or social structures). Articulating the principle of "what, where, and how" posits a different approach to methodology and to the way in which musical cultures are represented. Here, I advocate an ongoing continuum between inner experience and outer forms, be they technical, stylistic, or cultural, a continuum applicable to the given culture under study as well as to the researcher him or herself. Finally, study of Balinese vocal music has led me to propose the idea that many different *tembang* 'sung poetry forms' have their own distinct *tekep*, scalar arrangements and variations of intervals—conceived in an intuitive, not consciously systematized aesthetic practice—reaching beyond standard notions of *pélog* and *sléndro* tunings.

I sometimes wonder when we ethnomusicologists are casting our nets amongst schools of red herrings or when we are swimming up to the spawning grounds at a river's source. We can choose to take an intuitive step and leave behind many assumptions. Within the creative process we know that one should never be too sure about what is music, hearing, listening, seeing, or what are boundaries of culture and humanness. My early mentors at Bennington College never trusted work that lacked the imprint of personal creative process. Revered Balinese teachers repeat again and again that all one need understand is a very small entity (as one might study a nerve or blood cell), but one must learn everything essential about what enables it to live. All else is irrelevant outside of a very specific aesthetic context and must be recreated continually.

A note on language and orthography

❀

My research was conducted in the Indonesian language, supplemented with Balinese, without the use of interpreters. Translations of text from Kawi or Balinese to Indonesian were made with the consultation of various Balinese colleagues, credited in my introduction and in the text. Particular help in translation and spelling for the CD notes was provided by Ketut Kodi.

In this book, Indonesian words follow the system of spelling introduced in 1972. Balinese words generally follow the dictionary *Kamus Bali-Indonesia* (Panitia Penyusun Kamus Bali 1979). *C* is pronounced *ch* as in *chess*. Accented *é* is pronounced as in English *hey* and *e* as in English *third*. Word-final *a*, such as *pragina*, and *a* within a prefix, such as *panasar* or *gaguntangan*, are also pronounced as in *third* or *first*. Otherwise, *a* is pronounced as in *father*. Since 1972, some proper names, of people and places, have adopted the new spelling, substituting *j*, as in *jolly*, for the earlier spelling, *dj*. But most people have retained the original spellings of their names. I follow whatever spelling is currently being used by a particular person or place. *I* or *Ni* preceding a name is a rough equivalent of Mr. or Ms. respectively. I generally reserve their usage to photograph captions and the CD notes, as they are not generally used in everyday conversation.

Finally, I have chosen to spell *gambelan* with a *b*, which is the way Balinese people generally spell it, unless they are writing for an outside readership, in which case they have adopted the Javanese spelling *gamelan*. With the soft *b* is indeed the way the word is pronounced in Bali (but not in Java), and it seems to me, and to Balinese scholars with whom I have discussed the issue, that the "Javanization" of some Balinese music terminology, which is occurring in contemporary institutions of learning, need not extend to such a key word.

A note on musical notation

❀

I have chosen to devise a new staff for my musical transcriptions, rather than using either the standard Western staff or Javanese *kepatihan* 'cipher notation'. Western notation is useful for indicating irregular rhythms, semitones, and generally to convey vocal melodies to non-Indonesian readers in the most informative manner possible. But I am uncomfortable representing irregular Balinese pitch intervals through the grid of Western music's equidistant lines and spaces. Instead, I have developed a staff system in which the spaces come closer to reflecting Balinese intervals, and the lines represent a generalized Balinese series of pitches. My ultimate and quite simple intention is that the reader can still utilize his or her familiarity with a standard staff, adjust a bit, and then be able to hum a tune to facilitate an immediate musical impression, and to have some visual representation of melodic shape and variation, based on the transcription.

For the convenience of Indonesianists who are used to thinking in terms of the *kepatihan* system's pitch numbers, I always link them with their corresponding Balinese names for *gambelan* or vocal pitch in this manner: *nding* (1), *ndong* (2), *ndéng* (3), *ndung* (5), *ndang* (6). Instrumental *gambelan* pitch names are often spelled without the *n*, as *ding, dong, déng, dung*, and *dang*. The *kepatihan* system using numbers is not commonly used in Bali, so it would not be appropriate to have that system dominate.

As I will discuss later, there is great variety of tunings from one set of instruments to another and no two *gambelan*s are tuned identically. McPhee asserts, "In the last analysis, the tones *ding, dong, déng, dung* and *dang* are not fixed tones at all, but tonal zones which allow for endless modification of pitch . . ." So when I assign approximate Western pitch equivalents to the Balinese pitches, this is even more of a generalization, but one in which contemporary Balinese musical scholars also engage. As I will suggest in this book, even the traditional Balinese notation and terminology of *ding*, *dong*, *déng*, *dung*, and *dang* represent a highly generalized concept in the context of vocal music. Any notation system, particularly when applied to an oral tradition, has its limitations in representating musical form but still can provide insights into particular aspects of a music.

Again, lines represent the pitches of the standard *pélog* or *sléndro* tunings, as played on *gambelan* instruments. Notes in spaces (and in parenthesis) indicate *paméro*, in-between pitches or miscellaneous deviations from the standard tuning, and their Western pitch equivalents are included (in parenthesis) with the other pitches at the left of the staff lines. The corresponding cipher pitches are indicated at the right end of the lines. An arrow just to the left of a note indicates a chromatic quarter-tone higher or lower, depending on the direction the arrow is pointing. The staffs vary from example to example, with lines added here and dropped there, according to the melodic range of the given melody. One reason for this is that some melodies require ten lines, and with all the large interval spaces, the resulting staff would get cumbersome for most other melodies, some of which require only three lines. The more obvious reason is that I am representing different versions of *sléndro* and *pélog* by differently spaced lines. My suggestion is that, just before the reader approaches each transcription, he or she get oriented by humming (starting from the bottom) the sequence of pitches arranged vertically on the left or right, depending on one's choice of Western pitches or *kepatihan* numbers. When syllables in the lyrics are in parenthesis, they are not part of the word *per se*, but are meant to suggest a singer's way of shaping, extending, or transforming a vowel sound as it is vocalized.

The use of Western rhythmic indications is not intended to imply a metric system. Notation without bar lines is used in much twentieth-century Western music and is more appropriate for Balinese vocal music, which does not generally follow either a regular pulse or the colotomic phrasings of instrumental music. As is common with oral traditions, each rendition of a given melody can vary considerably. Consequently, my rhythmic and melodic notations represent only one of many possible ways of rendering a tune.

My first experiments with flexible staffs were carried out by hand, before I knew that the *Finale* computer program has a feature for creating custom staffs. Once I began using *Finale* with musical colleague José Evangelista, it seemed incumbent upon us to utilize the program to its full potential, which meant reaching for a new level of accuracy and a particular kind of "objectivity." *Finale* enables the computer to play back one's notations. We used the playback to refine the rhythmic values in the notations, but did not concern ourselves with *Finale*'s played-back pitch values:

since the program is designed for midi keyboards and limited to Western-tempered tuning, we relied on our ears for evaluating melody and pitch. We would first refine my original transcriptions, entering the notations into the program. Then with the aim of complete synchronization, we would play back each transcription on the computer at exactly the same moment as the audio recording of the particular singer's rendition from which the transcription had derived. If there was any rhythmic difference or discrepancy between the two renditions, we would go back to *Finale* and change the time values to make the time values of rhythms and rests match. *Finale* requires that all notes be set in a given meter—even though my end results show no bar lines (with one exception) or meters, since the essential feeling of most singing is unmetered—and one line of a song transcription could contain ten different unseen meters, rigorously arrived at. Hearing a melismatic phrase in close synchronicity with the computer playback is indeed exhilirating. This interactive medium, for an ear musician studying in Bali's aural tradition, made the process of committing this music to the printed page more rewarding than I had anticipated.

In many examples, the reader can refer to the compact disc accompanying this book, viewing a transcription as one listens to a particular rendition being sung. Most of the selections on the CD are of individual singers, unaccompanied, singing for me in their homes. The intention is for listeners to be able to hear some of what I have heard in the process of learning. And without instruments, one can more easily become attuned to the "movement of sound through the body" of the singer.

Voices in Bali

Désa kala patra
place-time-context

❀

Diverse are the voices, energies, and perceptions, within and relating to performance, that Balinese people have shared with me. And, to be sure, ever more varied, even contradictory, are those which I have not experienced or witnessed. This book will suggest various ways of approaching the interconnectedness of spirit and acoustics, poetry in song, song in dance, dance in character, characters in myth/history, and myth/history in locale, ecology, and religion. A fluid sense of orientation and focus reflects my experience with many Balinese artists, whose ever-contextual mode of discourse and activity continually refers to the concept of *désa kala patra* 'place-time-context'. While these writings are "about" voices, energies, and perceptions (*bayu sabda idep*), they are also "about," as much as they are shaped by, this indigenous mode of discourse itself.

The concept of *désa kala patra* is essential to Balinese artists and is discussed in a philosophical way or in a very direct and practical manner just before beginning a performance. It is a way of putting human activity into the context of the world and nature; a way of interacting with forces greater than the human. *Désa kala patra* gives a "sense of place" on both a social and a metaphysical level. Basically, if something is not in keeping with *désa kala patra*, it is out of context, either socially, spiritually, or ecologically. *Désa kala patra* is where things come from, where meaning and life-forces are manifested. It is also applied to ethics and civil behavior, such as the use of everyday language to reflect status.

In the Balinese language, the composite meaning of the phrase implies more than the sum of its parts. When the phrase is disassembled, the meanings of each word are myriad, depending, always, upon the *désa kala patra* of the discussion and interpretation at hand. The whole phrase could well be translated into English as "context," and we might be more accurate ascribing the definition "circumstance" or "situation" to *patra*. Of the many different ways that Balinese apply the phrase, *désa* can in itself refer to the immediate "place, time, and context" of an event, the sense of an overall organizing structure. In this case, *patra* would refer to the "activity" or "energy" and *kala* to a more transcendent aspect of time.

The way many people explain it, *désa* 'village' refers to locale, the character of a community and land. What kind of genealogical, family descent groups are there? Are there *jero*, members of the gentry related to the former palaces or members of the *Brahmana* lineage, traditionally delegated as priests, theologians and literati? Or is the community made up of *jaba* 'non-gentry', literally, "outsiders," who comprise more than 90 percent of the population?

Similarly, some locales are characterized by their proximity to and connection with one of Bali's thousands of temples, sharing its history, spiritual energy, and connotations. Another aspect of *désa* 'place' refers to the land and its particular character, the quality of an area's ricefields or other agricultural staple. Or whether it is in a densely populated or forested area, by the mountains, by the sea, or in the hills in between those two extremes. The *kaja-kelod* axis, referring to north-south, but really toward the mountain as opposed to toward the sea, is a source of spiritual as well as geographical direction and orientation. Pura Besakih, the mother temple worshiped by all of Bali, sits by the side of the great mountain, Gunung Agung. Mountains are thought of as the dwelling place of gods and ancestors, and it is from there that the deities come for periodic visits, occasioning ceremonies and festivals.

The sea is thought of as spiritually dangerous, the source of demons and witchcraft, as well as sickness. So, beachfront villages are considered more vulnerable to black magic and ill health; their ceremonial and artistic activities reflect a need to deal with those forces. Rivers are thought of as potentially dangerous from a spiritual point of view. On the other hand, springs are often sacred spots, and holy springs have been the location of meditation caves through the ages.

The *patra* 'context' aspect generally refers to the specific activity that needs to be performed, to be done in keeping with specifics of time and place. Particular group activities, ceremonies, and performances vary according to circumstances, need, and availability of resources. And there are many times when nonhuman entities dictate *patra*'s particular necessities.

During an *odalan* ceremony at the small community temple in Siṅ-gapadu, someone in trance conveys an unexpected message from the spirit of a *barong landung*. This pair of sacred barong landung masks have been stored away in the temple for many years. The spirit of one of them speaks through the human medium to say that the *barong landung* wants to be included again in the temple's cere-monies, and must be performed. So, for the next *odalan*, two hun-dred and ten days later, eight-foot high Jero Gedé and Jero Luh are brought out to give the *odalan* some additional sanctity while they tease each other with sexual humor and silly songs accompanied by the *gambelan*, in the context of a drama including many other char-acters, serious and comic.

In the course of these writings, *désa kala patra* is used as a compass leading us into varied perspectives on voices, energies, and perceptions, within as well as outward from Bali, ranging from the musical to the pedagogical, performative, cultural, ecological, metaphysical, and theoretical.

Music as an activity of an entirely transient nature, experienced in time and space; hearing as an inwardly directed activity, a perception of assimilation, and listening as a process of differentiation, directed outward; a teacher's loaded question, "Where are you coming from?"; each word's resonance and each phrase's sequence of reso-nances as vibrations transforming from throat to nose, to chest, around the mouth, and so on; musical tunings alternating back and forth, reflecting qualities of attentive-ness, reflection, impulsiveness, and spontaneity within the course of a dramatized walk in the "wilds" of nature; poetic lines and melodic phrases, rearranged extempo-raneously to fit choreography, mood, and gambelan structure; a topéng mask dance performance commissioned to tell particular family histories; over coffee and cakes, deciding who is to dance each role and basic plot sequence; all the ingredients of artistic process coming together in movement, wind, earth, song, conflict, pleasure, in-toxication, and spirit; a historical sense of the past, transcendent time, and the pre-sent, focused in the direct encounter with unseen but immediate forces; the very quality that artists and anthropologists have called uniquely Balinese, the great vari-ety from place to place, undergoing change in modern Indonesia; singling out an as-pect of creation, such as "the mountain," not to separate it from all else as a symbol but to unify the activity of attention by incorporating other aspects of creation into the quality of "highness"; phenomena taking on form, while shape is considered as a dynamic quality, in a time-space sense, manifested as neume, gesture, color, etc.; structure (désa) suggesting "a place for something to happen"; both method (note-to-note procedure) and material (the sounds and silences of a composition) as patra, also telling us "where"; and kala 'time' or in another sense, "flow," telling us "how" things happen.

Aji nusup *'lessons in penetration'*
the *désa kala patra* of experience

❀

A lullaby and its levels of meaning:
tembang Pucung *(CD selections 1 and 2)*

> *Bibi anu lamun payu luwas mandyus*
> *Antengé tekekang,*
> *yatnain ngaba masui*
> *tiuk puntul*
> *bawang anggon sasikepan*

> Restless baby, if mother should go bathing,
> she'll tie a scarf across her breasts
> bound up within it a piece of *masui* wood
> a dull knife
> and garlic for protection

The underlying, implied meaning of this lullaby has to do with magic and protection from witchcraft. Rivers are a common place for dangerous spirits to congregate. *Masui* wood, besides being used medicinally, wards off malevolent sorcery. A dull knife also repels harmful spirits as, of course, does garlic.

Another translation gives each phrase a corresponding didactic interpretation, sometimes offered by Ketut Rinda as *panasar*[1] in his *topéng* performances.

> To stay well and clean in this world,
> keep what you learn held close to your heart,
> be careful always to be learning from life-giving sources,
> for a confused mind,
> knowledge is all that is needed to live in this world

---

1. Comic attendant to the royal characters, the half-masked *panasar* provides much of the verbal throughline in *topéng*, including narration, humor, and philosophy.

Bawang 'garlic' is transmuted into *ngawang* 'knowledge' by means of *kirta basa*, the *panasar topéng*'s creative and playful practice of etymology-within-performance. In this kind of *kirta basa*, the implication is often that a closeness of meaning follows a closeness of phonetics. In other contexts, *kirta basa* is applied in a more formal linguistic sense.

The house is located on the eastern edge of the hamlet, just bordering the wet-ricefields. The door facing west leads into the family compound, a domestic area for a Balinese family comprising three generations. The door facing east looks out onto a wide expanse of terraced hills, the great volcanic mountain Gunung Agung, in the distance. Over a period of months, the fields change from mud into countless ponds of young green plants, and then into a blanket of gold awaiting harvest. It is clear where the Balinese find some solitude away from their closely knit social fabric, and one can observe the fieldwork from this porch, stage by stage as the seasons change.

Just by the house, a little way into the ricefields, is a holy spring, an ancient place of pilgrimages and meditation, with stone carvings dating back to the eleventh century. Between that spring and the house is another spring, where the people of the hamlet bring their ceramic and plastic pails to get drinking water, and where everyone bathes and does the laundry.

There are three sections, separated by stone walls, each containing a couple of stone figures, some of which are heads of supernatural beings out of whose mouths the water flows. One set of water spouts is for females, another for males, and the other section is reserved for ritual needs, very common in the Balinese Agama Tirtha 'religion of holy water'.

This village is situated between the Petanu and Pakrisan rivers, the area in which the great Balinese dynasties of the eleventh to fourteenth centuries flourished. From the higher hills of Tampaksiring to this village of Bedaulu and nearby Péjéng, are a series of ancient shrines, tombs, and meditation caves. The closest has a history thought to go back at least to the sixth century A.D. The demon-king Maya Danawa was jealous of the gods and did not let the people give them offerings. Indra finally subdued the demon, and his blood flowed into the river Petanu. Up until this century, I am told, water from the Petanu could not be used for irrigation because it was still tinged with Maya Danawa's blood.

But once Indra had killed Maya Danawa, he brought him to life again, dividing his soul into male and female twins who would marry and rule the island. This king and queen, located in Péjéng, had twins, as did each succeeding generation, until the seventh. This king chose not to marry his sister, and instead concerned himself with meditation and magical practices. While meditating, it is said, his head would leave his body and soar into the heavens. On one such occasion, his impatient and impulsive minister began to panic when the head did not return as soon as he had expected. So, as he saw a farmer walking toward the market with a pig, the minister, thinking a pig's head was better than none, cut off the head of the animal and placed it on his king's head. The king continued to rule but had himself installed on a high tower, forbidding everyone to cast their eyes on him.

As history tells us, this was the last of the line of Balinese dynasties before the advent of Javanese rule in the fourteenth century. This village bears the name of this king, Dalem Bedaulu, which means "He Who Changed Heads." [2]

After hiking up through the hills to my house in the *gambelan*-forging village of Tihingan, Klungkung, I indulge myself in a midday nap. When I awake, there is a strange sensation in my head. I boil some water for coffee, figuring that a little caffeine will clear up this hazy mental buzz. But after a cup, I realize that I am not merely experiencing a vibration within my head but a sound coming into my ears. I try to focus my listening, to identify the nature and direction of this sound, but wind up wandering in one direction and then another, out of my hosts' family compound and into the nearby dirt paths. I finally gaze upward and see a flock of pigeons circling overhead. Realizing this to be the source of the sound, I ask around and learn that little brass bells, *grondong* or *gongséng*, are commonly fastened to the legs of pigeons, as an aeolian sonic presence. The soundwaves do not travel to the ears of the behearer in any ordinary manner, but are diffused by the fast movement of the birds high up in the air. The sound does not issue from any one source or location, and that in combination with the high-pitched quality of the brass bells gives the resonance more of an all-embracing quality of air, or gentle wind, than of sound.

It was many years ago, and Tempo[3] had been living with his teacher for only one week. They would bathe mornings at a waterfall and listen to the sounds water makes. One time, as he was coming back

2. This episode as well as the defeat of *Dalem* Bedaulu at the hands of Patih *Gaja Mada* are popular themes for *topéng* mask dance performances, commemorating the advent of Majapahit dynasties in Bali.

3. I Madé Pasek Tempo was a singer, musician, and dancer from the village of Tampaksiring, *juru tandak* vocalist for *légong*, *dalang* for *séndratari* dance dramas, and *panasar* character for *topéng* and *arja*.

from bathing alone at the spring, his teacher asked, "Where are you coming from?" "The spring," he answered. "What was it like there?" "What do you mean?" His teacher continued, "What are the trees like by the spring? Who else was there? What color was the sky? How is the spring designed? What is it made of?" He was confused and did not know how to answer. His teacher said, "Alright, go home to your own village and think about it until you understand what I am asking you." For a year, he says, he would go to sleep at night wondering what his teacher had been getting at. That was the teacher from whom he later learned the "art of flowering."

Wayan Diya explains buana alit *'microcosmos' as a process of "letting them (qualities) enter into you."* Buana agung *'macrocosmos' is "to be able to enter into things." The world, cosmos, and our inner worlds are not places or entities. They are ways.*[4]

Activities, contexts, and implications of buana agung *and* buana alit *are diverse; sometimes corporeal, other times psychospiritual, still other times spatial, directional, and so on. Pangider-ider is a system relating various* déwa *'deities' with the different cardinal directions and their associated colors and weapons. A common feature of an* odalan *'temple festival' is* pangider buana *'traveling around-the-world', an activity in which members of the congregation process along the outer perimeter of the walls of a* pura *'temple', carrying sacred weapons or objects temporarily inhabited by divine visitors, possibly performing a processional dance with or without* gambelan, *and singing* kidung *verses.*

As we sit around, gathering momentum to begin the session, her husband and friend offer advice on teaching. She[5] is quiet, however, trying to really understand what it is about Balinese *tembang*

---

4. Pak Diya's perspective comes from learning from and performing with Pak Pugra and Pak Kakul, his uncle Wayan Rindi, and his father, Wayan Saplug, a musician at Radio Républik Indonesia. He also spent nine years in India. He currently lives in Jakarta, where he teaches dance at Jakarta Institute of the Arts and performs Balinese *wayang*.

5. Ni Nyoman Candri is a performer with the *arja* troupe of Radio Républik Indonesia (RRI), specializing in the role of *condong*, for both *arja* and *Calonarang*. She is currently (since my work with her) a teacher at the government-sponsored STSI, Indonesian College of the Arts.

singing that I wish to learn, and how she should begin teaching it.

Singing is an activity always intertwined with some other mode of aesthetic expression: dance, instrumental music, characterization, poetry, storytelling. It is in these contexts that much of its meaning, inspiration, and purpose arises. To read poetry is to sing. In all poetic genres practiced in Bali, the identity of a given poem is comprised not only of characteristic syllabic form, use of vowels, verse shape, and other "linguistic" and "poetic" features, but also of a characteristic melody. Even someone reading alone will be humming the melody of the poem to him or herself, though more quietly, syllabically, and quickly than when singing for others to hear.

To act is to dance and sing. The same word, *pragina*, denotes both dancer and actor (there is no differentiation, except in terms of specific characters or genres). *Masolah* is what a *pragina* does, and that means "to perform" or "to characterize," although in everyday usage, *ngigel* (from the root "to bend") denotes the activity of dancing. And although some roles are not vocal, any experienced performer is expected to be able to vocalize, in dialogue, stylized speech and song.

It is difficult, especially for the best Balinese performing artists, to objectify an individual activity such as singing, and to teach "it" outside of its context. The issue in this instance is not my being a foreigner so much as there not being an easily objectified purpose of study. If I was preparing a particular role for a performance group of which I was a member, my teacher would choose the appropriate songs for that character, and would teach how the vocal and dance phrasing and choreography express the character and interact with the instrumental *gambelan* music. If my aim was to sing poetry in the literary style, she would not bring in characterization, which often stretches words to their limits of recognition, but instead deal with ways of phrasing to enhance the meaning of the text. Or if I was just "collecting" songs, as both Balinese and foreigners sometimes do, she would simply sing into a microphone.

We come to an understanding that my aim is to learn not just the "rules of *tembang*" but the creative process of vocal characterization in song. She suggests that we start with the character of *mantri manis* 'refined prince', who has a large repertoire of songs in *arja* dance drama.

So she begins singing, and continues through all ten lines of *tembang Sinom lumbrah*. I expect her to sing it phrase by phrase, allowing me time to "get it"; but, rather than telling me what to do, she continues straight through the entire verse, again and again. I realize that her intention is for me to sing along with her, straight through, until the basic melodic flow becomes internalized. Singing together allows the student to follow the teacher's subtle facial, head, and neck gestures, shaping the sound by forming a kind of sympathetic resonance in each tone and inflection. Movement of the head and neck "helps the breathing and at the same time follows the course of the breath." Each leads the other. Dance gestures are intricately interwoven with the melodic and rhythmic flow of the song.

According to her style of teaching *tembang arja*, children should know the song before studying the dance. They begin by following the four-syllable phrasings of *macapat* poetic meter, and their gestures and steps are synchronized with the singing. As the style "enters" the student, and technique becomes less self-conscious, a more fluid and flexible sense of phrasing is learned, allowing the form "to be alive." Slow steps, for example, still follow a long, ornamented vocal phrase, but neither is counted in *macapat* meter's fours, allowing each to flow somewhat on its own. When a synchronized moment or phrase occurs, it is a bit unexpected. And although the dancer can alternate between ambiguity and clarity in his/her relationship with the *gambelan*, an inner cohesion should exist, in which the dancer is continually "touching upon" one or another of the various musical pulses or accents.

I have a paraphrased translation of the particular lyrics we are using for a *tembang* but do not understand it word for word. As we pause, after singing through it once, I mention that it is a little difficult to remember the verse without knowing the meaning of each word. Candri agrees that literal meaning is very important, "but," she says, glancing up toward her father's photograph on the wall, "the intent of the song is most important"; its use in conveying mood, character, or bringing a new angle into a story.[6]

Another day we are starting out on a new *tembang*, but Bu Candri's concentration seems unfocused. Friends are sitting around, making puns and teasing each other. She recites a set of lyrics for *tembang*

---

6. Candri's father, the artist/scholar I Madé Kredek, was the renowned Wijil character in Radio Républik Indonesia's *arja* troupe, an authority on vocal music and the seven-tone *gambelan luang*, and performer of *topéng, Calonarang, jangér, cak*, and so on.

Ni Nyoman Candri at home
in Singapadu (1992).

Sinom, which I write out, but she soon wanders off to eat lunch. While munching on rice, she asks her ten-year-old daughter to sing her rendition of the *tembang* for me.

In little Wayan's singing, certain phrases are filled with subtlety and nuance with expressive inflections, while others betray a child's unsureness and self-consciousness, on and off with intonation. It is clear, in listening, that she has not been taught any diluted or simplified "children's version" of the music. Rather, because of family background, she has been exposed to the living phenomenon of song; and although she has not yet grasped the techniques of the form, the essential qualities of *tembang* are already in her heart and gut, and the *tembang* can already sing through her.

Soon everyone is in the family temple, knocking oranges out of a tree. As the kids circle around, chasing after the flying oranges, Candri glances at me and starts to sing. I laugh, embarrassed, hesitating. She responds, "Come on, this is the way you get to know *tembang*. Sing everywhere, while you're picking oranges, while you're bathing.

I Nyoman Kakul teaching
granddaughters Ni Nyoman
Netri and Ni Nyoman Ganti
(1972). Photo by Beth
Skinner.

That's why you always hear children singing." As I begin to intone,
even the seven-year-olds are reciting the words, before each phrase
or along with me. They continue to knock oranges out of the tree,
and we sing together, loudly.

Candri absolutely insists that one follow through, once a melody is
begun. If I make a mistake, such as beginning in too high a register,
and stop in the midst of an intonation, the kids will break out in
laughter, jumping up and down; they laugh the same way when an
embarassed Balinese student hesitates or stops in midphrase. Stopping is just not done in *tembang*. She says that one must be able to
transform something unintentional into something good without
hesitating to think or reconsider.

Madé Sija's unique approach to teaching is to limit the study to the essentials: *arja* in twelve sessions for a group, *wayang* in five, *panasar topéng* or *Dalem*, *topéng*'s refined king, in three.[7] He says that one shouldn't study a dance in its entirety, from start to finish. That puts the emphasis on the teacher; it's like the teacher's rehearsal. The student should be taught what's most difficult, the most complex sections, the essence of a particular character, and then work on one's own to develop the rest, by watching and creating. The steps in his particular curriculum for the study of any particular *arja* character entail *mungkah lawang* 'opening the door, entranceway' (in performance, the *langsé* 'curtain'); movement of head and eyes; movement of arms and hands; the walk; and *mimik* 'gestural movements' such as pointing, or touching the *gelungan* 'headpiece'. Five aspects.

An image Pak Rinda uses to describe one of his students is that of having many sources, *sumur*, but having "not yet penetrated deep enough."[8] This is a play on words characteristic of his *kirta basa* style of etymology as a *panasar* character. *Sumbur*, with almost the same pronunciation, is a well or spring. He sums up the student's creative development with the analogy "water is not yet flowing."

The late Cokorde Oka Tublen[9] played *limbur*, the strong female role, in Singapadu village's *arja* ensemble in the 1930s, and he told Anak Agung Bawa[10] about Wayan Geria's early experience in the role of Punta.[11] The group performed at a religious festival in the village of Blahbatu, and after the performance their Blahbatu friends commented unanimously that everyone in the group was good except Punta, who was so bad he should be dropped from the group. As the performers walked the long distance home to Singapadu

7. I Madé Sija, known as *Dalang* Bona, "the *dalang* of Bona village," is a conspicuous innovator within the tradition of *wayang*, *topéng*, and *arja*, and an authority on religious offerings and performance literature.

8. I Ketut Rinda of Blahbatu performed *arja* since the early 1930s but was best known as a *panasar topéng*, continuing to perform into his seventies. A traditional scholar, he was an authority on history, literature, and many aspects of performance theory and practice.

9. Most esteemed of mask carvers, specializing in the spiritually charged Rangda and *barong*, he was an authority on the art of performance. *Cok.* is often used in conversation as a shortened version of his title, *Cokorde*.

10. Leader of the *gambelan gong* of Peliatan, and son of Anak Agung Gedé Mandera.

11. Punta is the name given to the *panasar* character in *arja*. Wayan Geria of Singapadu was the renowned Punta to Madé Kredek's Wijil, and *panasar* to Kredek's *kartala*, at RRI and in village performances throughout Bali.

from Blahbatu, Geria told Cok. Oka, "I'm so terrible, I should really quit the group." But Cok. Oka supposedly set him up with a series of teachers, one for vocal style in Denpasar, another for dance, another for literary sources, and he subsequently became *the* prototype Punta for *arja*.

The Balinese family compound is not the private enclave that one might occasionally wish for. And in turn, the rigorous activity of practicing, in the sense of working alone on one's artistic discipline, is equally public. As I practice out on the porch (the little "indoors" that exists being deficient in light and space), family members and neighbors tend to gravitate, from time to time, in my direction. The senior female member of the household passes by more frequently than do others. Within the community, she is known for an eccentric, giddy sense of humor, an abundance of nonsequiturs for any subject or context, and a wit that never lies dormant for too long.

In any case, as I begin to sing, strange echoes reverberate in other corners of the compound, sometimes here, sometimes there. Howls, as well as snatches of melody, issue from the open-walled kitchen area, then again from the pigpen out back, and again from a nearby porch where she is sweeping. Peals of laughter follow, as I continue through the verse.

Seeing the present opportunity, passing children join in from time to time, sometimes comically, other times in pure empathy of mood and sincere interest, but always with pleasure. It is always done with a certain sense of respect and politeness, but also with the instinct that activity cannot be truly alive unless it resonates in a body larger than itself. And then, there is the love of laughter, not restricted to whatever is particularly "funny." Rather, it is used to punctuate a sequence of time, or fill in a space that needs a little lightness.

I begin to lose my sense of embarrassment, realizing that the laughter is not directed at my activity, but along with it, in harmony and support. Theirs is an instinct to help me out of my isolation, insisting that one not be too seriously preoccupied with his or her own individual process but, rather, flow with the ambience of the surroundings and reflect the mood of the day.

In truth though, this kind of situation is not so much typical as it is an exaggerated testing of one's fortitude. For I have seen how members of a Balinese community, complementing their collectivity of experience, can also be adept at providing each other breathing space and quiet. And while there is a prevailing sense of humor, artistic activity is respected as a discipline of the mind and spirit. Most often, when I am singing at home, people in the family compound and in the adjacent ricefields quietly go about their business. But my voice (as does any sound issuing from within the confines of any family dwelling) traverses the high stone and mud walls to be heard by anyone within proximity.

And as I pause for a while, someone nearby may begin to sing the same or another song to him or herself, extending a thread of continuity. Children, as almost anywhere in the world, are more often awed than boisterous in the presence of artistic activity; and their additions to the auditory environment are less often making fun than they are trying out some sound they have been carrying around in their heads. And occasionally, when I am finished rehearsing by myself, grandmother, at our other home by the ricefields, politely offers me her version of the *tembang* I have been singing.

Morning of continuous rain, a sky overcast in all directions since dawn. Now it's 7:00, with only the crickets, rain, irrigation water flowing through bamboo pipes, birds, and occasional dog barking or rooster crowing. To sleep amid a stream of frog, cricket, and *cicak* lizard calls, pulsating ceaselessly over the rumble of flowing water, does something to one's inner rhythms. Sonic acupressure, patterns and vibrations being repeated, though shifting subtly, striking points of resonance in the perceiving organism and psyche. This sound input becomes "the state of things," incorporated into oneself, as one enters into it. It's in this sense that silence is not the absence of sound, but a complete acceptance of sound. Stillness can be discovered in the midst of motion, as momentum, energy takes off on its own. Hearing is an inwardly directed activity, a perception of assimilation. Listening is a process of differentiation, directed outward. Silence, then, is not in or about sound, but in what we bring to sound.

During my singing or tape-recording sessions with various performers, some ambient sounds are considered acceptable to them while others are considered intrusive. A rooster crowing is not noise. Neither is a distant dog barking or baby crying, as long as proximity and persistence do not increase. A motorcycle is noise. Rain is most often not noise.

My sessions with Pak Tempo may last from 9 A.M. until 4 P.M., while his family and friends put up a new thatch *alang-alang* roof, and his daughter paints a new costume with *perada* 'goldleaf'. Our conversation ranges from the correlation between the post and beam structure of the traditional house, laws and spiritual levels of society, creation of story and improvisation of poetry and song, to an acoustical-character-word-music analysis of the *panasar*'s vocal repertoire.

Opening a *geguritan* manuscript, Pak Tempo sings its first few verses using *tembang Pucung*, the poetic meter most often associated with didactic content. These particular verses follow that mode of thought, dealing with the process of study and the proper relationship between teacher and student. He reads a line in Balinese and then translates for me into Indonesian, paraphrasing. All of the images keep leading to the importance of faith: faith in oneself, student's faith in teacher, teacher's faith in student, and faith in the processes of experience and growth. These are all threads that weave a fabric of knowledge. Growth occurs in accord with nature; things are not completely within our control, and we alone cannot make things happen. He uses the analogy of bearing children. We do not know how a child will develop in the womb, or what the child will look like; but forces of nature take over from us in the situation we have initiated. Growth has to take place outside of purely human references; it must seek communion with nature and spirit. No growth can be solely concerned with human life or generated and controlled solely by humans.

He describes the attitudes and conditions that both teacher and student should be aware of. Neither can have ulterior motives in the learning process; art cannot be sold. A teacher cannot equate teaching with money; material things are necessary and important, but they should not bear directly upon the artistic or spiritual process. His paraphrasing also stresses how one must teach as one learns; since one must spend one's entire life learning, one must be able to externalize and pass on knowledge, share, learning as one teaches.

"To feel helpful, to have a feeling of giving, is impure. To have the feeling of being helped, of receiving, is good. This is because nothing is ours to begin with; everything belongs to nature. The only 'wealth' that humans truly possess are joys, sorrows, sickness, and death, *suka, duka, lara, pati*. To feel helped is fine; it effects a sensitivity to one's environment."

This echoes the attitude of the master dancer I Nyoman Kakul, who once told us, "this is not my knowledge; it does not belong to me. If it was (which is impossible), it would have to be of the pettiest significance, because nothing profound can be owned by an individual. So it *must* be continually passed from one to another."[12]

Tempo discusses the five senses, the fallibility of each, and the need for each of us to overcome our weaknesses. The lowest sense is taste, because it's so unadaptable and narrow. If you want your senses to be open, to perceive deeply the totality of an experience, you cannot filter out what you find unpleasurable. You cannot reject it or be upset by it. You must be prepared to hear what you do not want to hear, smell unpleasant things, taste unpalatable tastes, feel uncomfortable, see ugly sights. Sardono told Pak Tempo in Europe, "listen, you're not going to like the food here at first, but you have to transcend it. You can't always be desiring some familiar, ricey food, because you'll be anxious and alienated. To be creative you must be healthy and emotionally calm, and to be that way you must eat whatever is available to you and be satisfied." Tempo says the stomach doesn't care about the taste of what was eaten, only the tongue does. So he bypassed his tongue for a month or two in Europe, accepting the unpleasant tastes, and eventually came to like French cheese and bread.

Another big theme is materialism, Pak Tempo freely quoting from the *Ramayana, Dharma Prawretti*, and other texts. When the elephant dies, he leaves behind his tusk, ivory, and when the tiger dies he leaves behind his beautiful skin. Two exemplary animals. But what do we leave behind? *Dharma Prawretti* and the *Durma* verses, "*dening kecatri . . . ,*" suggest that we develop whatever can be taken with us when we pass on: spiritual knowledge, the fire and water that clean out negative tendencies. What, he asks, is the use of material things, such as *gambelan*, since the really important things are transcendent. I answer that material things can be valuable tools

12. I Nyoman Kakul of Batuan was Bali's foremost *topéng* dancer for many decades and an authority on *gambuh, wayang wong, Calonarang, baris*, and other forms. Beth Skinner and I studied and lived with him, his children, and grandchildren for seven months in 1972.

that facilitate the development of spiritual, aesthetic progress. He agrees, and adds that we should leave behind something of beauty that other people can appreciate. But all desires lead to more desires, and that takes us away from awareness and sensitivity to the forces of life. We must be striving to perfect what is deep and transcendent, while accepting our material circumstances, as long as we have a basic quality of life: food, shelter, clothes. We need not reject things, but cannot be caught up in acquiring things.

With emotional charge, he tells me, quite personally, "Don't feel that you must learn this, this and this, music, dance, and so on. All you really need to learn is the inner feeling of a single dramatic entity and understand how it encompasses all these aspects. This is what you need in order to create in America, not, 'I learned this dance'. Anyone can learn dances and musical pieces. What we're working with now is the *aneh* 'strange' or 'subtle' aspect of art, character and *perkembangan*, how the art lives.

"To think of end results while studying makes it boring and monotonous. One must not quantify what one one wants to learn; we must simply enjoy the very process, the very moment of learning. If you're clever and your thoughts are bad, all your accomplishments will be bad. If your thoughts and intentions are good, all that you do, great or small in scope, will be good."

Tempo runs out to get a couple of audio cassettes. He asks, "Why is it that these two *gambelan Semar Pagulingan* ensembles are so different from each other? One's pieces are the classical, beautiful compositions and the musicians are serious old men. The other has just two real classical pieces, the rest lifted from *gambelan gong* or *gendér wayang*, and the musicians are mostly less experienced youngsters. But whenever I hear this *gambelan*, I'm transported, my mind is calmed, I'm in bliss. Whoever made this *gambelan* must have been a very good man. He must have said as he hammered, 'how can I make a beautiful, resonant *gambelan*?' not, 'how much can I sell this for?' This *Semar Pagulingan* can play any melody, for any occasion, and the spirit is always subtle, unique, pure, beautiful."

I slowly realized that either all the visits we had had until then were deliberately geared toward testing and orienting me, or that Pak Tempo just operates on a subconscious but very consistent level. Ever since our first visit, he progressed in a manner

I Madé Pasek Tempo at home in Tampaksiring (1980). Photo by Beth Skinner.

balancing my intent with his concept of the art of performance. In our first discussion, he had dealt with performance as reflecting nature and cosmos, integrating the diverse levels of knowledge, psychological state, and experience into a pleasurable community interaction. The next visit was his teacher-student initiation, emphasizing "faith." He also touched on the unities of music and dance.

The next time, he tested my patience and disposition, since he had scheduled something else; but he set a propitious time for the "first session," and talked extensively on déwasa, his own astrological chart, and one's place in the flow of history. He spoke of adversity, remaining true to one's nature, dedication, and not surrendering to the negative forces of society.

The next session dealt with the Balinese universe, sense of the sacred, amerta, the water of life (or nectar of immortality), one's personal place, geographically as well as historically, in relation to ancestors and tradition. He challenged us to recognize our own traditions and place in the world, and to see the pitfalls in superficial learning (studying techniques), reinforcing the necessity of internalizing Balinese experience and knowledge in order to create within the désa kala patra of our own culture. The next session tested my disposition, to see if I had anything like the patience of the venerable wayang character Twalén. But we then got into the physical reality of vocal performance, a challenge to the organism, giving me a taste of the sensory pleasure of the art, and the dramatic basis of all sound.

The next session was to see if I had the intuitive sense to understand Balinese characterization. And then began the study of craft, in terms of improvisation, and the depth of performers' orientation.

The first five sessions now seem to have been meant to both test me and pave the way toward the study of a subtle and extensive art and spiritual discipline. He had to feel a firm grounding, personal purity of purpose and orientation, to be disposed toward laying out his art. The artist in life-cosmos-nature; the student-teacher relationship and the learning process; the life and times of the artist; cosmos, history, and priority of désa kala patra; patience, disposition, and the challenge of physical exertion; and after those five initiatory stages, we move on. It's as if we had to cover the area suggested in the first talk, all of the levels of study necessary for the development of the artist, before he could really feel comfortable interacting freely and creatively.

I question a Balinese performer friend about his decision to remain at a distance from esoteric spiritual teachings. For example, many dalangs deal on a level involving formal traditions of protecting the secrets of esoteric word meanings, and the inherent psychic dynamics associated with specific sound qualities.[13] My friend answers that his concern is with manifestation. When anyone does their art or activity in a state of concentration, attuned in mind, body, and spirit, the unknown becomes present, manifested as taksu. Any performer, in order to be good, makes himself open to nature's forces. One doesn't have to go out, or even search within by meditating, doing mantras, because the deep qualities will be drawn to your activity, will flow into your forms. He explains, "Whatever you get, you can lose, and however much you learn about spiritual practice, there are always people who know more and can challenge or hurt you, seeing your position and vulnerability."

He sees it as better not to enter that realm, or fray, and to work with what one knows, what one has perceived and felt directly. Then, the idea is that as one is active in a flowing, open manner, one comes to know, to perceive more and more. Let the mysteries find their way, take form and shape as they inhabit and breathe life into activity.

For some Indonesian and non-Indonesian educators, teaching begins with the "basic movements, out of which grow all dance forms." Other teachers

13. *Dharma Pawayangan*, the major written text of esoteric teachings relating to *wayang*, advises the student and reader to secrecy: "Keep in mind the lessons of this treatise; they must not be revealed. Do not speak about them, for there would be a calamity caused by the DI-VINE GOLDEN RULE. There would be no rebirth if they were revealed. If you do not reveal, and complete all according to this treatise, you will find a refuge in the World of Voidness with your forebears, you will find a divine heaven, you will be far from suffering and from Hell, you will not have to face the smoke of the cauldron of Hell. It is clear that the enlightened *dalan* will have enjoyment" (C. Hooykaas 1973: 73).

are skeptical of this interpretation of "basics," *pokok*, *dasar*, which when put into practice usually leaves the student knowing a good many rules but nothing of the artistic process. *Pokok* translates as "fundamental, basic; or the trunk, root of a tree." McPhee (1966: 57) further elaborates, "*pokok* is used in various ways, all referring to origin. *Pokok yeh* is a water source or spring; *pokok kayu* the living stump of a tree from which new shoots may sprout. *Pokok* may also refer to the founders of a family, origins of a village, etc." When institutionalized dance or music teaching takes "basics" to mean some sort of elementary regimen from which aesthetic forms arise, it operates under a misguided notion. Since the learning process has been taken out of the traditional context, this is thought to be necessary for the sake of expediency.

The real basics are *derived from* the experience of those living, complex forms. The emphasis on basic movements on the elementary level involves a misleading objectification of certain qualities, out of their context, creating a false sense of knowledge. The other approach is to let the student see the broader vision of the art form as a dynamic process, and fill in the details as one goes along. The real basics are only learned in a cumulative manner, when the aesthetic activity is in a social setting: rehearsal, performance, ceremony, play.

I've tried to be self-effacing about "getting something," a little role to play, a knickknack or knack to bring back, or a scholarly "something" to unwrap in the lab at home. In discussions with several of the venerable older generation of masters, I have been asked the purpose of my study. Part of their concern has had to do with the issue of objectification and exploitation of aesthetic processes: is their knowledge being taken out of the intuitive artistic context and delimited, or is it fertilizing new regenerative growth and reinvention? The deeper levels of spiritual-aesthetic exchange often followed this kind of discussion.

The issue is played out in varied scenarios. A teacher at one of the government performing arts schools was taking some singing lessons from my friend. As is becoming common nowadays, he made tape recordings of her renditions of various *tembang* songs, to complement the sessions with her. The variations were sung in successive levels of development for the student to comprehend the process of *perkembangan* 'flowering'. Sometime later, my friend heard from students that this schoolteacher was making copies of the recordings and distributing them to his students as part of their classes with him. She was distraught.

The feeling of having been violated had to do in part with the personal issue of someone with the status of a teacher using her knowledge instead of his own. But the lingering feeling had to do with something much deeper and raises broader issues. Had this person just played the recordings of her songs for his class and then gone on to teach them on his own, she would have had no objection. He could have studied the recording she made for him, learned the songs, and then recorded his own rendition for his students to take home. This process of direct transmission is part of learning the creative process of Balinese song, and my friend felt that, her creative process had been polluted and misrepresented. She felt that the recording of her voice was not the song, and that those students would be given a false impression that, because they are hearing a simplified version of the song, they are somehow keying into the creative process of *tembang*.

Playing a recording of her singing is just one step removed from the source, and this would have been valid for his class as a listening session. But to make second generation dubs for the purpose of someone else's analysis creates too great a distance from the source. As I have found with other teachers, my friend was extremely generous with her knowledge, but was equally upset when the teachings were objectified and taken out of the context of kinesthetic transmission. The phenomenology of first and second generation dubbing becomes an ethical issue of Balinese aesthetics in a somewhat related way to the use of digital sampling in music composition elsewhere.

I think of data as stones indeterminately arranged in a stream of water we are walking across. The stream is the flow of phenomena. We walk on just as many stones as is necessary to get across. The water is experience, and awaiting our arrival on the other side is a vision of the world. We may also choose to wade or swim in the water, or hop from stone to stone as frivolous sport. But the vision we ultimately derive is shaped by our means of crossing.

Wayan Diya speaks of the role of sleep in all-night performances of stylized, commonly known and shared forms. As the audience drifts in and out of sleep, they see the characters in their imaginations, creating their own images and scenarios as creative participants. Just as with small boats in a great harbor, the general area of imagery and plot to be circumnavigated is known, but there is ample freedom of movement, reflective of the winds, ambient mood, and points of interest along the way. Pak Diya also equates the performance process with wariga, *the calendrical accounting of* time. Each déwasa, or auspicious day, rather than being something to be counted along a linear path, is more a confluence of myriad qualities and energies. The wariga process of reckoning déwasa is an interpretive skill, though Diya likens it to that of a chemist, mixing the many qualities to clarify the spiritual nature of a particular day. Similarly, the performer's sense of kala involves creating a space-time continuum within a given number of hours. This art emphasizes how, rather than what, leaving a maximum amount of area for deep interaction.

A long discussion with Sardono[14] is inspired by his depiction of the Solonese practice of late night discourse. He suggests that as one drifts into and out of sleep one perceives on a deeper level. One does not always tune into "what" is being said, because one is more open to a totality of experience; what one gets in a conversation includes the ambience of the moment, an occasional breeze, a dog barking, a rooster crowing. We do not just hear and perceive things with our critical, dualistic senses, which delimit them: "this is such and such a series of tones" or "that bird's flying north to south." But some things spoken go right to the heart, resound in the recesses of the mind. Deep things are perceived with acute sensitivity, and others not at all.

He suggests that my reading of Pak Diya, placing the imagination so strongly into the sleep-performance-perception experience, is not complete. The really active aspect is the direct experience of subtle energies, a deeper, clearer process of transmission; not an image, representation, or suggestion, but an internal quality. It's an extension of the priority Balinese performers give to being open to penetrating energies (and ancestral visitations), not just "creating" or "using one's imagination." Now, Sardono explains this angle in terms of audience and late-night discourse. Even as one speaks from this drowsy place, one can, at times, communicate clear, direct qualities, like sending arrows to the heart or mind of the perceiver. In this transmission process, one can speak from one's intellect or from one's heart (a deeper, inner place), just as one can perceive intellectually or with the heart. As we describe a performance of ours at a psychiatric hospital, he is most struck by the account of empathy and resonance coming from the audience, echoing our sounds, gasping and laughing. Their understanding of themes, arising from a heightened perception of the dramatic process and an ability to immediately internalize imagery and kinetic qualities, had showed us what worked kinesthetically and what didn't, but this beyond the imaginative process idea adds a new dimension.[15]

14. Sardono W. Kusumo was trained in the court dance of Solo, Java, as well as the martial art *silat*. Since 1972, he has collaborated a great deal with Balinese performers, touring his company throughout the world. He teaches at Jakarta Institute of the Arts. Sardono commissioned me to compose and perform experimental vocal music for his productions in Switzerland and Mexico (*MahaButa*) and for a film in Indonesia (The Sorceress of Dirah).
15. Sal Murgiyanto (1990: 351) writes: "Sardono looks at his development as a dancer and choreographer the way a Buddhist looks at the cosmos which can be differentiated into three

In dealing with the world, "universality" often suggests seeing oneself in everything. Penetration is quite different. Entering into things may dissolve the dualistic attention to detail.

A Ch'an Buddhist story tells of a monk trying to empty his mind of all thoughts for the purpose of meditation. But whenever he closes his eyes, he sees a nest of snakes. His meditation teacher suggests that the next time he sees the snakes, the monk should look close enough to be able to describe to him the patterns and markings on the snakes. The next time he closes his eyes to meditate, the snakes are there. But as he approaches them and focuses his attention on the details of their form, they disappear.

Similarly, focused attention to stylized artistic or meditative forms can dissolve dualities and open one up to other energies and states. Letting things enter you creates fluid self-identity.

When Nyoman Candri was first learning from her father, she would sit in the river with water up to her neck and sing in her high register as loud as she could. After half an hour or so, she'd lose her voice. A few days later, the voice would return and she'd be back at the river. After either a few times or one month (she has said both) of this practice, the voice was strong and relaxed. As a daily regimen for a good voice she drinks cold water when she arises in the morning, but I believe that, rather than this being a traditional practice, she got the idea from the medical doctor Moerdowo's radio program.

---

regions: the region of sensuousness (the lowest), the region of form (the middle), and the region of formlessness (the highest)." The actual practice is not one of discrete and separable areas but, rather, a continuum varying in emphasis and focus. In Tantric Buddhist ritual performance, the kinetic, corporeal aspects are fundamental paths into the more subtle realms of consciousness.

Vocal qualities

❊

One quality of the standard *dalang* and *panasar* voice is *suara ncah* 'broken, shattered, fragmented', a quality that might be described superficially as coarse or hoarse. One can be relaxed with this style, but it is generally believed that this is achieved only after a training period entailing much forcing, pushing the voice and throat to their limits. Young *dalang*s are often instructed to practice singing full volume at the ocean shore, facing the loud waves, until hoarse. Or, sitting under the spout at a spring, one lets the rushing water pour over his throat as he sings loudly. This is another way to intensify the sensations in the throat and develop a strong voice. Some *dalang*s use a throat-conditioning drink of fresh red peppers soaked in oil.

Yet other *dalang*s, such as Wayan Nartha, say that *suara ncah* should not be forced, but worked on gradually. Supposedly, two of the great *dalang*s of the earlier part of this century, Granyam and Rawa, had voices that were not very loud and strong, but conveyed *ncah* qualities with less force and tension. A basic consideration is not to be pushing the sound out of the mouth, but keeping it resonating within the body. With *suara ncah*, the throat is the most crucial area (whereas in *arja*, the mouth is most prominent).

One aspect of warming up involves letting low tones resonate quietly in the throat. There is a specifically vocal aspect to the standard *mantra*s, invocation, and *Panyacah Parwa* stanzas that begin *wayang* performances. These preparatory, opening verses invoke the sacred world of the *wayang* as the shadow puppets come to life. At the same time as they manifest this macrocosmic order, these stanzas have a physiological, microcosmic role in preparing the voice through the use of coarse, moderate, and sweet qualities (low, middle, and high ranges). Each vocal quality and body organ has an associated cosmological counterpart. In this way the *dalang* is warmed up in each range in a lyrical context—less urgent or forced than if he dived directly into the story. One does not want to go into the *keras* 'strong' voice cold, or without the *taksu* 'inspiration' accorded by prayer.

Dalang Madé Sija's speaking and singing voice is *ncah* to the extreme, but it's so accustomed to embodying, conveying character and spirit that it's a gestural voice, shaping sounds and phrases not so much melodically as in deep sweeps of feeling, like broad brush strokes.

SENDON PANASAR TOPÉNG WITH PAK TEMPO'S INTERPRETATION[1]

Bléng mbang bléng mbong, carikan tahun
Bléng mbong carikan lemah
Manuk muni maurahan
Sawang ghajita ring prabata
Céng koro aka kuwu angalun-alun
Sawang rawi meh rahina semubaang Hyang Aruna
Kadi netraning rogorapuh
Munihang tabeh–tabehan sinaméring raja dauh néng tenun
Mwang wina rawana suaranya merdu aganti

mist and clouds clinging together over the ricefields
mist clinging to the earth
shows that the day is almost breaking
birds are warbling as they fly here and there
just as if they are all glad this morning
(at the moment) a rooster is crowing continuously
it is like this every morning, as the sun glows, reddened
a little like someone's sore eye
the pulsing noises are like the sounds of a queen
weaving at her loom
like a flute and lute, sweet and refined

Pak Tempo touches on the physical techniques and characterization of voice for the *panasar*'s *sendon*, "*Bléng mbang.*" Chest, throat, mouth, and nose sounds require specific focus. Each word's resonance and each phrase's sequence of resonances determine how vibrations will transform from throat to nose, to chest, around the mouth, and so on. The word *lemah* at the end of one line is sung as an inflection gradually becoming more nasal as it slides up an interval of a fifth.

Bléng is drawn out as *bléh—yéh—wéh—ng*. The *yéh* and *wéh* shape the expiration of breath, shape the mouth as well as following the melodic contour. But the initial articulation of *bléng* as well as its *y* and *w* do not really occur in the lips but in the throat. The intense energy involved in

---

1. *Sendon* are the poetic lines or verses sung by a *panasar topéng* as he comes out from behind the curtain. Often containing a series of brief snatches of *Kawi* classical poetry strung together, the melody is generally improvised over the *bapang* 'ostinato' phrases of the accompanying *gambelan*.

the dispersion of breath helps shape the sound. A subtle example of this is *mbang* and *mbong*, in which a *w* is gently articulated between the *b* and the vowel *a* or *o*, creating just a hint of *mbwang* and *mbwong*.

When I try the back-of-the-throat *getaran* 'vibrations', he explains I am making it happen, not allowing it to happen on its own. "It sounds close to the sound but it's not the correct process." After I try it for a while he says, "now it is the right process, I can tell, but it will take you six months to really do it." The force of the throat resonance is prodigious. In Tempo's conception of the learning process, relaxation of the voice comes after forcing.

Breath may shape melodic phrasing to be "separate but as if continuous," "spaced apart but as if joined," or "continuous but as if broken up." One version of this last one is produced by a kind of glottal punctuation, creating a staccato series of exhalations. In the lower melodic phrases of the *panasar's tembang Durma*—the word *manusa* in CD selection 5 for example—the feeling of the melodic phrase is smooth while the exhalations are articulated by vowel changes, subtly enough to be felt but not consciously noticed by the listener (fig. 1). Generally, a singer takes enough time for breathing "to absorb the meaning of the *tembang*." But *ngunda angkihan* 'continuous movement of the breath' is referred to here as *nguaca angkihan* 'stealing breath' because it should go unnoticed. Emptying one's breath at the end of a phrase with an open vowel, the old air is expelled and inhalation made in a single motion.

Luwung means "simple but good" to some, but other performers use the word as the highest praise. *Lebeng* means "cooked to proper consistency" (with food preparation and art), and aesthetically indicates something very

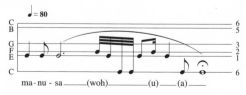

Figure 1. *Panasar's* (Punta's) *tembang Durma*.

good. It often suggests that a song "fits" the character of the musical form being played by the *gambelan*, of the dance, and the *rasa* 'feeling' or 'range of emotion'. Another, more specialized meaning of *lebeng* refers to a seven-tone *gambuh* and *gambelan luang* tuning and the subtle use of semitones. *Matah* 'unripe' or 'uncooked' suggests something as yet unprepared.

Contrasts in vocal qualities are sometimes expressed as *lalah-manis* 'spicy-sweet', or *galak-manis* 'fierce-sweet'. Pak Tempo asserts that when a sound is "too sweet, it's beautiful"; when sound is "too spicy, it's fierce." Spicy or fierce qualities are usually associated with phrases in a high or rising register and amplitude, while sweetness often fits with a descending or level melodic contour. Fierce and sweet qualities should be balanced within each phrase of a song. Shifting back and forth keeps the audience interested and "reflects the truth that everything in life has its sweet and harsh aspects."

With each character in *arja*, the throat is closed in varying degrees. Sweet prince *mantri*,[2] princess *galuh*, and maidservant *condong* use nose, mouth, and throat in fairly similar ways. But for the *limbur*, the forceful mother, *mantri buduh* 'crazy prince', and *panasar*, *ah* often becomes *uh* or *eur* as in French; that's a very common vowel sound, especially for *limbur*. She shapes *eu*, *ah*, and *eee-ah* most distinctly and stridently, exaggerated by her use of the lips. The voice is most concentrated in the throat, with a quality referred to as *boh* 'very open, relaxed'. This aspect of vocal characterization is intertwined with timbral shading and melodic phrasing, expressed by way of *nyutra suara* or *gedong céngkok*.

Gedong céngkok has been defined in the liturgical as well as performance context of vocal music as "the movement of sound through the body." *Gedong* is the word for house or building. *Céngkok* in this case means hole or space, although in Javanese music it refers generally to short melodic phrases. In Bali, *gedong céngkok* can also refer to the shape, jumps, and spaces within the flow of the melody, *ilegan*, or within the singer's body. The terms *gregel* 'melisma' and *luk* 'slide' or 'glissando' are also used to describe melodic phrasing, although I have heard that *gregel* was adopted from Javanese terminology by Bali's government arts schools in the 1960s.

Central to Nyoman Candri's *tembang* language is *nyutra suara*, the subtle shaping and transforming of vowel sounds, and its interplay with

2. Depending on the particular story being performed, *mantri manis* may in fact be a prince or whichever refined young man (though performed by a female nowadays) is a principal character. Likewise, *galuh* may also be the refined daughter, and not necessarily a princess. Either way, they are generally referred to as *ratu* 'royal' characters.

melody, meaning, and physical qualities. *Nyutra* derives from Sanskrit *sutra* 'silk' and refers on an aesthetic level to smoothness and delicacy of the sound, *suara*, also derived from Sanskrit, *svara*. Taking into account the considerable assimilation of Tantric Buddhist practices, concepts, and terminology in Bali, *nyutra* may conceivably refer on a mystical level to the silken thread of which *tantra* is woven.[3] Mary Zurbuchen (1987: 62) writes:

> . . . inherent in verbalization is a force associated with our vital organs. The Balinese concept of the *dasaksara* [group of sounds and written symbols important in Balinese mysticism; from *dasa* 'ten', *aksara* 'letter'] links the physiological fact with a multitude of linguistic symbols, each of which reiterates the relationship between language and various levels of universal truth. In Burke's (1970) terms, there is a "logological" relationship between Balinese metaphysics and linguistics, in that the nature of transcendent reality is expressed as an analogue of written symbols. These symbols stand for sounds that are successively "born" and "dying" in speech, while themselves remaining in "imperishable" (*aksara* 'not perishable') testimony to the eternal quality of divinity, cosmic order, truth, and so forth. . . . Possible logological patterns can be seen in the meanings of words like *nyutra* . . . and *sandhi* 'merging, becoming one'. Both are used extensively as metaphors for mystical transformation and are based on linguistic terms for sound assimilation.

Nyutra is based on the sounds of the language, but it takes off from there. It's done subtly, except by *panasar, kartala,* and other comic characters who exaggerate it for humorous effect. *Nyutra* does not involve pushing vowels for all they're worth, but often softening, tempering, or letting them ring (*ng* . . .) after the meaning is conveyed by clear enunciation. The face and mouth contours reflect the *nyutra*, but it's more internal; it must be to remain purposefully "vague." As the melody is developed, *nyutra* is employed even more subtly, with the mouth and lower jaw less active. Clear, distinct pitches and enunciation accompany less melodic development, more literal meaning and strident physical shaping. A long *u* is tempered into a kind of *uh* trailing into and then out of the nose. *Nyutra* practice involves a dynamic flow, a movement of resonance through the body expressed in subtle variations.

Nyutra suara contains within it *ilegan* 'melodic flow', but *ilegan nyutra* implies a particularly smooth contour. Another quality, *nyutra nyerod*, is to have *serodan* 'swirls of melody' within *nyutra*. *Tembang Adri* possesses abundant *nyutra*, partly because it is slow, but also because it is associated with the character of *galuh*, the ultrarefined and reflective princess. The actual sound quality alternates most often between throat and nasal cavities, and the chest for breathing, of course. The use of face and mouth is not to

---

3. An interesting link is provided by Chogyam Trungpa (Rinpoche), Tibetan Buddhist teacher (1973: 219): "*Tantra* is synonymous with *dharma*, the path . . . The word *tantra* means 'continuity.' It is like the thread which strings beads together. The thread is the path."

produce sound but is a result of the sound's process. But just to use transformations of nose and throat does not result in *nyutra suara*; *nyutra* exists only in the melodic context, especially in combination with *serodan*, hence *nyutra nyerod*, swirls of melody within the body.

Though Candri and I have given it much time, it is very difficult to categorically pinpoint the nuances of *nyutra suara*. It's not enough to say that *eeee* changes for a time into the upper palate, softening it; that *u* is pushed to the front of the mouth at times and softened to something like *uh*; or that the last vowel of *punya* is a Balinese version of *oh!* with an extreme nasal quality. The most beautiful and elusive quality of *nyutra*, which is so difficult to analyze, involves the *way* in which the melodic flow and vowel sound are totally but subtly unified expressively in an internal (physiological) and external (acoustical) way.

Sound cannot be too loud; it must be subtle. *Ilegan nyutra* can be an aspect of *nyutra nyerod*. As we go through *tembang Adri* and *Sinom lumbrah*, Candri sings a phrase with nasal transformations and *serodan*, but explains that this is not *nyutra suara*. Then she sings the phrase with it; the difference is subtle, but basically it is that the *nyutra* shapes the melody; the *nyutra* and *serodan*, swirl of melody, are as one. Another aspect of *nyutra suara* involves slow slides leading into *serodan*. Candri says that she often cannot really use the subtleties of *nyutra* suara in performance because of her "lack of skill" in combining it with dance and louder projection.

What others refer to as *gedong céngkok*, the late Pandé Madé Kenyir called *manyingén*, a kind of amorous "sweetening." His rendition of princess *galuh*'s *tembang Adri* agreed with Tempo's, with regard to the more demonstrative role of the mouth in shaping sound, in contrast with Bu Candri's subtle *nyutra suara*. This may reflect a male style, since Pak Kenyir's experience went back to the early part of the century, before female performers joined *arja*.

For Pak Tempo's *suara ngilik*, a slight rise in pitch in the high register such as the semitone between pitch *ndang* (6) and the upper-octave *nding* (1), one must bring resonance to the nose. To shape the *u* in *metu*, the tongue must carefully articulate the *t* touching the upper palate, gum, or teeth to distinguish the two syllables. Pak Tempo feels that the real beauty people find in *tembang* singing comes from the expression derived from movement of sound within the body. *Galuh*'s *tembang Adri* has the lyrics *kenyung manis* 'sweet smile', which characterizes the feeling, with singing more sweet and with mouth less open. He insists that the term *ilegan* was not used earlier, but *gedong céngkok* was used to express the unity of melody, and placement of sound, which again, are always intertwined with words, mood, and character.

For *panasar* and others, *i*, pronounced *eee*, may become *ay*, especially at the end of a phrase, and *a*, pronounced *ah*, may become *u*. This kind of weaving or oscillating back and forth between the two vowels "keeps the sound alive" as well as projecting the voice into the audience by keeping the resonance in the throat, not in the nose, as befits a *panasar* character. *Panasar* style also tends toward *aw-ah* in the mouth, throat, and jaw. *Ngengkuk* is a related melodic device sometimes used for drawing out a phrase with an accelerating series of "waves," such as the repeating pitches *ndung-ndéng-ndung-ndéng* or *ndung-ndang-ndung-ndang-ndung-ndang*, as in the word *beli* in CD selection 14 (fig. 2). With the last words of *panasar*'s *sendon*, *merdu aganti* 'sweet and refined', the melody is developed not on *merdu* but on *aga . . . nti*. Extending the *ah* is much more in keeping with his character than would be drawing out the *u*. However, comic use could be made by extending the *u* at the end of a word, such as *uu-ah-uu-ah-ee-ah-uu-ah-uu-ah-ee-uu*.

Phrasing can be intentionally "vague" to create "melodic movement without the feeling of movement," often by slow, gradual change, similar to a superlegato. "Melodic continuity" can be affected where the pitch jumps, even dramatically, as long as the internal flow is not cut off. Tempo pays great attention to whether a succession of tones should be "connected" or "separate." *Nyambung* 'continuity' is in part made effective by a rapid succession from note to note. Certain phrases have many jumps between pitches, creating a "bumpy melody." Momentum can overtake the shape and energy of a melodic phrase, expressed by terms like *useran*, as water circles down in a *swush* or whirlpool, and *nyimbang* 'to toss up'. In this rendering of *metu* (fig. 3), from *galuh*'s *tembang Adri*, on a different take from CD selection 4—hence a different phrase but similiar style—the series of pitches *ndang ndung ndéng ndung* (6 5 3 5) suggests a simple swirl and tossing up amidst melodic calm. While composing *tembang* in performance, the singer must link both the sounds and meanings of words with the melody without "going astray." The most common problem is when the flow of melody precedes the flow of meaning.

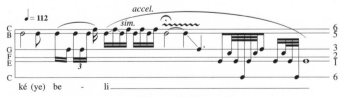

Figure 2. *Tembang Durma* with *ngengkuk* "waves."

Figure 3. *Adri* with *nyimbang* "tossing up."

In discussing *wirama kakawin*, the classical Old Javanese poetry, Pak Rembang, Pak Gerana, and Pak Naba[4] each present a different idea about the meaning of *reng*, most often interpreted as *getaran* 'vibrations' or 'resonance'. They find this definition insufficient, but they have difficulty finding another word for *reng*, agreeing though that the closest term might be *rasa* 'feeling'. It is the characteristic feeling of a particular *wirama* 'poetic meter with its associated melody', and so the *reng* of *wirama Aswalalita* can be contrasted with, say, *wirama Perititala*. With Pak Gerana's examples, it is a unified combination of melodic flow, shaping of words, vowels, placement of sound, and general sound quality. It's very moving to hear a quality expressed so completely and clearly, basically like Nyoman Candri's use of *nyutra nyerod* but a bit more bound to the particular style of each poetic-melodic form.

I have heard from many singers that *tembang macapat* uses more head and nose, the Middle Javanese poetic form *kidung* uses more throat, and *wirama* more chest and throat.[5]

Discussing laras

Pak Tempo does not generally use the term *lebeng* to describe semitones, but refers to each variety in a different way. He calls a high-register semitone rise *ngilik*, the meaning of which he gives as "water passing through a small hole, such as bamboo irrigation pipes." One example (from CD selection 17) is the tone (7) in between *ndang* (6) and high *nding* (1), approximately a quarter-tone above a D, sung at the *gongan* 'end of the phrase' of the *tandak* praising the king, *Dalem* (fig. 4). Or also, instead of *paméro*, he sometimes refers to *suara mirip* 'resembling the sound' as subtly transforming the sound of a word and pitch together.

---

4. Nyoman Rembang is an authority on *gambelan*, having taught at SMKI, the Indonesian High School for Traditional Performing Arts, in Bali, and is the author of numerous books and articles. The late Pak Gerana was a respected singer of *kakawin*, teaching at SMKI. Pak Naba is Pak Rembang's brother, and was a singer on the staff of RRI, performing all varieties of Balinese vocal music.

5. *Wibhawa*, the term most often used to describe the vocal quality characteristic of *wirama*, "implies a sound that is full, low-pitched, and reverberating, originating in the diaphragm" (Wallis, 1980).

Figure 4. *Tandak Dalem* with *ngilik*.

At the conservatories and elsewhere, one often hears that *tembang* (except for those in *sléndro* tuning), along with *sendon* and *tandak*, follow the tuning system of *laras pélog selisir* for *gambelan gong*, with the recognition of a good deal of variation from *gambelan* to *gambelan*, even within this general "system."

The example shown in figure 5 uses approximate Western tempered-pitch equivalents that do not correspond to any particular *gambelan*; for the *selisir gambelans*' corresponding intervals may vary from one to another by as much as a Western chromatic half-tone.

Based on comparison of numerous *gambelans*, Colin McPhee rendered a generalized *selisir* tuning of C♯, D, E, G♯, A (1966: 46). For ease of reading transcriptions, in this book I use the generalized standard provided by Madé Bandem (1992), E, F, G, B, C; in practice, the important musical factor is intervallic relationships rather than fixed pitch frequencies, with singers adjusting (transposing) their song (and the actual pitch equivalents of *nding*, *ndong*, and so on) to suit their own comfortable vocal range, unless they are bound to fixed *gambelan* pitches, which is often not the case.

McPhee (following A. J. Ellis and Jaap Kunst) suggests that *sléndro* tuning, the pentatonic scale used in *gendér wayang* and *tembang*, is distinct from *pélog* in that the intervals are generally more equidistant, each somewhat approximating 240 cents, the "ideal" interval of an equidistant scale (see glossary). But *sléndro* can vary widely from one *gendér* set to another, and within any individual *sléndro* tuning the intervals are of recognizably different size and character. Mantle Hood corroborates this view, that "in actual practice all gamelan sléndro tunings are non-equidistant" (1954: ch. 7 and 1966: 30). McPhee (1966: 51) even provides an example of a particular *gendér* that has two distinctly different intervals, 293 cents (close to a tempered minor third) and 195 cents (slightly less than a whole tone).

Figure 5. A Western chromatic approximation of a "generalized" *laras selisir*.

Figure 6. A Western chromatic approximation of a "generalized" *laras sléndro.*

McPhee's generalized chromatic approximation of *sléndro* is F♯, G♯, B, C♯, E, starting on the pitch *ndong* (2), as is the general practice. Bandem's, which I shall follow, is rendered as D, E, G, A, C (fig. 6). But in many vocal renditions of *sléndro*, the E *ndéng* is instead sung closer to an F (following *gambelan angklung* rather than *gendér wayang*, according to singers), creating a very different modal equilibrium, or what McPhee describes in another context as "a very different tonal atmosphere" (1966: 45).

I have heard the assertion that most deviations from the *selisir* standard are unconscious, undeliberate mistakes, arising from a lack of theoretical systematization. This view admits that there are some deliberate tonal shadings used, as in the upper-octave *nding* (1) of *tembang Adri*, flattened about a half-tone (100 cents), or the semitone slide up from the pitch *ndéng* (3) sometimes used in Punta's *tembang Durma* (CD selection 14), which Pak Rembang calls *palungut* or *ngelungut* 'sweetening', like *paméro* (fig. 7).

The use of *lebeng*, Pak Rembang says, is really something peculiar to the village of Singapadu and Pak Kredek's personal style, possibly influenced by the seldom heard seven-tone *gambelan luang.* Figure 8 suggests how Pak Kredek's *tekep lebeng* can be used to "weave" in and out of *tembang Pucung* (CD selection 1, translated in "*Aji nusup* 'lessons in penetration'") by means of the *paméro* (7), rendered here as a D.

One Balinese music scholar has suggested to me that the often shifting pitches of Gusti Windia's *panasar topéng*[6] might not be deliberate, but I assume otherwise. These *lebeng* phrases were intentional and shared in common by the major *topéng* performers, such as Nyoman Kakul and Ketut Rinda, who influenced everyone and were well versed in the various

6. Gusti Windia and his ensemble are generally referred to as *topéng* Carangsari, denoting their village and genre. They are especially popular for the *panasar* and *bondrés* characters, verbal humor, and circuitous plot deviations and embellishments.

Figure 7. *Durma* with *palungut* "sweetening."

Figure 8. *Tembang Pucung* with *lebeng*.

*tekep*s of *gambuh*.[7] And the fundamental point comes up concerning artists who are less analytical than others: an element that is not always consciously planned or analyzed is no less a part of a developed aesthetic. If one is dealing on the level of *rasa* and *masolah* characterization, one does not always isolate an individual factor, such as pitch variation, as something in itself.

Pak Rembang does not feel that a different *tekep* for each individual *tembang* or *wirama* is a consistent aesthetic. He feels that most performers do not fit their *tembang* singing to the *laras* 'tuning' of *gambelan gong* because they don't know how to, or at least are not aware of the aesthetic practice. But he believes that those who are good do. Even since the beginning of this combination of *gambelan gong* with *tembang*, during the 1930s *prémbon* era, there were those whose *tembang* fit with the *gambelan* and those whose *tembang* did not.

When I play them an audiotape that I made of Pak Tempo's singing, Pak Rembang and friends like Tempo's rendition of *Durma panasar* and think that his basic musical, tonal sense of *tandak Dalem* is good but that he fills in too much with *tandak*. (Anak Agung Rai Cebaang, an esteemed dancer of *topéng Dalem*, also told me that Pak Tempo's version on tape [now CD selection 17] is excessive—overzealous.) Singing should come in just before the *gong*, or *kempur*, and trail off just after. Indeed, in this rendition Pak Tempo was showing me all of the possibilities, rather than how he would sing within a given performance. In the actual performance tape of *Dalem*, they feel his voice is too low and deep for *tandak*, where the words and melody must rise above the *gambelan*. The ideal range is with the *kantilan* 'upper-octave metallophones'. Pak Naba says that he and others generally work off of the high *ndung* (5) pitch, and get higher up to the *ndang* (6), but can rarely use the still higher *nding* (1) of *gambelan gong kebiar*. Some *gambelan*s, such as that of Radio Républik Indonesia in Denpasar, are tuned a bit lower, giving a singer more freedom. Pak Rembang also says that ideally one should fit the tones in between *ngumbang* and *ngisep*,[8] the two tones of any given pitch, paired about seven cycles per sec-

---

7. See the melodic sketch of Pak Rinda's *sendon* in the "*Panasar*" chapter.

8. Each of the many-keyed metallophones in a *gambelan* ensemble is one of a pair (with a few exceptions, such as *selonding*). *Pangumbang*, literally "mason bee" or "hummer," is the lower-pitched of the pair. *Pangisep* 'sucker' is the higher-pitched. The acoustical beats resulting from the precise, synchronous striking of the matching keys of each instrument, are what gives Balinese *gambelan* its unique, shimmering quality. The acoustical spacing (*penyorog*) of *pangumbang* and *pangisep* varies from genre to genre, and according to the tastes of the *pandé krawang* 'bronze-smith' and his patrons. Generally, *gendér wayang* is six beats per second, *gong kebiar*, eight, *Semar Pagulingan*, seven. Some contemporary research (Alvin Lucier, personal communication, 1978) into the movement of acoustical beats in space confirms the accuracy of the Balinese seemingly "poetic" terms "hummer" and "sucker."

ond, or beats, apart. To favor one or the other would eventually create a clash. Of course, the range they prescribe is quite high, and most *juru tandak*, solo vocalists, and *panasars* cannot use it. They cite several singers able to use that high range, but their preference might reflect their regional (Badung) taste. Because *tandak* must be high in pitch and loud enough to rise above the sound of the *gambelan gong*, one cannot get into as many subtleties as one can with *arja's gaguntangan* ensemble, where the *suling* follows the singer-dancer.

Regardless of today's common institutional usage of the general terms *pélog* and *sléndro*, the venerated musician Madé Lebah still thinks of *pélog* as specifically referring to the seven-tone *saih pitu* system employed by *gambelan gambuh* and *gambelan luang*.[9] Otherwise, he refers to *tekep selisir* when speaking of *gambelan gong kebiar* or the five-tone *Semar Pagulingan*.

It is Nyoman Sumandhi's recollection[10] that the terms *pélog* and *sléndro* were not in common use in Bali until Pak Rembang introduced them at the Konservation Karawitan Indonesia Bali (KOKAR) in 1961, after he returned from studying and teaching in Java. And a recent manuscript written by STSI director Madé Bandem (1992) has suggested the general idea that *tembang macapat* does indeed reflect both five-tone and seven-tone *pélog* systems (with *paméro*), as well as two *sléndro* systems, following some variation (and there are many) of either the five-tone *gendér wayang* or four-tone *angklung*.[11] Wayan Dibia (1992: 182) also discussed *tembang arja* as employing seven-tone *pélog*, and the playful ambiguity between *pélog* amd *sléndro*. The question is, in what ways are individual *tekep* tunings still an expressive element in the creative rendering of *tembang* melodies in practice?

9. Personal communication, 1992. I Madé Lebah was Colin McPhee's chauffeur and a key musical informant. Since the 1930s he has been a highly regarded musician and teacher of *gong kebiar*, *Semar Pagulingan*, and *arja's gaguntangan* ensemble.

10. Personal communication, 1992. I Nyoman Sumandhi, *dalang*, musician, and dancer, is Director of Sekolah Menéngah Karawitan Indonesia (SMKI), the Indonesian High School for Traditional Performing Arts (formerly KOKAR) in Bali.

11. Dr. Madé Bandem, ethnomusicologist, dancer, and musician, is Director of Sekolah Tinggi Seni Indonesia (STSI), the Indonesian College of the Arts in Bali.

Tembang

❁

Tembang *terminology*

Tembang macapat are the songs used in *arja* and other performance genres such as *Basur*,[1] *topéng prémbon*,[2] and sparingly in *wayang*. The verb *nembang* means simply "to sing," but *tembang* generally refers to a specific poetic form called *sekar alit, sekar macapat,* or *pupuh.* Another general word for singing is *magending,* although *gending* by itself may also refer to an instrumental composition. Actually, *pupuh* means tune, or melody, and sometimes refers to *kidung,* another poetic form, *sekar madya* in Javanese terminology. Pedagogically, *pupuh* can also refer specifically to the poetic or melodic structure of a given *tembang.* Both *macapat* and *sekar alit* are originally Javanese terms and the poetic form is found in Javanese manuscripts dating from around 1550 (Wallis, 1979: 34). *Sekar,* literally "flower," refers to poetic meter as well as melodic form. *Alit, madya,* and *ageng* refer to small, medium, and large meters, the latter applied to *wirama kakawin.*

Geguritan are poems and stories set in the *pupuh* style, most often in either the common or refined Balinese language, but occasionally in classical *Kawi* or *Jawa Tengahan* 'Middle Javanese' (see p. 90 for the origins of *geguritan*). The "rules" of the poetic form, varying with each *tembang,* are most generally referred to as *padalingsa.*[3] *Guru wilang* commonly signifies the

---

1. A dance drama genre of intense romance and magic, named after the lead character, Basur. It is performed in *arja* style, but with its own versions of various *tembang,* both textually and sometimes melodically. With a transformation into the powerful witch sorceress Rangda, *Basur* is often considered a *tenget* 'highly spiritually charged' genre, and the combination of that with the element of thwarted love makes it an emotionally moving experience for Balinese audiences.

2. A popular form since the 1930s combining *topéng*'s mask male characters (performed by males) with nonmask *arja*-style characters performed by females.

3. I Gusti Bagus Sugriwa (1978: 3) has written that, in this poetic style, *pada* refers to the number of syllables in a line and *lingsa* to the particular variety of vowel sounds at the end of the lines. Others define *padalingsa* as the rule governing the number of lines in a given stanza.

Figure 9. *Pacaperiring* for *tembang Pangkur*.

number of syllables in each *carik* 'line', and often the number of lines in each *pada* 'stanza', as well. *Guru ding-dong* is the rule governing each *tembang*'s particular arrangement of final vowel sounds for each line. There are eleven commonly used *pupuh*, each with a general number of lines, number of syllables, and final vowel for each line. In Balinese pedagogy, *pupuh* are listed in the following manner, with the number referring to the number of syllables, in each line, and the vowel indicating the final vowel sound of that line:

Pucung 4–u, 8–u, 6–a, 8–i, 4–u, 8–a   6 lines

Ginada 8–a, 8–i, 8–a, 8–u, 8–a, 4–i, 8–a   7 lines

Sinom   8–a, 8–i, 8–a, 8–i, 7/8–i, 8–u, 7/8–a, 8–i, 4–u, 8–a   10 lines

Durma 12–a, 7/8–i, 6–a, 7/8–a, 8–i, 5–a, 7/8–i   7 lines

The term *macapat* derives from the fact that the poems are composed and read with an emphasis on groups of four syllables (*maca* 'to read', and *pat* 'four'; hence, "to be read in fours").

Within the parameters of *padalingsa*, there are varieties of each *pupuh*— refer to CD selection 10 for *condong*'s version of *Pangkur*, its first line shown in figure 9, in its skeletal form—each with its own characteristic melody. Some *geguritan* narratives and texts have their own melodic version of a *tembang*, and some *tembang* have both a *sléndro* and *pélog* variety. *Pacaperiring* (figure 9) is a syllabic style of reading with just the skeleton of the melody, most often used when one is reading to oneself without the need for extended melodic development. Even with *pacaperiring*, there is some variance from person to person with regard to pitches within each line, but the last pitch of each line is fixed (yet still manifests some deliberate exceptions in actual practice).

In any given *tembang*, each fourth syllable, *macapat*, may be pitch-set as

---

But most generally, it refers collectively to *guru wilang* 'counting' and *guru ding-dong*. Even as the terminology varies, the actual usage of vowel endings and syllables per line is flexible.

Figure 10. *Durma manis* 'sweet' (CD selection 3).

Figure 11. *Durma polos* 'less florid'.

well. If the line is long, often the second *macapat*, or eighth syllable, may also be pitch-set. If a line is being sung "sweetly" or the word is too long for tonal *macapat*, the principle is disregarded in favor of the word and melodic variation. In the refined prince's flowery version of *tembang Durma*, the melody can seem so carried away with pleasure as to be oblivious to even the final obligatory fixed pitch. Almost as an afterthought (but really part of the style), an appropriate last melodic flourish is added (even repeating the last syllable of text), landing finally on the fixed pitch. An example, shown in figures 10 and 11, is line 2, "*nguda manampokang*," from *Durma*, ending on *ndong* (2).

Several varieties of tembang context

Specific variations of *tembang* are commonly associated with particular moods and characters. However, within a dynamic interaction of characters and shifting moods, almost every *tembang* may take on a greater variety of qualities.

The regal themes of *tembang Sinom Wayah* may be sung by the *panasar topéng* preceding king *Dalem*'s entrance, for which the more elaborate *tandak* style is sung. *Arja*'s *limbur* uses *Sinom Wayah* or *Sinom Lawé* in lecturing the younger generation, and any character may sing it for giving advice. *Sinom Lawé* is sung by the *kartala* to describe the beauty of the kingdom. *Tembang Sinom lumbrah* is used for a romantic mood but also for bringing in or clarifying the story. *Mantri manis* uses it for coming through the curtain, as does the *limbur*, while the *condong* uses *Pangkur*. *Tembang Durma* can be angry, sad, sweet, instructive, or used for *angkat-angkatan* 'entrances and departures' (*pakaad* more specifically refers to a character's exit). It is Punta's "coming out" song, and also used by *mantri buduh*. *Tembang Adri* is used by the *galuh* for "coming out," with a mood of romance, desiring, wishing for the presence of her lover. *Dandang* may be *galuh*'s song, but it may also be used to deal with country, state, rule of law. Versions of *Ginanti* can be happy, silly, reflecting a climate of peace, or sad, even anguished. *Basung* uses text from *Arjuna Wiwaha*, and may be used dramatically by *mantri*, or another character, in a quiet forest. The role of *mantri manis* is also often associated with *tembang Sinom Wug Payangan*, happy and romantic, and *Semarandana*, sad and reflective.

Ginada can be sad and melodious, very sad with emotive, sliding phrases, or sweet for romance. For story development *Ginada* has a basic melodious style, and it can even be angry by growing emphatic and syllabic. It is commonly used for sung dialogue between *galuh* and *condong*.

There is an old version of *Adri* that refers to how the different divinities are present in the human body, referring to the various organs, their associated *betara* 'deity' and spiritual color. But it is easier for a *panasar* if the *galuh* sings the standard *tan pendah* lyrics rather than having him explain the more philosophical lyrics well.

Style: Shaping the melody with flexible laras 'tone series' and intonation

Balinese refer to high and low pitches as small and big, respectively. This reflects the physical characteristics of *gambelan* instruments, of which the size of a bronze key or *gong* correlates with its pitch. But the *gambelan* smiths I know are indeed aware that lower pitches are made up of longer vibrational periods (*getaran*), less frequent sound waves (*ombak*), and higher (frequency) pitches with shorter vibrational periods and more frequent waves. In any case, for the purpose of clarity, I shall keep to the terms high and low.

In contemporary systematized pedagogy, as discussed earlier, it has often been assumed that *tembang* follows a fixed set of pitches corresponding to *laras pélog selisir* or *laras sléndro* tunings, except in the case of specific, occasional *miring* 'slanted' or 'in-between tonal shadings'.[4] In *pagambuhan* (*gambelan gambuh*), the varieties of tunings reflect a formal system, with specific tunings and modal configurations being associated with particular dramatic characters. Outside of this context, however, the use of *paméro* may reflect an individual performer's style of expression. Often,

---

4. The original use of the term *paméro* is within the context of the *saih pitu* 'seven–tone tuning' used in *gambelan gambuh* and *gambelan luang*. They are secondary tones found in between *ndéng* (3) and *ndung* (5), or *ndang* (6) and *nding* (1). *Miring* is a less context-specific term applied to many varieties of tonal shading and bending.

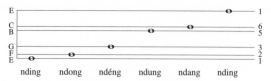

Figure 12. *Pélog selisir.*

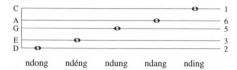

Figure 13. *Sléndro.*

performers will call these pitches *lebeng*, the name of one of the *saih pitu* seven-tone tunings. And sometimes, the use of *paméro* or *lebeng* does not really reflect character or situation specifically but just musical *kréasi* 'creation'. Using these semitones, a singer may playfully introduce a modal ambiguity, where listeners are not sure whether the *tembang* is in *sléndro* or *pélog*.

But in traditional practice, an even greater variety exists in an aesthetic that is not consciously systematized. One might even propose that many *tembang* have their own characteristic *tekep*, in the sense of either scalar arrangement or mode. Some versions vary from singer to singer, but most are shared. When one considers the actual practice of a variety of vocal *tekep*, or even the tunings within the realms of *laras selisir* and *sléndro*, as well as the selective use of *miring*, *paméro*, and an even greater preponderance of unnamed *kréasi*, it is clear that Balinese tembang tunings are much more complex than a fixed five- or even seven-tone conception of *pélog* and *sléndro* implies.

Again, an approximate and "generalized" *laras pélog selisir gong* and *sléndro* could be rendered as shown in figures 12 and 13. But, in the *pélog tembang Sinom lumbrah*, the "standard" upper-octave *nding* (1) is not sung at all. Instead, an "in-between" pitch is consistently sung in its place, either a whole or half chromatic pitch flatter than *nding*. The normal *nding* is "not pleasant enough" for the melodic context. From a Balinese perspective this is interesting in that there is no other *nding* in the *tembang* except this one. Candri also speaks of two varieties of *ndang* (6). In *tembang Mijil*, for example, a melody descending to the lower-octave *ndang* (6) may come very close to a B rather than a C, or a pitch wavering between the two. This B is still considered a *ndang*, rather than a *ndung* (5). The next phrase is likely to maintain this intonation of *ndang* (6), but it is not

Figure 14. *Punta's Durma* with sharp *ndang*.

maintained for the entire *tembang*, and a later phrase will contain the more common *ndang*. Candri confirms that *ndang* and *ndung* are often lower-pitched in the lower octave than in the higher one.

Punta's lower-octave *ndang* (6) is often a half-tone sharp, or wavering between a D♭ and the standard pitch, C. This imitates the airy, wavering, lower-octave *ndang* of the bamboo *suling*, so prominent in *arja*. For example, in figure 14, *déning*, the first word of one version of *Durma*, can be drawn out with a wavering sharp *ndang* (6).

In *tembang Sinom Wug Payangan*, *sléndro* tuning (CD selection 9), the higher- and lower-octave *ndings* (1) are often sung a half chromatic tone flat. Even in the most basic *pacapeiring* 'skeletal melody' version, the descending phrase of pitches *nding ndang ndung* (1 6 5) is compressed, being sung:

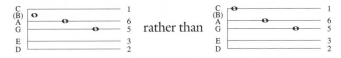

Upper-octave *nding* (1), as the *tembang*'s first pitch, figures prominently in the melody, with many phrases touching on *nding* from various strategies of melodic contour (fig. 15). But the oddest characteristic is that the pitches above the flat upper-octave *nding* (1) may sometimes conform to their

Figure 15. *Tembang Sinom Wug Payangan*.

Tembang / 43

intervallic relationships with the flat *nding*, not their lower-octave equivalents. It is as if the scale begins anew with the standard intervals as it ascends from this *nding*, B, to C♯ and D (or D♯), rather than treating the flat *nding* as a *paméro* 'false' tone and jumping up to a normal D and E. This may alternate, reflecting the mood of each phrase, with a just slightly flat *nding* leading to a normal *ndong* (2) and *ndéng* (3) phrase, B (quarter-tone sharp), D, E. This modal treatment creates a more open, bright mood in the upper octave and a reflective, subtle feeling as the melody descends. But then, in other phrases of this *tembang*, the normal *nding* (1) is restored, allowing even greater shifts in mood and quality by the contrast.

When *arja*'s *condong* character sings *tembang Pangkur* in *pélog selisir*, *ndéng* (3) varies between G♯ (half chromatic tone sharp) and A, what some would call "high *ndéngs*," and others, *paméro*. Again, many of the melodic phrases revolve around and play off of this *ndéng*, coming at it from various curves and twists. Two examples, shown in figure 16, are *pamuluné nyan-*

Figure 16. *Condong*'s *tembang Pangkur*.

dat gading 'her forehead golden yellow' from line 2 and *mangenah kukuné lantang* 'you can see her long fingernails' from line 4 (CD selection 10).

Galuh's tembang Adri (CD selection 4) has an upper-octave *nding* (1) that is consistently flattened a quarter or a half chromatic tone, as performed by Candri and other adept singers. This shading, slightly "narrowing" the interval even less than a normal *paméro*, suggests the delicacy and fragility of a shy princess. A normal "major third" interval to high *nding* (1) might be too brazen. I am told that this *paméro* is not necessary, that one can use a normal *nding*. But I'm not sure that I have ever heard Bu Candri use it, except when her STSI (College of the Arts) students repeatedly use the normal *nding* and she gradually adapts to their fixed notion. Or, if one's voice is weak or hoarse, one can avoid high *nding* altogether and develop the melody elsewhere.

In *tembang Semarandana* and the "sweet" *Durma*, if a pitch or slide is used in between *ndéng* (3) and *ndung* (5), it is sometimes called *lebeng*. An important pitch in this range is a half chromatic tone above *ndéng*, sometimes highlighted by approaching it with a slide from just below *ndung* or from one whole tone above *ndéng*. That slide works with the sad *Semarandana*. In *Durma*, Punta's *ndéng* often wavers around a pitch flattened by a half chromatic tone to add subtlety to the subtlety of the *paméro*, or in-between pitch. Rather than

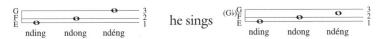

Tempo asserts that this is just "variation," not a distinct *tekep* 'tuning'. Similarly, the late Madé Kredek's Punta's ways of wavering both a half and a whole tone above *ndéng* (3) are sometimes simply referred to as *kréasi* 'creations', more in a personal expressive style than something as formal as *lebeng*.

A whole other realm of modal ambiguity and shading comes into play with a different version of *sléndro*. As mentioned earlier, in addition to the *sléndro* tuning for *gendér wayang* is the *sléndro saih angklung*, often described as the same *sléndro*, but without the *ndong*, rendering it a four-tone scale (*gambelan kembang kirang* 'lacking a flower'). There are many different versions of four-tone *sléndro*, and even within any given classification, an endless variety of tunings from village to village.[5] CD selection 12 is an example of the unusual genre, five-tone *angklung*, mostly found in North Bali. Uncommon as it is, the fifth pitch makes it resemble the vocal version of *saih angklung*.

5. McPhee (1964: 53–54) provides analysis of a wide range of *gambelan angklung* tunings.

In the singing of *tembang*, the scale is never limited to the four pitches of the common *gambelan angklung*, and the *ndong* is used regularly. One significant aspect of *angklung*'s *sléndro* is that the scale begins on *ndéng* (3)—but this is a *ndéng* so sharp that in relation to the next ascending pitches, *ndung* (5) and *ndang* (6), the series can sound like another *sléndro*'s *nding ndong ndéng* (1 2 3). The two varieties of *sléndro* are often interchangeable, and singers regularly transpose pitch names from one *sléndro* to another, with subtle differences between them. Since the *tembang* tradition is not based on fixed-pitch instruments, singers are free to create a fluid, shifting sense of mode, where a given pitch can be known by *ndéng* or *nding*, depending on one's preference at a given moment.

Ginada lumbrah, because it is normally based on *saih sléndro angklung*, uses this *ndéng* (3), which is generally a half chromatic pitch sharper than the *ndéng* of *sléndro gendér wayang*. Rather than a progression from *ndong* (2) being:

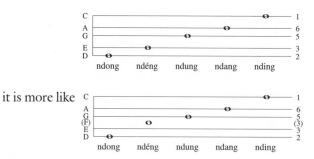

(Again, even though the normal instrumental *saih angklung* has no *ndong* (2), the sung *tembang* version includes *ndong*).

As with many versions of *tembang* in *sléndro* (and in the *condong*'s *tembang Pangkur*, in *pélog*), a sequence of intervals that might be heard as *nding* (1), *ndong* (2), *ndéng* (3), is really intended as *ndéng* (3), *ndung* (5), *ndang* (6), more in keeping with the tuning of *gambelan angklung*. (In other renditions, the reverse may also be true.) *Ginada lumbrah* uses two kinds of *ndangs* alternately, the most common one being something like a chromatic minor third and the other a major third from this "high" *ndéng* (3). The "higher *ndang*" (A) is used for more uplifting, romantic moods, the other for the introspective or sad qualities associated with *Ginada*. As with other *tembang*, the intonation can shift from phrase to phrase, expressing ambiguity and subtle shifts of mood, often reflected in the lyrics as well as in the first and last lines of *Ginada lumbrah* (fig. 17) and CD selection 11 (see CD notes for lyrics).

Figure 17. *Tembang Ginada lumbrah* with alternate *ndang*s.

For a sad mood, upper-octave *nding* (1) may be flattened, if it is being approached from below. Rather than *ndung ndang nding* (5 6 1) being:

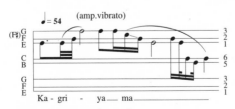

In this mood, the descent from the B *nding* is done with a gradual, melancholy slide, sometimes called *luk* 'curve' or 'bend'.

A completely different version, the *pélog Ginada Éman Éman* (fig. 18), is often sung for extremely lovesick or heartbroken states. This *tembang* can use a low *ndéng* (3), altering 1 2 3 from E, F, G to E, F, F♯ within the same breath.

Nyoman Candri's *tembang Pucung* using *lebeng* has a *pacaperiring* form that differs from normal *Pucung*, even using different tones at the end of some lines such as line 3, ending with *masui* (fig. 19 and 20). She explains that one cannot bring *tekep lebeng* into *Pucung* and have it come from the usual tones in a musical way. The rules may give way to peculiarities of mood and melodic context. And one line following another must re-

Figure 18. *Ginada Éman Éman.*

Figure 19. Common *Pucung selisir*.

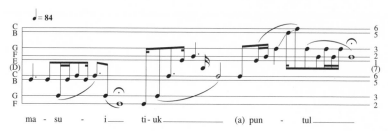

Figure 20. *Lebeng* version (on CD selection #1).

flect the first line's choice of ending, however peculiar, so they are "companions" not just for the first word, but for the whole line.

In another example of playful ambiguity, *tembang Sinom Cecantuman*, or *Cecantungan*, sounds to Balinese listeners as if *laras selisir* is being interwoven with *tekep lebeng*, although in actuality its true distinction is a resemblance to the unusual *tekep tembung* tuning, with a flat *ndung* (5) and unusual phrasing of intervals. When one hears the descending phrase approximating C, B, G, F, it may sound like *ndang* (6), *ndung* (5), *ndéng* (3), *ndong* (2). But in this *Sinom*, that phrase is really *ndong* (2), *nding* (1), *ndang* (6), *ndung* (5).

As discussed in an earlier context, the traditional *arja gaguntangan* ensemble, where the only melodic instrument is the *suling*, allows more freedom to transpose. The *suling* player has several differently tuned flutes, and he adapts to the range of each singer, so the actual pitch frequencies of a scale are relative. With *gambelan gong*, the intonation of a vocal *nding* must correspond to the *nding* pitch of the *iringan* 'accompaniment'; but in *gaguntangan*, the *suling* player will shape tones to adapt to the singer's *ndong*, *nding* range and intonation. CD selection 4 evidences this close relationship, while selection 15 shows how, perhaps more in rehearsals, tonalities can contrast sharply between *suling* and singer. This clash of tonalities is not altogether rare in instrumental ensembles such as *gambelan gong* or *angklung*, where *suling* can sound quite out of tune with the precisely tuned bronze metallophones.

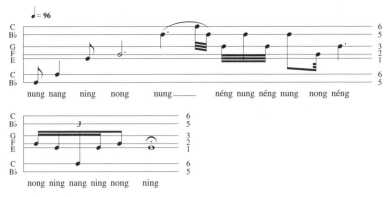

Figure 21. *Sinom Cecantungan* with *low ndung*.

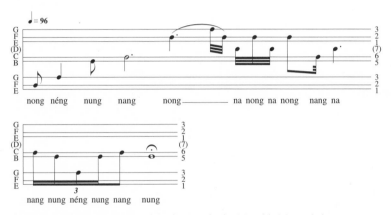

Figure 22. *Sinom Cecantungan* heard as standard *selisir* with *lebeng* pitch.

In any case, *Sinom Cecantungan*'s intervallic relationship of the flat *ndung* (5) to the other pitches, especially *ndéng* (3)—a chromatic interval of a minor third instead of a major third—and the *ndung* (5) to *ndang* (6)—an interval of a chromatic near-major second—makes it sound like a *paméro* (7) vocalized as *na* within that different modal configuration. Figures 21 and 22 offer a glimpse of a melodic phrase, accompanied by the two different ways of hearing it (CD selection 13).

When this *tembang* is adapted to *tandak* or *sendon* with *gambelan gong*, the pitches are indeed transposed. The intervallic series *ndong* (2), *nding* (1), *ndang* (6), *ndung* (5), becomes 6 5 3 2. With the *ndéng* (3) now heard as the in-between pitch, *paméro* (7), a genuine second *tekep* 'modal configuration' is used to weave in and out, sometimes joining, sometimes departing from the *tekep* of the *gambelan*, but referring back to the basic pitches.

Tembang / 49

As long as one keeps referring back to certain *gambelan* pitches, one is said to be "following the *gambelan* pitches," even though the vocal *lagu* melody is in a different *tekep*.

In *arja*, what sounds like weaving into and out of *tekep lebeng* is used romantically when *mantri manis* is walking with someone in the woods or garden, with a stream here, statues there, trees all around, a beautiful setting, and as he gazes around, he comments on the scene. The feeling of changing *tekep* back and forth dramatically reflects the quality of attentiveness, reflection, impulsiveness, and spontaneity of the somewhat "wild" context.

Ilegan, *shaping the melody*

Bu Candri asks me to sing Pak Tempo's version of *Durma* Punta, and as we sing through it repeatedly, she gets into Punta's voice and elaborates, subtilizes, criticizes, and augments the melody. She has me develop melodic variations on my own, while she analyzes whether or not it is an appropriate variation on the form, offering various alternate melodies for different phrases. She suggests an alternative to the normal intonation beginning with the first word. The *ndong* (2) is repeatedly sharp until the very last melodic flutter at the end of the breath, when it returns to the normal pitch (fig. 23 and CD selection 14).

As I sing certain lines she will say, *sudah nembang* 'that's *tembang*-singing', indicating a certain grace and departure from the *pokok* structure. She uses this expression with her own renditions as well; an unadorned version may be just *Ginada*, but a fully melodic version is *Ginada nembang*. When *tembang* are free of *macapat* phrasing, the meaning of the words can be made more clear and emotive. During dramatic characters' initial *tembang* (*papeson*), however, the elaborate play with melody and shaping of vowel sounds may completely obscure the actual words. Once their *tembang* connect directly with the drama at hand, performers are more careful to balance sound, melody, and meaning. If the first word or words of a *tembang* line are two or three syllables, the melody can be developed there. The fourth syllable may be sung quickly, as part of the next phrase, to balance out the

Figure 23. Punta's *Durma* with sharp *ndong*.

time spent on the first part of the line, or because it's a prefix, such as *mang*. In *makelap mangalap*, *mang* is the fourth syllable, but in *arja* performance, the drawn-out or melodically elaborated syllables are most often the first, third, and sixth. The fourth syllable may even be dropped altogether, changing the word to *ngalap*, stressing the *lap*. CD selection 10 reflects a bit of the reading style, with a slight pause on *mang*.

While *macapat* phrasing may remain a reference point, the singer may create a balance with a word occurring later in a line by instinctively drawing out the melody that precedes it. Figure 24 shows melodic development on the fourth and eighth syllables, as sung on CD selection 13. But in *arja* performance, *bi* and *lang* would be elaborated and *ngi* grouped syllabically with the other syllables of *ngilehin*. A singer may draw the fourth syllable out a bit, not pausing or elaborating so much as idling, saving the greater development for the end of the line (figure 25 and CD selection 3). Angry verses will disregard any pause around the fourth syllable. Figure 26 gives a glimpse of the same line from *Durma*, but angry this time. Just as *macapat* is not really adhered to as a rule in performance, the set tone marking the four-syllable phrase may be flexible or disregarded altogether, both in performance and reading.

Although some *arja* performers do not place any great importance or weight on the fourth syllable, *macapat*, of a line, Candri uses *macapat* phrasing for beginning students. Her children's *arja* ensemble even phrases their *tembang* in *macapat* within the performance context. The advantage of this is that students can concentrate on melody and voice quality without having to think about word phrasings and meanings, which is

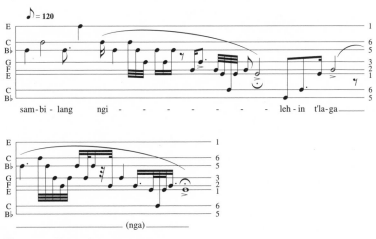

Figure 24. *Sinom Cecantungan.*

Figure 25. *Durma manis.*

considered the next step. When one finally begins singing in performance style, free of *macapat*, the meaning of the words, as is to be expected, is more clear and emotive. Even then, fourth-syllable phrasing is used stylistically for specific characters and moods.

Madé Sija, on the other hand, thinks the only place for *macapat* phrasing is in *mabasan* (poetry readings emphasizing translation) or *mamaca geguritan* (reading the narrative verses while sitting); *macapat* is not even used in teaching children *arja*. He elaborates different ways of singing *tembang*, according to mood, situation, and character. *Mantri* phrases *tembang* syllables in twos: *yan sang . . . nata. Limbur* phrases in fours. *Mantri*'s phrasing in twos is in keeping with the sense of *dharma*, considering things carefully, little by little. *Limbur* is more didactic and persistent, a forceful mother set on persuasion.

Tempo's primary concern with word phrasing is to avoid obstructing

Figure 26. *Durma.* "Harsh, angry questions confronting the messenger."

Panji, *gambuh*'s prototype of refined male characterization, performed by Ida Bagus Nyoman Ceta of Batuan (1972).

the words, even when using elaborate melodic phrasing. *Mantri*'s *yan sa . . . ng nata* is only acceptable if *nata* is included in the same breath; even then, Candri's version is a bit obstructive, but acceptable. *Galuh*'s phrasing is very *polos* 'simple', and vowel-shaping is subtle. A princess who is really beautiful doesn't have to be garish; she says what is true and necessary, straightforward, and that is enough, she need not overstate things. There is an older, "truly authentic" version of *galuh*'s *Ginada*, which is not used anymore in performance. It was associated with the *gaguntangan* ensemble and is distinctive in the use of sliding tones and high register, not so much rolling up and down or swirls of melody.

Generally, the refined *mantri* will create flowery melodies almost anywhere in the phrase, following melodic and language sense, still gravitating toward the fourth syllable. *Limbur* elaborates less than he does, tending to sing phrases in the range of eight syllables, though not counted strictly. It's basically so that her point is gotten across before she elaborates melodically, having time for politeness or play. The meaning of her words is primary, though there is more blatant shaping of vowels than with *mantri* or *galuh*.

Some performers have the *mantri buduh* 'crazy prince' phrasing in all different ways and never holding to any one melodic style. His role is difficult, because he must alternate between Javanese and Chinese singing style, using different variations of *gedong céngkok*. But the *mantri buduh* also phrases words emphatically, in groups of eight syllables, when practical. As with the *limbur*, he is too emphatic to pause on an early word to sweeten the sound and message, and he gets to his point before elaborating at the end of a line or phrase. Of course, if either character has a contextual reason for putting on the charm, he'll elaborate more often within the phrase, still maintaining his emphatic pulse. And conversely, even a *manis* character needing to come quickly to the point will leave out melodic flowering, *kembangan ilegan*, until the completion of an idea or line—if angry, urgent, or otherwise emphatic, or just in a hurry to leave—simplifying his *tembang* with the barest, unadorned *pacaperiring* melody.

In the mood for motherly advice, the *limbur* might sing *tembang Pucung*'s lyrics, *Bibi anu* (see "*Aji nusup*: lessons in penetration"), to the *galuh*. Here she could use the *pélog* version, but the *sléndro* tuning is most often used for the *limbur*'s didactic instructions or tender admonitions.

Candri speaks of three versions of *Ginada lumbrah*, each of which, in quality and melody, expresses a different emotional state, though the basic melodic form remains the same. More elaborate variations are used for a romantic quality, while the *ilegan* 'melodic flow' for sad moods is quite simple. While the really sad quality is expressed with an even lesser degree of "bending and curving" of the melody, those variations are replaced by slow, microtonal slides and shadings.

The vocal technique for extremely sad states involves taking a quick, strong breath and storing it high in the chest, tightly. The sound produced is quivering, breathy, and the fluctuating but narrow melodic range stays within the gestural form of the emotion, almost like a sigh, or weeping (and also, if one looks into the glare of the lights, that encourages watery eyes). Closely aligned with emotion, but in a stylized way, it is somewhere in between the language of naturalistic expression and "musical language." This kind of phrasing is just on the verge of being pure gestural language, where the emotion is not explicitly "expressed"—as weeping, for instance—but is given the distancing of melodic stylization.

This distancing allows the space for a bit of air to enter, and us to take a breath or gasp. Gesture takes on the quality of a "where," rather than a "what," leaving us with a penetrable area of focus, rather than an "emotional property" to view. A natural tendency to refer to the melodic range as narrow really ignores the scope of the more subtle features. Broad can be limited, and narrow can be extravagant. Each measuring stick (if one desires one at all) must be designed anew for each thing to be measured;

then it might show the internal dynamics, as opposed to comparing the peripheral.

Composing Lyrics

When Candri asks which lyrics I would like to use for learning *Sinom Cecantuman*, I suggest we use whatever a *mantri manis* might sing while walking in the woods or garden, observing the trees and flowers (as she already indicated as appropriate for that *tembang*). She answers, "Oh, but I just compose that in performance according to what the *mantri* is seeing and what's happening in the story at that moment with the *panasar* or *galuh*."

I say, "If you really compose it that way, why don't you just do it now, so we have words to work with. Just imagine you are in the midst of a story." She is surprised at the idea of extemporaneous composing outside of the performance context, but laughs, and enjoys the new challenge once we discuss it.

If one is dealing with a story that is found in a *geguritan* text, one has to have memorized actual lines, images, discussions, and use of *geguritan* poetry. This requires a great deal of study, since performers often show up to perform and are told the evening's story right before going on. If the story is from *geguritan*, the organizer should not have to spend any time explaining plot, since it's already common knowledge. He just mentions the particular section of the story that he has in mind, and it takes shape in performance.

If, however, the story is not taken directly from a specific written text, but created anew—using some basic thematic material from *Panji* stories, for instance—only the basic plot is outlined beforehand, and the performers go out and compose their lines then and there. Still, the basic requirement is that the number of syllables to each line and the concluding vowel and pitch of each line should match the particular melodic line of the *tembang*. The *tembang* form, set syllables and vowels, serves as a focal point, pressure point, where certain attention is sent in order to free, release, the creative, flowing process of composition. The opening lines, *tembang papeson* in *arja*, or *sendon* in *topéng*, are set in strong poetic imagery, and from time to time within the story, already existing lines are quoted for *selingén* 'comparisons,' or *carangan* 'branching out'. So, there is still a balance between composing and free-associative recitation of existing verse. It is often for specific actions that improvised lines are appropriate, though one may also quote from a literary source. One may take a line from a *kakawin* poem to express an idea or clarify an action, translating or paraphrasing it from classical *Kawi* to *basa tembang* 'the language of *tembang*', Balinese.

A performer may take an entire *pada* 'stanza' and compress the relevant images for the situation into two *bait* 'lines', paraphrasing a bit to make it flow. The number of syllables can be one or two off. But each actor must be able to recognize the *tembang* from one line and answer with the next successive line, in conversation. In a casual situation within the drama, the words may be spontaneous, composed according to the feeling of the moment. But if a king is giving instructions to his son, lines would be quoted, to emphasize formality and tradition. So, something akin to a theatrical *haiku* tradition is being practiced here, built on cumulative experience (personal and artistic) and *perkembangan*. Candri uses her own personal experience of romance, anger, nature, to imagine the scene and create within it. The study of texts (Candri prefers learning from *tembang* directly rather than from texts) is a vehicle toward the goal of creating freely: resources built up, not for use in their entirety, or even directly, but for incorporation within an improvised style. The process of "composing" each *tembang* must have a smooth, spontaneous quality, as with performing and improvising a story. As Candri tells her students, the words have to be memorized by heart so that their recall becomes "unconscious."

If a performer begins with the second line of *tembang Sinom*, the other performers should recognize it and continue composing on the theme, often following the structure of *Sinom* line by line. When another performer comes in with an answer or elaboration, it can be a different *tembang* altogether, in dialogue, to indicate a very different perspective on a situation, or a change of mood or action. The first performer should follow into the new *tembang*, even if still in the previous mood, just adapting the new *tembang* to the previous mood. One may stay in the previous *tembang*, but it's not as good. In an exchange between the lovers, the refined prince may be trying to cheer up a sulking or weeping princess. The dramatic progression may lead from the *galuh*'s sad *Semarandana* to *mantri*'s sweet *Durma* to *galuh*'s sad *Durma*, back to *mantri*'s sweet *Durma*, resolving in agreement with *galuh*'s sweet *Durma*.

If two characters such as *mantri* and Punta are having a discussion, generally *mantri* sings one or two lines, Punta translates, then answers by singing the next one or two lines, translates those, and then the *mantri* answers again.

Although specific *tembang* are considered to be most appropriate for given moods and characters, a good performer should be able to express any mood in a given *tembang*. The flow of dialogue, melody, mood, and expression from one character to another in stylized stages is a refined and highly prized skill amongst *arja* performers.

Masolah

the *désa kala patra* of spirit

❋

Masolah is the kinesthetic and spiritual *désa kala patra* of a character. It may be translated simply as "characterization" or used in everyday Balinese conversation to mean "to perform." Amongst *dalang*s, it can refer to the movement or dance of a shadow puppet. But, *masolah* in its fullest meaning implies the inherent *taksu* 'spiritual energy' that integrates the state of a performer with the physical form of his own body, and/or that of a mask or puppet. As such, for many performers it involves no less than momentarily merging *buana alit* 'microcosmos' and *buana agung* 'macrocosmos'.

Masolah characterization is directly based upon kinetic (mask, puppet) and physiological (vocal placement) conditions, as well as spatial (*wayang* screen, dancer's gaze) and kinesthetic (inner force, outer restraint) sense. The qualities expressed are in some sense universal, objective qualities of human and other conditions. Characterization inherently possesses a toning and conditioning of the body from which sound and movement take shape. In Balinese performance theory and practice, macro- (world) and micro- (body) dramatic characteristics are all unified in a systematized but intuitive manner. The tight bond that links the macro and micro realms, like an aesthetic rendering of the very energy of matter, literally grips one by the guts and psyche simultaneously.

At the core of Balinese vocal characterization are the four *panakawan*, or *parekan* 'court retainers' of *wayang* shadow theater and the *wayang wong* mask dance drama. They are Twalén, also called Malén; Werdah or Merdah; Délem and Sangut. In one way, they function as comic servants or attendants to the principal royal characters, providing an earthy perspective on the drama's spiritual and philosophical themes, often spicing up

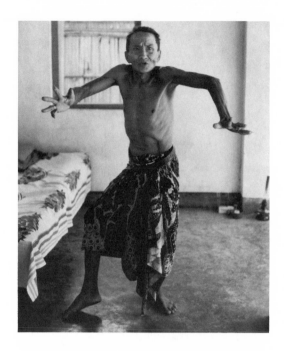

Pandé Madé Kenyir teaching *jauk manis* in Singapadu (1981).

highly charged arguments, tender love scenes, or esoteric mystical discussions with ribald humor and parody. While serving as advisors to the principals, they also translate and interpret those other characters' flowery, classical, *Kawi* discussions for the benefit of the audience.

The *panakawan* provide a bridge between the worlds of the *kawi* 'poet' and that of the contemporary audience, bringing in local gossip, critiques of a nearby coffee stall, or discussion of the government's family-planning program. Yet in another way, the *panakawan* are considered to be the most *sakti* 'sacred, magically powerful' of all the characters in the *wayang*, most related to Balinese ancestors and personification of sacredness.

In *wayang parwa*, episodes from the *Mahabharata*, Twalén, and Werdah are on the side of the Pandawa clan, while Délem and Sangut are with the Korawa clan. In the *Ramayana* the first two are with Rama and the *wanara* monkey army, while Sangut and Délem are with Rawana. In other words, Twalén and Merdah occupy the side of the protagonists, the right, while the other two occupy the side of the often monstrous antagonists, that of the left.

There is much discussion regarding a different origin of the *panakawan* from that of the other characters of the *wayang*, who inhabit the distant world of India's *Mahabharata* and *Ramayana*, with which Balinese people only partly indentify. It has been suggested that the *panakawan* may belong to indigenous ancestral rites predating the assimilation of the Indian epics. I Gusti Bagus Sugriwa (1963: 2) has written that the characters Semar, Bagong, Garéng, Petruk, and Dawala, Cepot, and others were already present in a pre-Hindu *wayang* tradition. The first four of these are the Javanese versions of the four Balinese *panakawan*.

Another common term for the *panakawan* is *panasar*, from the root *dasar* 'base, support'. This could merely refer to their omnipresent and prominent role in the *wayang*, regardless of the particular episode enacted by the *dalang*. But another interpretation relates the word *panasar* to *dasaran* 'persons often entered by spirits during ceremonies honoring the ancestors' (Panitia Penyusun Kamus Bali 1979: 146). This is one sense in which the *dalang* is said to make contact with ancestors via the medium of the *wayang* puppets. A common origin is often suggested for the words *déwa hyang*, both of which designate divinity—drop the *dé* and *h* and you have *wayang*.

> Twalén: seems as if he's stupid, but understands everything going on
>
> Merdah: thinks he understands and can explain everything, *but* misunderstands
>
> Délem: with wide-open eyes, thinks he's alert and sees everything around him, *but* doesn't see anything for what it is
>
> Sangut: eyes partly closed *but* sees more than Délem

According to *dalang* Madé Sija, Sangut is shrewd, honest, and cannot be deceived by trickery. His movement does not have to be funny; he is so funny naturally, the character and face, that whatever he does is funny; he doesn't have to make it so. Délem is also naturally funny, but he makes it even more extreme. The strongest quality of Délem is boastfulness and conceit. Twalén also can make things funny, and always likes to philosophize. Merdah, like Sangut, has a firm, resolute attitude and is stubborn. But he can't be funny, especially if he tries; he's too straightforward, although in the end, that's funny too.

According to *dalang* Nyoman Rajeg,[1] Délem's voice is shaped by the lips, with open mouth, but stiff, as if the inner lips are stuffed with chewing tobacco. Sangut's tongue is stiff and short. He speaks as if dumbfounded, his words resolute or slow, stuttering as an old person might do. Twalén's lower lip hangs down and juts out. His sound is in his stomach,

---

1. Nyoman Rajeg, also known as *Dalang* Tunjuk 'the *dalang* of Tunjuk village', has continued to perform regularly into his seventies, as well as teaching *wayang* at KOKAR, the conservatory in Denpasar (now SMKI). He is a respected philosopher of *wayang* and raconteur.

Wayang wong's Twalén in the village of Mas (1992).

an inner sound, "throat closed." The voice is described in different ways, as the texture of a scream but moderate or actually quiet, hot or hoarse. The "genuine" subtly hoarse voice for Twalén is too quiet to use in *wayang* performances, so in order to make his words understood, the *dalang* must "compromise." Merdah's teeth shape his voice, being prominently displayed.

Other *dalang*s say that Délem's speech is shaped by the middle of his tongue. Both *Sangut* and *Merdah*'s voices are sometimes described as nasal. Other *dalang*s say Twalén is *bisah*, his speech shaped by the base of the tongue.

*Dalang*s find basic guidance for vocal characterization in the *Dharma Pawayangan* text.[2] This guidance is followed in performance as well as personal study, a key to characterization as well as vocal technique. The *dalang*'s voice comes from each character, and each character is said to come from a specific part of the body. The ritual formulas quietly recited by the *dalang* at the beginning of each performance include actual mention of each character and where his voice comes from. After this, it be-

2. *Dharma Pawayangan* is the primary metaphysical treatise on *wayang*, generally considered an essential reference for the *dalang*. See Hooykaas (1973).

comes unconscious, just part of the state of performance (the *wayang* characters take over). The "*dalang*'s voice," *kawi suara*, is used for narration and at moments when not speaking as any character within the story. *Kawi suara* conjures up the transcendent, mystical world of the *wayang* and sets the scene for the action to follow.

In *wayang*, "the shadow screen is one single body." (At the same time, the screen becomes the sky, and the banana tree trunk in which the puppets are stuck becomes the earth.) Once the shadow puppet is in the *dalang*'s grip, his hands and arms serve as a connector, a lightning rod, through which the puppet's character, voice, and spiritual life-force, *taksu*, enter the *dalang*. In a sense, he serves as a medium. Nobody is speaking for the character; he speaks for himself in his own voice and language. *Dalang* and puppet become as one while the character is speaking or moving.

Tabuh suara, the rhythm and melodic contour of every sentence and spoken phrase, is prescribed in both the stylized *palawakya* prose *Kawi* as well as the *panakawan*'s common Balinese speaking. The *dalang* gives each phrase an inflection and overall shape based on formal linguistic style as well as on the particular rhythms and cadences of a character. Even each character's laugh has its own distinctive rhythm and timbre. Merdah's laugh, for example, is a more percussive and dental *ha-hahaha-haha-haha*.

Séndratari, a dance drama form evolved in the 1960s, has the *dalang* sitting away from the action with a microphone, either to the side of the dance drama, with the *gambelan*, or "backstage." He narrates, commenting on the scene from a distance, and, taking on myriad voices, speaks for each character being danced and mimed by a large company of performers. But the *dalang* does not attain that direct link with the characters in the same sense as with *wayang*. "Speaking for" the characters from a distance creates a less responsive alienation effect, and is different from "speaking in the characters' true voices," which enables him to *menjiwai* 'transmit spirit' through the character. And while the *panasar topéng* is said to *menjiwai* a king or prime minister being danced by another performer, it's one on one, not a whole cast of characters. But more importantly, the *dalang* in *séndratari* does not have the *taksu* of a mask or puppet with which to interact.

Problematic situations arise in other *padalangan* contexts. *Wayang*

Tantri, a form recently being experimented with, presents a challenge in performing animal characters.[3] How, some ask, can the *dalang* carry on dialogue, speaking "in the characters' true voices?" He doesn't; he may speak in Indonesian, Balinese, or even English, but it's not intended to be the voice of the animal. But in *wayang* the idea has been that each character really must speak for himself, with no distance between *dalang* and puppet.

In *wayang gambuh*, the *dalang* is joined by another singer who adds the musical modes associated with *gambuh*'s sixteenth-century *Malat* sources. Nyoman Rembang remembers that in *wayang gambuh* of old, often as many as four *juru tandak* joined the *dalang*. Not currently being performed at all, a *wayang gambuh* project was commissioned by the Balinese Arts Council, Listibiya. Wayan Nartha, who was commissioned as the *dalang* and puppet maker, articulates a problem here with regard to characterization. The *dalang* is in direct contact with the puppets, but the voice of the additional singer or singers is a distraction, disturbing the integrity of the dramatic universe as expressed through *kawi suara* and the all-encompassing voice of the *dalang*.

In the 1970s, Listibiya also initiated an experiment by commissioning the *dalang* Madé Sija to develop a new genre called *wayang arja*. He made all new *wayang* puppets rather than using *Mahabharata* characters and trying to adapt them to the *arja* chronicles of Daha, Koripan. "How can anything such as the character of a puppet really enter the hearts of the audience if they're seeing an Arjuna puppet as *mantri* and Twalén as Punta? They're seeing, but not believing." He used *arja*'s traditional *gaguntangan* ensemble, and followed the rules of *tembang* characterization, such as having the refined prince and princess, *mantri* and *galuh*, singing and not speaking. But *wayang arja* was a short-lived experiment, since it was too difficult to sing *tembang* and maintain the *dalang*'s style. Other *dalang*s have since experimented with the idea, but the obstacles have similarly discouraged them from continued involvement in the genre. One would have to be amazingly dexterous to intermingle the "sweet voice" of *tembang* and the coarse *suara ncah* of the *dalang*.

A well-made *tapel* or carved wood mask, has its own *taksu* and an inherent way of behaving, moving, or speaking. However, some *topéng* performers

---

3. *Tantri* is the Javanese version of the Hindu *Pancatantra*, which is a variant of the "Thousand and One Nights" theme. *Tantri* stories include many animals, although the main contemporary performance context for *Tantri* themes is *gambuh* dance drama, which does not include a great many animal characters. The recent idea for using *Tantri* stories for *wayang* was explained to me by *dalang* Wayan Wija, its main innovator, as an attempt to use animal characters to interest young people in *wayang* and its moral and ethical lessons.

use *kirta basa* etymology to say that a *tapel* is just a piece of wood, *kayu*, and cannot come to life without *kayun* 'desire, will, thought' provided by the performer's force and concentration. That play on words aside, all agree that any good mask has its own *jiwa* 'spirit'. A mask has its own sense of place, movement, time, and character, which can adapt only with an inner and outer technique, an understanding of the kinesthetic unities inherent in *désa kala patra*.

Where the particular piece of *pulé* wood comes from may determine the *taksu* of a mask. A tree felled by lightning, within or just outside a *pura dalem* 'temple of the dead', might be saved for a sacred Rangda or barong mask. Location in or nearby other temples, by a river or other place of spiritual significance, is also prized. Masks receive regular offerings, some as performance masks and others as *déwa* 'deities', as sacred entities kept within the temple but not danced. Spiritual energy within a mask is taken for granted, and even if not especially *tenget* 'magically charged', ritual care and deference are always due a mask.

In *topéng*, the half-masked *panasar*s *menjiwai* 'speak for' and 'transmit spirit' into principal mask characters, as a *dalang* does with puppets. When a character is being spoken for, he or she is coming from some other place or state, and his or her "voice" is distanced. *Palawakya*, the classical *Kawi* prose style, is used for these characters in *topéng* and *wayang*. *Arja*'s nonmasked *panasar*s, Punta and Wijil, speak for themselves and are relatively "right here," so they do not need that stylistic distance. They speak only the Balinese language, except in *cecelantungan* 'poetic quotations' or occasional polite conversation with royal characters. I have been told that it was only in the late 1940s that *arja*'s *limbur* began to talk common Balinese in an everyday inflection, instead of *tabuh suara* 'stylized speech'. This reflected a new earthiness and lack of stylized distance between characters and audience, and followed by only a couple of decades the inclusion of female performers in *arja*. This was a further step away from the stylized distance of characterization inherent in the female roles of the originally all male *arja* groups.

My old teacher and friend Madé Gerindem stops by the house on his bicycle one afternoon to chat over coffee and cake. Blunt as usual, he gets right to the point. "Okay, you've been studying *tembang* with Bu Candri and Pak Tempo for how long? Three months, already? Show me what you've learned." With some confidence I

I Madé Gerindem playing *gendér*, second from left and holding mallets, with *gambelan Semar Pagulingan* of Teges; Madé Dana and Madé Tantra play *Kendang*s in foreground (1980).

sing *tembang Sinom manis*, as sung by a refined, sweet prince. "Uh-huh, what else?" he asks. I proceed with several more *tembang* renditions, ending with *tembang Durma*, as sung by *arja*'s Punta, or *panasar*. "That's pretty good," he comments. "Now, how about the laugh?" "How about what?" I ask. "The laugh," he insists. "How's your *panasar* laugh?" "I can't do that," I explain. He scolds, "That's ridiculous. What's the use of singing the *panasar*'s *Durma* if you can't do his laugh? There's no *panasar*! Here, this is it. Like this—Hm—hm hm hm—hm hm hm—hm hm hah—hah hah hah hah hah ha hah." He's now pleased with himself, and chuckles. "Okay, okay—show me the dance," he continues more calmly, but just as if before the storm. "Oh," I answer, "I don't dance." He feigns incredulity. "Then, why are you studying *tembang* songs?" he asks. "To understand the relationship between vocal music and characterization," I reply, a bit shaken. "You can't do the laugh, and you don't even study the dance, and you think you're learning the *tembang*? What are those teachers doing with you? Here, listen, you can do it. This is *panasar*." He gets up from his chair, dancing and singing through a few lines of the *panasar*'s song. "Now, here is the *mantri manis*." He demonstrates a fairly foolish version of the refined prince's dance and song. "If you can't get the *panasar* and *mantri*'s movement and characterization before you leave Bali, you've got nothing. Don't even visit me to say goodbye before going home. It'll be too embarassing." Of course Pak Gerindem was being overly dramatic as usual, but he had made his point.

While some panasar *or Punta performers are praised for their dancing, others for their vocalizing, and still others for their literary, narrative, or comic skills, I am told of one performer who has the essence of* masolah *Punta characterization. When we finally get together, I see that for him, it's all in the face. What his admirers appreciate is the way he balances a sweet smile with a sense of concern and occasional alarm, and his subtle shifts of gaze; there is stylization, but it's so genuine;* lebeng *'well-cooked', so the ingredients are not tasted as strong, distinct flavors, but as a subtle brew.*

Another performer is said by many of his colleagues to be a prototype of masolah topéng Dalem, *mask characterization of the refined king. While other great dancers fill their performance with "choreography," his movement is remarkably minimal and subtle. Others would spend a short while at the curtain and proceed into various walks and patterns of gesture. This dancer takes an unusual amount of time at the curtain, just looking out, shifting gaze, slightly shifting his balance and stance, then again altering his gaze. But to many of his peers and students, what he is doing is beyond movement, as he is zeroing in on the quality of the character, and an altogether different sense of time. Refinement is expressed by most dancers as continuously flowing movement, whereas he merely gives us a glimpse of a character's presence, Dalem's state of being; nothing more, nothing less.*

Madé Sija discusses Ketut Rinda's skill at bringing the panasar *to life. Pak Sija explains that many people can dance. "This is called dance," and he demonstrates a sequence of* panasar *movements. "But this is* masolah. *This is the way the spirit of a character is embodied, which is what Pak Rinda can do." He shows a sequence with much less flourish, most of the movement coming from a flick of the hands, a nod of the head, a glance.*

Pak Sija's distinction between solah (masolah) *and* tari *'dance', is a recurring theme; he sometimes uses the word* tari *almost pejoratively. He speaks of four* topéng *styles, from the villages Batuan, Mas, Badung and Cebaang, and he demonstrates the difference just by the initial* mungkah lawang, *gesture of the hands open-*

ing the curtain. Solah *is most concerned with sensing the world around, while* tari *moves more on its own.*

The same subject comes up with dalang *Wayan Nartha, talking about his* prabu *'prime minister' character in the* Tantri *dance drama performances of Sukawati village. He asserts that his own dancing is not good; many people dance the* prabu *better than he. I answer, "but the character was so strong." He smiles at the flattery, and explains that it was Pak Kakul who taught him the* prabu *role for the village Sukawati's newly formed* Calonarang[4] *group at the* pura dalem *temple. From Pak Kakul he came to understand how to develop that unified manifestation of spirit in voice, movement, and characterization. Kakul taught how to make each gesture, voice, facial expression change with the emotion and content, from keras 'angry' to halus 'sweet'. Pak Nartha feels that it's similar to the* dalang's *art of characterization, but without the puppet.*

Creating a sense of space happens not through depiction and description (as with much mime) but through internal energies. The quality of the vibrations in the surrounding space comes to you, and you respond to it subtly, revealing its character, rather than its form. We see this as crystal clear flowing water in Pandé Kenyir's jauk *characterization, in his eyes (without the jauk mask) and movement—gestures not so much delineating space as sending out threads of energy, allowing us to "see" the invisible vibrations of performer and space clearly. At once limitless and small, without bounds or proportion, this energy may be perceived in myriad ways.*

These ways of dealing with invisible forces permeate all Balinese performance, including arja, *a form that is literal and entertainment-oriented, certainly "not sacred." But the kinesthetic and kinetic seeds of Balinese art were planted long ago in what has grown into many things, including* arja, *with winds blowing the seeds into fields of the "secular." One can still recognize the flowers.*

Some choreographic ideas do make reference to specific immediate factors. *Jauk* and barong have a sequence, *ngintip jangkrik*, following the sound of crickets, and then catching them. *Oyod padi* 'the swaying of rice plants in

4. The magic drama genre enacting the eleventh-century story of the Witch of Dirah, East Java, concluding with her manifestation as Rangda, the monstrous mask character. Village groups perform *Calonarang* most especially for their own and other villages' *pura dalem* 'temple of the dead' festivals. The performance genre is derived from *gambuh* and *arja*, as well as Rangda and *barong* temple ritual, and has seen an upsurge in interest amongst Balinese audiences in the 1990s.

the wind' is danced by groups of *jauk*s and their female counterparts, *san-daran*s. And as the *jauk* first appears through the temple gateway, he turns back and forth from the tall *pajeng* 'umbrella' on his left to the one on his right, suggesting a physical delineation and magic borderline between his world and ours.

And while some artistic traditions imply spirit and manifest a material world, Balinese manifest spirit while implying, suggesting the material world.

A key factor in keeping a character focused and energy strong and believable is *tebek*, literally meaning "to stab or pierce with a sword or pin," but referring here to eye contact, focused visual attention. One must *nebek* (the verb form) with the third-eye level of the audience; if the character is looking up, he should *nebek* with audience standing; if he's looking down, *nebek* with those sitting. If two characters are interacting, of course, they *nebek* each other, or at least the *panasar* will focus on his king, *Dalem*. *Tebek* is used even if *pandangan* 'focus of eyes' is not as strong as it would be in anger or anticipation. If the character is weeping, *nebek jiwa* is still focused, as the *tebek* changes from concentration on eye contact to focus on the *jiwa* 'spirit' and feeling. Madé Sija, like Nyoman Candri, uses personal experiences in acting sad emotions, thinking of when his child was sick, and so on. The actual focus of eyes, *pandangan*, is synonymous with *tebek* for experienced performers, but those less accomplished focus *nebek* with the spot in between their eyes, the third eye, so as not to be distracted by looking too closely at the audience and scene around them.

For Wayan Rangkus of Singapadu village, the feeling of *panasar* or Punta movement is *keras* 'forceful', but the actual movement does not appear that way; it's mostly kept inside the performer, not shown blatantly. The strength is even greater because of the restraint.

My six months of study with him were always illuminated by Pak Rangkus's foremost concern, that of *pandangan*, focus of eyes and energy. Focus must be held as if the object of your attention, or the whole world, would collapse at the release of your gaze. Whether in anger or humor,

I Wayan Rangkus teaching *arja*'s Punta characterization in Singapadu (1992).

focus is always strong. And once the gaze is set, it must not falter, at least until the completion of the opening verses of *tembang Durma*.

Another area of focus comes from the *tegak* 'taut' position of shoulders, neck, and head, and *bahu pandangan*, where shoulders may follow the direction of the gaze. *Tegak* poise is kept stylized throughout Punta's opening stylized monologue, *Béh! Déwa ratu agung* . . . and in any dance or dramatic transition sequence. But once Wijil comes out and *mekanda* 'dialogue' begins, Punta may drop his shoulders and his "fixed, energetic focus."

Pak Tempo asserts that *arja*'s Punta and Wijil are basically the performers interrelating and not totally in character, but in *topéng*, character is kept throughout. In *arja*, stylization is dropped for a more naturalistic level of drama during the dialogue after the opening verses of *tembang Durma* and the initial monologue establishing the dramatic world. And, in fact, many *topéng panasar*s pretty much drop character during comic interactions with their audience.

Anak Agung Rai Cebaang, a revered *topéng* dancer, reserves the expression *solah* for performance with masks or *wayang*. *Arja* and *gambuh*, with dancers singing and speaking, are half *solah*, half *ngigel* 'dance'. Agung Cebaang reaffirms the idea that in *séndratari*, the *dalang*'s voice "has nothing of *solah* to connect with," in contrast with the process of "spirit entering a mask" with the *panasar* and fully masked dancers in *topéng*. In his lexicon, the *baris* dance is *ngigel*.

Pak Tempo is talking about vocal style and movement and how all qualities come from the character and are not decided upon or planned out. The character takes over and gives life to the song and movement. What creates the character is the mask, and every mask has different qualities, temperament, age, and ways of communicating. Tempo leaves for a moment and comes back with several cloth bags containing masks. He brings out two *Dalem* masks and asks me to compare them. "What are their likes?"

I comment that one seems to be concerned with the world, governing, more experienced, while the other is more concerned with his own inner state, seeing the world from his own place. Tempo says that I am mostly correct but that the second is a weak character and a deficient mask. This is a *Dalem* interested in his own affairs, young, impulsive, preoccupied with clothes and women, and not experienced enough to avoid intrigue. The older mask, though less skillfully carved, is a deeper character, able to balance out situations and control his emotions. He takes out a prime minister mask and asks for comment. I hold it for quite a while before daring to appraise the character, then comment that this *patih* seems quick to anger, not able to take in the entirety of a situation, being too focused on property, power, influence. Tempo agrees.

Then he takes up the next cloth bag, a bit more ceremoniously. "Now you are ready to consider this," he says as he brings out a half-mask. This variation on Ketut Rinda's *panasar* is strong, reddish-brown, with whiskers, open cut-out, *mata bolong*, eyes, and many long, flowing wrinkles. Tempo asks, "What are his likes and dislikes?" After another long pause, I venture along safe terrain, that this character likes to size up situations, make comparisons, judgments, follow the actions of others analytically. Tempo asserts that I'm pretty accurate, but that what this character likes best is to have friends and to socialize. He explains that this mask can move in any style. A dancer does not have to be good, because the character of the mask will lead the way in a simple or more elaborate manner. He demonstrates the movement alternately as a strong but fluid *baris*-oriented energetic feeling, then a "pose and punch–style," and then a shy, limp style. All three distinct varieties of movement work with this mask. Tempo points out that sculptural skill doth not a good mask make, but spirit is what gives a mask flexibility and depth of character.

Pak Gerindem drops by at about six in the morning and stays for a couple of hours, sipping coffee and talking of life, death, and sickness. He says that during his performances of the dance drama *Cupak* he is possessed by *betara* 'deity' Brahma. His Cupak character is so rough that Wayan Retug, normally a wild and spontaneous *panasar*, felt intimidated and had to stop playing the comic *panasar* role for Pak Gerindem. Gerindem's Cupak kicks and hits his servants excessively. After consuming enormous amounts of food as Cupak, he can eat a normal meal when he returns home, as if he had not yet dined.

Pak Kakul served as a mentor to Madé Regug in the early stage of his career as a mask maker. Aside from being Bali's foremost dancer of *topéng*, Pak Kakul had also made some beautiful and profound masks himself (for his own use). One day, we all sat on the master dancer's porch, admiring some of Regug's latest completed maskwork. Pak Kakul was intensely examining the Orang Tua 'Old Man' mask, which must communicate a regal bearing along with the wistfulness and humor of old age. Without discussion, he picked up a knife and made two gashes into Tua's cheeks. Pak Regug gasped aloud in surprise, his horror undisguised. Although many glances around the porch revealed a slight concern over his sanity, all remained quiet as Pak Kakul continued his revision of the mask. Finally, he stopped and exclaimed, "There's the character." We and Regug inspected and admired the subtly altered face. The earlier version had been an acceptable version of the stylized characterization, but Kakul's incisive instinct brought out the unique spirit of this particular wood mask.

Panasar

❀

Panasar and *kartala* are the half-mask comic narrator/philosophers of *topéng* and other dance dramas. The performers' lower lip and jaw are not covered by the mask, enabling them to vocalize. Attendants to the *ratu*, 'king, prince' or to a prime minister, these two brothers, or close cohorts, speak for the fully masked royal characters.[1]

There are two basic kinds of *panasar* masks: *mata batu*, with bulging "stoney eyes," and *mata bolong*, with eyeholes cut out, leaving the performer's eyes exposed for dramatic effect. The *kartala*'s eyeholes are always cut out (*bolong*), but left as slits, so the actor's own eyes are not seen. This is different from most other Balinese masks, including *panasar mata batu*, which have the eyes painted in, with a slit just below through which the actor sees.

Ketut Rinda's mask is that of a strong *panasar* Délem,[2] so his eyes and basic composure must be a bit forceful, *keras*. But he's not the boastful, hyperenergetic type, only about 20 percent Délem, according to Pak Tempo, who describes Pak Rinda's *panasar* Délem as a serious character. Madé Sija sees *panasar mata bolong* as requiring more focus, since the audience observes your eyes. But Pak Rinda, who is the prototypical open-eyed *panasar*, has told me that he considers his *panasar* Délem more free to be funny and to connect directly with the audience.

Wayan Retug's mask is more the bragging, nervous Délem. With his particular mask, I am told, the movement cannot be anything but just like Retug's. One can't help it; the mask is uncompromising. A performer finds

1. See the "*Masolah*" chapter for a perspective on *panasar* characterization. The *kartala* is also called *panasar cenikan* 'the younger' while the elder is *panasar kelihan*. *Panasar* generally refers to the elder.

2. A style of *panasar* mask somewhat derived from the Délem character in *wayang wong* dance drama and *wayang kulit*. In one style, the performer's eyes are exposed, unlike *wayang wong*'s Délem, who has bulging wooden eyes.

Topéng's *kartala* danced by I
Wayan Teduh (1972). Photo
by Beth Skinner.

his hands always wandering around, in the air and on the body, picking his
nose and sniffing, after scratching inside his ass (conspicuously using the
same finger). This *panasar* is still only about 50 percent Délem—a funny
one, using Indonesian language a lot, but in a clumsy manner, such as in-
correctly using *begini, begitu* 'like this, like that' and bragging on and on.
He's sometimes more like a pure comic *bondrés*[3] than a serious *panasar*.
Tempo identifies his own *panasar* mask as more of a wizened Twalén character. But Pak Sardru's style is considered 100 percent Délem; his stance is
solid and square, with swaying head and body, coarse vocal style, shifting
balance of arms and legs, and an exhilarated air of self-satisfied mirth.

Pak Sija describes one of his *panasar* masks as human, the next as *dedéleman*, suggesting some differentiation. But he later indicates that Délem is

3. *Bondrés* are the half-mask characters, often in a reality one step further toward the audience and out of the time-sense of the story. They are responsible for the wilder and sillier antics least relevant to the main narrative, and may divert the story into long, involved, farcical
intrigues. One occasional strategy is that a completely loony, rambling, and irrevelant turn of
events winds up, after an hour-long diversion from the main story, to serve up as its dénouement, providing some key information sought by the more serious characters in the main narrative. Part of the punchline is the shock of two realities—the more immediate *bondrés* and
the historical time realm—colliding.

human, too, though perhaps on the edge in some respects. He takes on some animal-derived gestures such as sticking his head forward like a bird. As with *jauk*, some movements are like a tiger, and *dedéleman* has its own movement of a bear going after a wasp. He begins by coming out through the curtain the way a normal *panasar* does, then sees the wasp, takes three steps, hops toward it, grabs at it, then jumps back, waving his hands in front of his face.

All performers I know agree that the open-eyed *panasar* Délem style is more coarse in character, voice, and movement than the wooden-eyed *panasar*. The style is more emphatic, staccato, demonstrative, funny, bragging. You sing coming out, do an *angsel* 'rhythmic phrasing build and break', introduce the story, take a long walk, double *angsel*, and turn around to face the curtain and call to the lazy *kartala*.

In *arja* and other nonmasked dance dramas, the *panasar* and *kartala* become Punta and Wijil, changing the stylization in various ways. People generally think of Wijil's character as less intelligent than Punta, since Punta often translates *cecantungan* 'snatches of poetry' that are spoken or sung by Wijil. But that can be reversed. Wijil is most often the more comic while Punta relates seriously to the dramatic events. Usually it's the *kartala* or Wijil who does the exaggerated rendition of vocal shaping of sound, *gedong céngkok*; he's "free, smooth, and funny." Madé Kredek's drowsy *kartala* would sing with sleepy, yawning, descending slides, to ridicule the *panasar*'s seriousness. Wijil and *kartala* dance movement is loosely based on that of the *mantri manis* 'refined prince'. There is often a kind of dance contest between the performers of prince and attendant, with Wijil trying to outdo and parody the *mantri*'s sweetness and grace with improvised choreography.

Pak Rinda says that whatever *Kawi* phrases are chosen for the *panasar*'s opening *sendon* song, they should be "peculiar and funny," to arouse the interest of the audience. *Panasar* or Punta's first intention is to "enchant" the audience "with a feeling of just waking up." A *panasar* may sing an entire stanza or two.

PANASAR'S SENDON TOPÉNG VIA MADÉ PASEK TEMPO
(CD SELECTION 6)

Katkat taluklak saluklik
kelika lika lulut warwaning wiwalik
pupuk paksa ngipik ngipik kipijar tangkuak warwaning
Basundari Uma Durga Gangga guri
arsa sidi yang kemari

mantra mantra wija wija
tutur tutur mapuja gan tan pangguh péksa budining lén[4]

cockatoos and other birds
the proud *kelik* enjoying the pleasing company of others
pupuk, kutuku, night bird, careful not to dwell on others'
    faults, and always happy
Basundhari, [deity of] the earth, Uma, goddess of fertility
    Durga, goddess of death [and the graveyard], *Gangga*,
    goddess of holy water,
mantras, ritual rice offerings
moral teachings, prayers, and not making trouble for others[5]

Madé Sija reads the first three lines as *katkat luklat saluklik, likalika lu-luting larwani wiwalik, pupuk paksa ngupéksa ngipik-ngipik kipijar tang-kuak kupu-kupu*. An interpretation of these lines based on his insights follows as:

> a flock of cockatoos
> the *kelik-kelik* enjoys seeing the flying ants returning
> the gray stork wants to get closer to the heron
> who is closely observing the butterflies

P. J. Zoetmulder reads the second line as *lik-alik alulut ing larwan niwi walik* and translates it as, "sounding loud and shrill with desire are the nightbirds at the sight of flying ants."

Other *panasar*s, like Pak Kakul, might choose just a few lines, sometimes stringing together images from different literary sources. In one particular performance (CD selection 19), he used the verse shown above as a final *cecantungan* 'offshoot' to conclude a string of *sendon*, sung as brief poetic quotations, in the following manner: *Katkat luklak likalika lulut warwaning wiwalik pupuk paksa ngupéksa*. The phrase was intoned on one pitch, the lower pitch of the *gambelan*'s *bapang* 'ostinato', *ndung* (5). Coming after many long, melodic vocal phrases (including an excerpt from "*Méh rahina*" shown in figure 27), this line was a strong contrast, suggesting a mantra-like calm, only to be immediately followed by the first explosive, shouted words of the *panasar*'s monologue.

---

4. The first three lines are from the *Kawi Ramayana*. Zoetmulder's version (1982) is *katkat luklak saluklik lik-alik alulut ing larwan niwi walik*. Zoetmulder translates *katkat* as "a kind of bat?" Pak Sija believes *katkat* is *paksi pékat* 'cockatoo'; that the first *ipik* could be playing with *upik* 'gray stork', and the second *ipik* be "to look at something." Through collective use as well as individual performers' play with alliteration, versions vary over time. Translations from Kawi to Balinese, and interpretations, also vary among performers and scholars. *Dalang* Ketut Kodi interprets *kelik* as a small crow, *supéksa* (Kakul's *ngupéksa*) as wings, and *pupuk* as energetic fluttering of wings.

5. This is Pak Tempo's interpretation, given to me in Indonesian. He would translate some words literally, and paraphrase others to express the feeling and implication rather than a strict rendering.

Figure 27. *Sendon panasar topéng.*

Pak Rinda explains how funny-sounding *Kawi* phrases are quoted, the *panasar* even adding repetitive consonants here and there to create humor through alliteration (see translation in CD notes). In the following sketch of one rendition (CD selection 18) of Pak Rinda's first phrase (figure 27), an upward-pointing arrow indicates a quarter-tone sharper intonation on specific notes; (7) indicates *paméro*, when *tekep lebeng* is brought in. It should be noted that, on this stave, the opening *ndung* (5) is already in the singer's midrange, so the ensuing melody reaches into a high "tooting" quality with the upper *ndéng* (3), *ndung* (5) and *ndang* (6), exaggerated by the sounds of the words themselves.

Arja's Punta often chooses *Durma* themes relating to *karmapala* 'right-action, fate, spiritual cause-and-effect' and *dharma* 'spiritual teachings, responsibility, law'.

PUNTA'S *DURMA*, IN COMMON BALINESE,
AS TAUGHT BY MADÉ PASEK TEMPO
(CD SELECTION 5)

from behind curtain	*Déning kecatri dadi manusa*
dancer opens curtain	*pemragaté pacang mati,*
	Eda ampah teken awak,
dancer comes out	*dwaning twara ja tawang*
	buin pidan gantiné mati,
	Dadak-dadakan
	uripé tong kenéng esti

If we are born into this world as humans
we must all die eventually,
Don't be reckless with yourself,
because you will never know
when you are to die,
Unexpectedly! . . .
Because our souls cannot be sure
how much time we'll have . . .

For *arja*'s *Durma* Punta, and for a *panasar topéng* desiring to extend the literary content of his *sendon*, the first verse can be "broad and philosophical," setting the mood. His next verse may then be addressed more to the audience or contemporary world, dealing with the general context of spiritual and creative work, but still not getting into the story. The content of the opening verses of *Durma papeson*[6] or *sendon topéng* is generally not translated or discussed between *panasar* and *kartala* in their *mekanda* 'verbal exchange'; only when the opening stanza is relevant to the story at hand. Most often, the use of song in plot development begins after the two have completed their initial songs and dialogue.

According to Pak Tempo, "*papeson panasar topéng* is like walking in the woods without a path, but knowing the signs, trees, flora, lay of the land, so you can get from one place to another desired place."

Tempo feels very free to deviate from the pitches of the *gambelan*, and is not willing to affix specific tones, *ndong nding*, to his *sendon topéng*. But there are consistent melodic contours, pitch patterns, and colors, as well as a touching of *gambelan* pitches, at the *gongan* 'end of a phrase', on *bapang* 'ostinato' tones, *ndung nding ndung nding*, or *kotékan* 'higher register inter-

6. *Papeson* 'coming out' refers to the first vocal music and dance a character uses to come through the curtain or gateway.

locking pitches'. He chooses the first pitch of his *Bléng mbang* song as *ndéng* (3), a minor third above the higher pitch, *nding* (1), of the ostinato, *ndung nding ndung nding* (5 1 5 1).

Pak Rembang's distinction between *sendon* and *tandak* differs from Tempo's and Candri's. *Sendon*, he says, is derived from *sendu* 'sad' and is associated with any kind of sadness, love, longing. In performance, *sendon* are done fairly "straightforward," without too much interference or discussion from *panakawan, panasar*, except for simple translation. No joking. The *sendon* is basically entrenched in the emotion of a scene. *Tandak*, which Pak Rembang derives from *candak*, meaning "to block or create an obstacle," is more commonly attributed to the word *nandak* 'to assist' or 'fit'. So, he would call the opening *papeson panasar* "*tandak*," while others may call it "*sendon*." Tempo and Candri say *tandak* follows, and plays off of, the instrumental melody, while *sendon* is free of the *gending* 'instrumental composition', usually used during *batél* or *bapang* 'ostinato' sections, and still keeping (or relating to) the *gambelan* pitches.

Madé Sija sometimes sings what he calls *selisir* (referring to the common *gambelan* tuning) instead of what he considers real *sendon* for *topéng*'s *papeson panasar*. He says it's easier and more closely knit with the *gambelan*, rather sweet and flowing.

When *arja* is performed with *gambelan gong*, Punta's *sendon* may involve a tonal feeling of *Sinom Cecantungan*, but less fluid, more emphatic and syllabic, with the *nyutra* more open. The voice adheres to the pitches of the *gambelan*, except for some *paméro* and unnamed semitones. But unlike *tandak*, *sendon* does not follow the *gambelan*'s *ilegan gending* 'melodic contours'. As explained earlier, this "tonal feeling" is actually often called *tekep lebeng*, similar to the style used by many *topéng panasar*s.

Arja's Punta uses a movement style comparable to that of the *panasar topéng*, but with a different feeling and sometimes more interconnected with the *gaguntangan* ensemble. The song's rhythmic and melodic phrasing is not directly coordinated with the instrumental music. As the dance "follows" the singing, the *gambelan* is led by the dance. Vocal phrasing is stretched out over the simultaneous, overlapping melody of the flute, the vibrations of the *guntang* 'one-stringed bamboo zither', and the undercurrent of rhythms from the drums and other instruments. However, the dancer should have the instrumental music thoroughly internalized so that his dance is coordinated with it, leaving room for improvisation and the feeling of the moment.

Gambelan mulut 'mouth *gambelan*' is the way teachers vocally transmit all relevant musical information to the student. It is a fluid, informal style of singing during a dance lesson, continually shifting emphasis according to the structure and energy of the dance, as well as adapting spontaneously to the student's particular needs. CD selection 7 provides a rendition of *gambelan mulut* for the dance of *jauk manis*, and selection 8 the corresponding instrumental *gambelan* music.

In *arja*, the first strata of vocables is composed of the names of the pitches of the flute melody,[7] *nding, ndong, ndéng, ndung, ndang*, pronounced without the *d*. Some teachers use the names more associated with the sound of bronze-keyed *gambelan: nirrr, norrr, nérrr, nurrr, narrr*. The vocal sound for the large bamboo *guntang* is a rolled *pur*, sounded *pur-r-r* (deriving from *kempur* 'medium-size gong' stroke), *gir*, or *sir-r-r* (deriving from the large-size gong stroke). It is played, and sung, on the last beat of each phrase, which means every eight beats for the slow phrases of *adéng* 'slow' Punta. The small bamboo *guntang cenik*, vocalized as *tit* (pronounced teet), is the pulse, theoretically struck on each beat, but in this case struck, or sung, on every other pulse beat, on two, four, six, and eight. But instead of the *guntang's tit* sound, for more distinct vocalizing, Pak Tempo generally uses the sound of the bronze hand-held *ketuk*, vocalized as *tok*. Woven into a vocal phrase, *tok* is sung as *toka* to weave the rhythmic phrase tighter. A teacher may vocally fill in every *tok* to call attention to a specific detail of dance phrasing. Or he may replace it with the colotomic vertical gong, *kenong*, sung as *tong*, on the fourth beat of each phrase. Actually, for *gaguntangan*, a *tawa-tawa* is used, vocalized as *pung*. Every other *tok* (or *tit*) is also played on the little hand-held *klenang* (sung as *yang*) on the first, third, fifth, and seventh beats, creating a more even (*malpal*) emphasis on each of the eight beats of a *kempur* phrase. As with much traditional Indonesian music, the main beat, or pulse, is counted on two, four, six, and eight, with phrases reaching resolution with a gong stroke on eight. The actual pitch or pitches intoning each *tok, yang, tong, pung, pur-r-r*, or *gir-r-r* will be sung following the *suling* melody. For a more flowing melodic rendition, each pitch is sung with its vowel (*nding-ndong*) name. "Mouth *gambelan*" will also include the drum rhythms, as the teacher chooses. *Ping* is a high-pitched open ringing tone produced by hitting the edge of the skin with the smaller two or three fingers of the left hand, while dampening the lower-pitched skin with the right hand. *Plak* (rhyming with rock) is a slap on the higher-pitched skin. *Tut* (rhyming with fruit) is a middle tone made with a stroke of the right hand to the middle of the skin. *Dag* (pronounced with an *ah* sound) is the low tone produced by the right hand hitting at the edge of

---

7. In *arja*, the flute provides the main instrumental melody, but in other genres the *gangsa* 'metallophone' does this. Pitch names remain the same.

the lower-pitched skin. A *tut* stroke may be vocalized as *ke* (or alternatively pronounced *che*) as in *ke-plak* (or che-plak), when the emphasis is being put on the flat slap of the *plak*. Often, in this context, the actual stroke muffles the tone, so it does not ring out as *tut*. Or the muffled *tut* may also be de-emphasized with a vocalization of *te*, as in *te-dag*. The higher *ping* stroke may also be vocalized as *pléng* for vocal sonority, and a series of *pings* can produce a vocal rendition of *kom-pléng-kom-pléng-kom-pléng*. In *gambelan mulut*, the drum strokes are sung out as the vocables of the melody, replacing the *ndong-nding* vocables indicating pitch. So the voice maintains the flute melody, while vocables constantly shift to indicate—in addition to pitch names—drum patterns, colotomic phrases of gongs, or pulse keepers filling in the eight-beat phrase. In this way a single voice can encompass all instrumental strata of a *gambelan* piece. All of the interweaving threads of sound are internalized by the dancer, and in turn woven into the dance.

Feet may step on any *tok* (or *tit*), with a one-step or two-step, or on a shift of weight. Gaze shifts simultaneously with, but contrary to, weight shifts (generally, every three weight shifts). Of course, that's only a *patokan* 'standard form', and once that is internalized, one plays off of it.

Four phrases of the slow section, *adéng* Punta, in *tabuh telu* form (*arja*'s slowest meter), may be rendered by *gambelan mulut* as shown in figure 28. (This style is demonstrated in CD selection 16 although this not a direct transcription of that particular rendition.) While all of these musical undercurrents are flowing into and out of the dancer's consciousness, the actual vocal line is still *tembang Durma*. As mentioned earlier, the *tembang* singing only occasionally connects directly with these instrumental strata. But each poetic/melodic phrase has a corresponding synchronous gesture or choreographic sequence. In other words, the dance is relating to each of the differing musical aspects in differing ways, simultaneously. There is one choreographic connection with the dancer's own vocalized poetic phrasings, and quite independently, another choreographic pattern weaving in and out of intimacy with the complex instrumental currents.

As mentioned earlier, the eight-count colotomic structure detailed in figure 28 is the slowest, and only one of four in *arja*. In practice, there is greater variety according to dramatic context and also from group to group, or village to village. In brief, the lively *tabuh batél*[8] is composed of phrases of two, with a *pung* on each *tit*, and every other *tit* additionally

---

8. *Tabuh* has several meanings: a *gambelan* composition; a mallet used to strike a *gambelan* instrument; stroke; *menabuh gambelan* 'to play *gambelan*'; *Tabuhin!* 'Strike up!' In the present context, it refers to any one of several compositional structures used by the instrumental ensemble for *arja*.

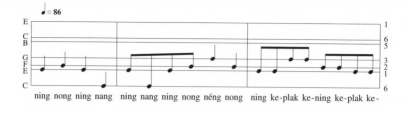

Figure 28. "Mouth *gambelan*" for Punta's "coming out."

sounding a *pur-r-r. Tabuh besik,* also in two-beat phrases, has *pung* and *pur* alternating on each *tit.* These are used for *papeson* 'entrances', or more literally 'coming out', when the dancer wants to grab the audience's attention with strong, tightly phrased movement. The slower and quieter *tabuh dua,* which accompanies speaking sequences, is phrased in fours, with *pung* on two and *pur* on four.

Sir, or more often pronounced as a rolled *sir-r-r,* is the mouth *gambelan* sound for the large gong. The colotomic instrumental phrasing of the *bapang* 'ostinato' entrance music for *panasar topéng* is "*sir tok pur tok tong tok pur tok sir.*"

A simplified explanantion of one *angsel* in the *panasar*'s dance is as follows. After *pur* is a rapid three-foot *de-de-dét* (right-left-right) or *de-de-de—dét* (left-right-left-right), the last right falling on the last *tok*; then left foot sidestep, grab *saput* 'cape'—right hand on *sir,* then right foot sidestep forward, gaze out again as left hand grabs *saput,* all on *pur;* then *de-de-dét* on *tong; dét,* left foot lifted up comes down on toe, on *pur; seledét* 'glance up and to the side' *(dét), sir-r-r.*

When Punta or *topeng*'s *panasar* finishes his song, his laugh begins in the chest, mouth closed, and then rolls out as the mouth opens in a smile. *Hm-hm-hu-hu-huh-huh-ha-ha-hah-hah-hah* . . .

The five areas that Pak Tempo says a *panasar* must be able to draw from are (1) religious and poetic literature, history, philosophy; (2) likes and dislikes of the audience; (3) sense of time, being able to extend the story or keep to its basics, "shorten without cutting up"; (4) sense of movement; (5) sense of *gambelan*, fitting with, adapting to *iringan* 'accompanying instrumental music'.

The late Madé Kredek's process of teaching *panasar* followed a sequence similar to the performance itself. That's significant inasmuch as penetration of form and the dramatic world by the performer as an individual is reflected in the process of penetration by the audience, community. Before even beginning *panasar arja* work, an aspiring performer had to know the *tembang* most often used for developing and clarifying, "composing" the plot. Then he would begin with basic dance sequences, coming out of the curtain, specific walks. *Sendon topéng, Durma arja*, and *tandak* come next, with proper vocal quality. Then, standard verses and lines with inflection, stylized speech with gesture, for both monologues, *Béh! Déwa ratu agung titiang* . . . , dialogue and literary sources, poetic verses, stories, and tangential episodes.

It is always said that a *panasar* must be adept at all aspects of his multidisciplinary role. But over the course of time one hears how each of the great masters had identifiable strengths as well as weaknesses. One was skilled at text and verbal exchange but was not a proficient dancer or singer. One was a good *bondrés* comic and skilled at dialogue, and another was skilled at dance. Someone else was adept at vocal music, text, and dialogue, but had less strength as a dancer. One is considered excellent at *panasar* dance characterization and another best at linking eye movement and facial expression with song.

It is often said that if one accepts an invitation to perform *topéng* or *arja*, he or she is expected, upon arrival, to be told which story is being performed, which character he or she is to portray, and then be able to do it. Performers will go over the basic events of the story, especially if it is not well known. If one asks too many questions, he might be told politely that before accepting another invitation to perform, he should go home and study the texts and dramatic sources. Improvisation is free and smooth only after a vast amount of study and experience.

However, when Pak Rangkus would perform Punta with Pak Kredek's Wijil, or anyone else for that matter, the important dialogue and quotations of sung poetry were discussed just before performing. They would go over the interpretation of various lines and themes to be used in the story. Sometimes, they would prepare the material days before a performance. I ask if the Wijil would ever come up with some *cecantungan* 'brief poetic quotation' that the Punta has never heard before. "How could I possibly know how to answer him or translate, if we hadn't ever rehearsed it?" For humor and general story development, dialogue can be free. But for the keys, Pak Rangkus needs preparation. His greatest strength is as a dancer.

Although singing is always considered an important aspect of the performer's craft, it is said that most *panasars* hardly sing anymore within the story, but just for their entrances and *Dalem*'s arrival. They do use *Sinom Wayah* for *Dalem*'s entrance or for giving advice. They may quote a line or two of *wirama kakawin*, sung relatively quickly as a *selingan* 'allusion' or *cecantungan*. *Kidung* musical phrases from *Malat* stories can also be used for quotes or for introducing royal characters.

Literary sources may be transformed into *tandak*, following the instrumental melodic flow and leaving behind their original poetic meter and melody. In *wayang* performance, quotations from *wirama kakawin* or *tembang* may keep their distinct melodic and poetic phrasing, but they all leave their original literary identity to become part of the story at hand. In *arja*, verses from *wirama* and *kidung* may depart from their musical identity and be sung in *tembang* style.[9]

Tembang Ginanti is sometimes sung by Wijil, with a giddy feeling of rapture and sweetness, meant to express his own joy and pleasure.

> *Brakutut muni angunggul,*
> *mincok ning taru marunggi,*
> *cacagan muni lan alon,*
> *talungan muni lan suling*
> *bamban,*

9. Some of these printed literary sources are *Ramayana*, *Panaséhat*, *Sutosoma*, *Arjuna Wiwaha*, *Dharma Prawretti*, and *Malat*.

bamban bawu rahina,
tembangin antuk Ginanti

Doves calling out loud and clear
perched in the tree, singing
their sounds repeated slowly over and over
like the sounds of *gambelan* and flute
slowly,
slowly as the day breaks
the *tembang Ginanti* is sung

Within an especially sacred performance of *barong landung* in the hamlet, *Banjar* Kebon, Singapadu, the humor is no less evident, in its proper place within the story. One *bondrés* comic character poses the riddle to another:

> "What's the difference between riding a woman's bicycle and a woman?" After inordinate quibbling over the meaning of the question comes the answer:
> "A bicycle you pump up first and then climb on, but . . . "

The rest of the answer is interrupted before too much is said.[10]

In expectation of *Dalem*'s arrival and appearance from behind the curtains, the *panasar* gives a verbal cue for the *gambelan* to begin *Dalem*'s theme, and may clap his hands together to emphasize the cue. The *panasar* begins his *tandak*, fitting his song to the *gambelan* phrases, leaving much of the freer vocal play to the end of each phrase. *Panasar* and *kartala* are trying to "uplift the hearts of the audience" to make the feeling of the king's arrival more beautiful. At the same time, the performer has a chance to show the subtleties of his vocal prowess as demonstrated on CD selection 17.

Sekar emas ngararoncé
sekarang mangigel gambuh

10. Endo Suanda, West Javanese ethnomusicologist, has told me that he heard this joke on Indonesian radio years ago, and Clifford Geertz thinks *he* remembers first hearing the same joke in high school (both, personal communication, 1992). What may seem like an incongruity—imported, lewd humor in a sacred context—is in fact not at all inappropriate to much Javanese and Balinese performance.

Figure 29. *Tandak Dalem* (CD selection 17).

gambuh di rejang kendran
gagambelan mangasih-asih
manisé ngasorang madu

adorned with gold flowers in his hair
worn for his regal dancing
gambuh and *rejang* danced as if in heaven
the *gambelan* music flowing in waves
sweeter than honey

As a brief suggestion of the melodic style (in *pélog selisir*), a sketch of the second line is shown in figure 29.

Once *Dalem* has come out and done his initial dance, the *panasar* changes from song to *palawakya ngaturing Dalem* 'homage to the king'. This *ilegan ucapan* 'melodic and rhythmic speech' is a stylized prose style in the flowery *Kawi* language (interpreted by Pak Tempo), with gradual, swooping melodic contours, intoned rather than sung with discrete pitches.

Pangaksaman ing ulun ring pada hyang mami
sang ginelaran sarining ongkara ratna mantra
werdaya sulayem yogi swara
sira ta nugraha ring purwaka wus lepas
luputé mami ring upemedi
namastu sekula gotra santana dirgeyusa dimatemahan ayu anarwati

I kneel in obeisance before the one supreme divinity
who already embodies the essence of the holy Vedic scriptures
whose existence is of the highest order
in order that no obstacles may obstruct your blessings
free from temptations and any other misfortune
as the one supreme divinity bestows mercy abundantly, as our inheri-
tance, and for all, long life, and spiritual purity

As *Dalem* again takes up his dance, the *panasar* launches into song, lively and quite syllabic, except for long drawn-out vowels at the end of each line.

simsim alit mungwing tuding
tangané lemet maléngkung
inggek inggek sadanayog

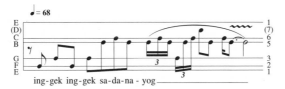

ing-gek ing-gek sa-da-na-yog

Figure 30. (CD selection 17).

makebeh ida mekeber
nyerégség tur nyaliog
kemikan bibihé manis
kudiang titiang ngelayarin

little rings on his fingers
his hands are graceful and pliant
heel step and shuffle, arms slowly sweeping down
like a peacock about to take flight
feet making fast side steps, head tipping side to side
his lips form a sweet smile
how could I ever leave him?

Another brief sketch of a melodic phrase, line three above, using *paméro* (7), is shown in figure 30. As the *panasar* observes *Dalem*'s dance, he composes the song, taking cues from specific gestures, such as *gulu wangsul* 'head tipping left and right', *ngelo* 'figure eight of the head and neck', *ngunda* 'one or both arms raised', *nyambir* 'picking up *saput* cape'.

On CD selection 17, Pak Tempo offers another version of spoken text. He often performs with people from different villages or regions whom he does not know, and so he must follow their choreography of *Dalem* and compose the *tandak* as the dance progresses. Each line or phrase reflects or describes either the mood, appearance, or movement of *Dalem*. Tempo's approach to *tandak Dalem*, as well as *tandak* for the *légong* dance, is somewhat unusual. As is usual, the flow and pitches of the instrumental melody are followed with embellishment. But in his style, the vowel sound of the last syllable, *suku kata*, of the final word in a colotomic *kenong* (*tong*), *gong* (*sir*), or *kempur* (*pur*) phrase is matched with the vowel in the name of the melodic pitch. For example, if the melody of a short or long instrumental phrase is about to end on the pitch *ndong*, he chooses a poetic phrase or single word that will end with the vowel *o*. And so forth for pitches *nding*, *ndéng*, *ndang*, and *ndung*.[11] The *nding* pitch at the *gongan* 'gong-stroke' is

11. This technique is also found in some *kidung* (*sekar madya*) poems, but only at the beginnings and near the ends of stanzas (Wallis 1980: 199).

sung in between upper-octave *nding* (1) and its lower neighbor, *ndang* (6), ending the vocal phrase at the stroke of the *gong*, or just before. Because the *juru tandak* vocalist is "only singing" (not dancing), Tempo feels it incumbent upon himself to get to something deep and subtle, so he uses this style whenever possible. One must have a reserve of poetic lines and *ilegan* 'melodic phrases' memorized, which can be rearranged extemporaneously to fit the choreography, mood, and *gambelan* structure. *Tandak* must be "energetic, smooth, and spontaneous."

The space after each *gong* is where performers may steady their breath and pause to regain a sense of orientation, since one can lose one's sense of time and place while being carried away by and swept through the melody. Going through the melody again, Tempo indicates the ways in which *gong* phrasing and changes in the energy of a melody provide phrasing cues for performers.

We go through many, many *gong* phrases of *Dalem*, with Tempo freely improvising poetic phrases and melodies, I following with voice and mirroring his mouth shapes, trying to imitate his "flow of sound through the body." A single word can be extended over an entire instrumental phrase, *gedong céngkok* transforming the eeee sound of *simsim* into ee-*ah-oh-uu-ah*-ee . . .

He begins to dance while describing what *Dalem* is thinking or saying, along with each change of movement or music. "Oh! What is all this before me? Let me view the landscape and situation. Oh, my *panasar* is here. Good. I wonder who else is here. Oh yes, quite a few people are gathered. I should approach them and see what's going on. Oh, my *patih* is here. I must give him instructions what to do."

He explains, "music, dance, *tandak*, and dramatic situation are one entity, completely unified. *Dalem* encompasses all of these aspects; everything is *Dalem*. Whenever I see *Dalem*'s dance, all is calm, and I forget all my worries and troubles. I can't conceive who might have composed such exquisite music, and all I can do is try to comprehend it and feel it as deeply as possible."

Désa kala patra *within performance*

❀

A Balinese character or dancer is said to "come out" from the curtain or gateway to perform, and to "enter the curtain" to exit. This contrasts with Euro-American performance in which a character makes an entrance to perform. The Balinese terms suggest the notion of coming from some-where, another realm, invisible but no less real. They also reflect the fact that traditionally performers would often come out through a temple gateway and down the steps to begin their dance. Choreography and sub-text for dances such as *jauk*, derived from magical ritual drama, include sequences in which the character comically studies this gateway that de-marcates a boundary between his world and ours. Before coming out to dance, he hovers in the liminal, in-between space, gazing from side to side as if trying to decide whether to manifest. Similarly, before bringing his shadow puppets out, the *dalang* raps on his puppet box to wake up the spirits of the *wayang*, the ancestors, as the *topéng* performer recites *man-tras* before opening his mask basket, to invite the ancestors, spirits of the masks referred to as grandparents, to be present and give him a charge of *taksu*.

Characters are often clearly crossing a gap between worlds. Instead of a make-believe world built on suspended disbelief, characters may actually call attention to stylized distancing. A sense of invisible demarcations of spatial factors is occasionally expressed in stylized utterances by characters. A character appearing from behind the curtain or stone gate may sing out, *Mijiiiiil . . .* 'I'm coming out!' Or *iwasin, iwasin!* 'look out, look out!' cre-ating a mood of expectancy that something is about to arrive out of ether.

It should be mentioned at the same time that, in another more obvious sense, the physical realm of backstage is occupied by everyday behavior, ca-sual conversation and joking amongst performers, eating and drinking cof-fee or soft drinks. Looking at it from this vantage point, as they step

Children sleeping by curtain as I Nyoman Kakul dances *topéng*'s Orang Tua in Batuan Kakul (1972). Photo by Beth Skinner.

through the *langsé* 'curtain' or gateway, they are moving from the everyday world into a dramatized historic realm.

Within a *topéng* performance, different characters embody different aspects of *désa kala patra*. Fully masked characters such as king *Dalem* relate to *kala* 'time' in the sense that they are coming from, and create a feeling of, another realm of historical and spiritual time. The speaking and singing *panasar* and *kartala* intermediate between this realm of ancestral time and that of the present. They interact within *Dalem*'s world, speaking for and with him, translating the poetic dialogue of *Kawi* and refined Balinese into everyday language.[1] In this way they tie the story to the *désa* 'place' of performance and the contemporary world.

Another reflection of *kala* is the feeling of *kalangén*, savored by performers and audience alike. This is a state of rapture, in which all aesthetic, kinetic, and spiritual elements have come together to create an atmosphere

1. Discussing Javanese *wayang*, Alton Becker refers to alternating dramatic uses of classical and everyday language as "speaking the past" and "speaking the present" (Becker, 1979). Similarly, in Balinese performance, the language being used at any given moment, whether it be Sanskrit, Old Javanese, Middle Javanese, High Balinese, Low Balinese, or Indonesian, suggests or invokes a realm with its own historical, spiritual, and contextual associations.

of timelessness, in which personal place/time orientation is temporarily "lost."

The role of the *bondrés* half-mask comic characters extends into the *patra* 'context' of the performance event, in that they deal with the most mundane issues, often not even related to the dramatic plot. They generally speak in the language and voice of the contemporary community, though of course with an exaggerated comic style. They also are free to enter the "real time" of their audience, joking about members of the audience or even extending the actual performance space by wandering out into the audience.[2] In the following chart, the words on the top, going horizontally, refer to aspects of orientation, the middle horizontal line refers to dramatic characters, and the bottom words signify the corresponding conceptual realms.

Time	Space	Activity, Context
Dalem	*< panasar >*	*bondrés*
kala	*désa*	*patra*

Désa kala patra and themes in performance

According to Madé Sija, a *dalang* or *topéng* performer will choose and develop the story to suit the occasion. If the audience can personally identify with some activity or aspect of the story, they will be more involved and attentive, and the story will "enter the hearts of the audience." It's the *dalang*'s way of giving the public a way of seeing their situation or experience in a wider perspective or in an ideal model. The narrative is definitely didactic in this sense, though an aspect of the performer's motivation toward offering instruction has to do with the performer's own need to engage the audience in the play, by means of seduction. As a macro-micro aspect of *patra*, the *dalang* extends his narrative out to bring the audience in. He empowers them by teaching, they empower him by succumbing to his seduction.

For instance, if the ceremony has anything to do with constructing a new *balé* 'building' of a *pura* 'temple', *banjar* 'hamlet', or *pekarangan* 'family compound', the *dalang* could choose the section from the *Mahabharata* when the Pandawa princes are building their abode in the forest. The way they organize the project and interact, the composition of the offerings and prayers, the attitudes, the actual materials and layout of the architectural

2. Since the late 1980s, *bondrés* scenes have grown more prominent in *topéng*, responding to a certain impatience contemporary audiences have with some traditional forms. *Bondrés* behavior has also filtered into some *panasars'* style. The informal style of *bondrés* is more easily suited to dealing with the rapidly changing way of life in Bali (Nyoman Catra, personal communication, 1994). In fact, a "real time" genre of performance involving only *bondrés* has evolved, mostly composed of topical humor and physical "clowning."

Bondrés character of *padanda* 'Brahmana priest', *patih* 'prime minister', and *kartala*, performed by I Nyoman Kakul, I Madé Ruju, and I Wayan Teduh with *gambelan Semar Pagulingan* from Teges (1972).

form, all "give the audience a reflection of their own present experience." This again is a device that is didactic as well as dramatic and entertaining.

Topéng is often expected to deal with a particular family's history. For instance, during the course of royal intrigue and conflict, a curse intended to last for seven generations was placed upon a *Satria* high-caste family. As this spell came to an end in 1980, a *topéng* performance was commissioned to tell this particular family history and celebrate the moment of its dénouement.

Although the lyrics of *geguritan* poems are not improvised in *arja*, there was a time when they were composed to express a changing *désa kala patra*. According to Adrian Vickers, *geguritan*, as a new genre developing in the latter half of the nineteenth century, came to define the differences between commoners and aristocrats. Themes concerned commoner heroes and heroines and were about love, black magic, spirituality, and day-to-day life within their contemporary society and political system. *Geguritan* poems were written by commoners or aristocrats and priests in the voices of commoners.[3]

Often, *désa kala patra* is expressed with particular lyrics throughout the

3. Vickers (1989: 72) associates the birth of *arja* as a performance genre with the birth of *geguritan*. However, Dibia (1992: 20–21) sees the primary literary source for *arja* as always

course of a performance. Ketut Rinda's *tembang Pucung* addresses *patra*. He begins with a lullaby within the story, and expands the meaning to address the audience on the issue of spiritual knowledge and the learning process. *Sinom lumbrah*, as sung by the refined prince, often deals with *patra* by discussing statecraft and rule of law. *Désa* and sense of ecology may be expressed by *Sinom Lawé*, describing a royal dwelling, or *Basung* and *Sinom Cecantungan*, dwelling on flora and fauna. The *sendon topéng* verses *Katkat taluklak saluklik* . . . deal with *kala*, time, depicting an era of joy and common decency. Or a dimmer *kala*, or era, may be presented by *arja*'s Punta.

> PUNTA'S *DURMA* IN COMMON BALINESE,
> AS TAUGHT BY WAYAN RANGKUS
> (CD SELECTION 15 OFFERS A STUDENT'S RENDITION)
>
> *Tuwuh jatma né jani tigang benang tiban,*
> *Jatmané gangsar mijil,*
> *Wong laré (k)enggal tua,*
> *Wong tua (k)enggal pejah*
> *sesayan sebudi-budi*
> *Panengan punah,*
> *Pangiwané sakti magendih*
>
> Nowadays humans only live to about seventy-five years
> More and more souls fast being born
> young people are too soon to grow old
> Old people are people soon to die
> confused and not knowing what to think
> the truth is not believed
> Sorcerers' magic ignites in flames

Within the dialogue of a performance, one strategy for expanding or contracting the *patra* 'context' of a situation is to place it in the light of the intrinsic qualities of numbers. This can throw a mundane situation into cosmic proportions, or bring the most theological discussion back to basics, as the number triggers a whole new "branching out" of the subject for anywhere from half a minute to half an hour.

The Balinese use of numbers reflects a phenomenological concern with oneness, twoness, threeness, and so on, at least up to nine. The number one suggests unity, Surya 'the sun deity', or nature, as well as Sang Hyang Widi 'all encompassing divinity'. Two is duality of all varieties, night and day, sickness and health, male and female, life and death. Three is *bayu*

---

having been *Malat*, the classical Panji Romance earlier associated with *gambuh*, and places the earliest stage of *arja* around 1904, with *arja doyong* 'simple *arja*'. But Dibia, like Vickers, sees the development of *arja* as reflecting a democratizing process, replacing the formalized music and dance structures of *gambuh* with improvisation. Bandem and de Boer (1995: 79) write of an earlier version, *dadap*, performed in 1825.

sabda idep 'energy, voice, and thought'; Brahma Wisnu Siwa, 'creation, preservation, destruction'; *désa kala patra* 'place-time-context'; *bumi langit akasa* 'earth, sky, heavens'. Four is the deities *betara* Brahma-Wisnu-Siwa-Iswara 'north-south-east-west' or 'earth-water[liquid]-fire[light]-wind [air]' *suka duka lara patih* 'joy-sorrow-sickness-death'. Five can be north-south-east-west-center or earth-liquid-light-wind-ether. Nine is three threes, compounding the mystical connotations.

As I approach the family compound of the *gambelan* maker Pandé Gableran for my first visit in eight years, I hear *topéng keras* music coming from a *gambelan gong* next door. I walk over to discover *dalang* Bona (the *dalang* of Bona village) performing ritual *topéng pajegan* for an *upacara mesangih* 'tooth-filing ceremony', with ritual *wayang lemah* just beside him. Once the *dalang*, Pak Sija, sees me enter, I know I will be staying until the *topéng* performance ends (it hasn't really begun as I come in). His dance is quite simple, yet very much attuned with the *gambelan*, and most concerned with characterization, at least with the introductory *pangempat* (*panglembar*) dances, including a strong, wide-eyed *Dalem*-type and orang tua, 'Old Man.' For the opening *papeson panasar*, he sings what he later describes as *selisir*, easier, he says, than real *sendon*. And more than *sendon*, it fits very closely with the *gambelan*'s melody, unusually sweet and flowing for a *panasar*, whose vocal style is more often staccato, jagged, and strident.

In his monologue, he veers in and out of character, coming from this world more than from another. This is clear in his use of *mata bolong*, the mask with hollow eyes, leaving the performer's eyes exposed. One can observe Pak Sija's eyes, strong and steady in gaze, then wandering without stylization as he surveys the surrounding audience. His *panasar* character tunes into individual members of the audience, addressing statements to a boy here, a girl there, discussing the ceremony and performance at hand. He points over to the *wayang lemah* in progress and discusses its role in religion. He directs some discussion toward me, looking and gesturing directly at me, concerning the fact that I am in Bali to learn, because Balinese culture and art are so "strong." His progression of *kirta basa* 'etymology' leads to "*Bali* means strength, strong religion, strong culture." His emphasis here is on educating more than storytelling, and making people consciously aware of whatever they are seeing. His combination Délem-pig-faced comic *bondrés* mask performs two dances, the male *baris* and female *rejang*. But first, he discusses the fact that dance plays an important role in ritual and that therefore he will broaden the *topéng* performance to include these other forms.

The *topéng* master Pak Kakul could slip out of character for a moment and have his *panasar* or *bondrés* character refer to someone in the audience as part of a humorous aside, and a *panasar* or *bondrés* might discuss issues of spiritual or ethical significance relating to the particular ceremony taking place. But with this style of perfoming *topéng pajegan*, Pak Sija is working for something else quite specific. He's working on a rational level, as a teacher, trying to help people look at and think clearly about, and with a present-day world view, art and religion. He is trying to deal with the fast-changing people and culture by experimenting within a traditional form and context, using *topéng*, and performing constantly at temple, house, and community ceremonies.

When he performs in this fashion, he's taking a new approach to bridging worlds and satisfying his contemporary community. He tells me that he sees this community becoming less entwined in the roots of their spiritual and artistic practice. And so, in order to commune with them (and instead of his *wayang* approach of weaving a story that draws them in and, along the way, reflects everyday realities as well as spiritual, philosophical values), he concentrates on sensitizing them to the present moment, situation, using the story as a simple reference point, giving them some personal sense of orientation in the world and cosmos. In this way, *désa kala patra* predominates over *masolah*.[4] And *désa* and *patra* are incorporated more than *kala*, at least in its transcendent sense.

This even extends to his final Sidha Karya character, who comes out with a tray of *sajen* ritual offerings. In doing the offerings and *mantra*, he (not the character) has the *gambelan* stop playing, so the audience can hear and understand what he is saying. These offerings are for this purpose, for this family. After that, as the *gambelan* resumes, he gives out the offerings, one by one, to kids and

---

4. Dealing with a very extreme form of *désa kala patra* within performance, Hildred Geertz (1991: 165) discusses a particular performance of *topéng* that took place in 1947, within which *panasars* are described as having engaged in "ritual dramaturgy," establishing very direct and weighty connections between events in the play and particular individuals in the audience. She suggests quite another performative function, involving real physical punishment as well as extreme public humiliation.

Daytime ritual *wayang lemah*
in Peliatan (1981). Photo by
Beth Skinner.

adults—mango, egg, coconut, the obligatory old Chinese *képéng*
coins—giving each person a piece of fruit and a few *képéng*, very
methodically and self-consciously (in contrast with Pak Kakul's deep
state of altered consciousness). Then he puts down the tray, picks
up a child, and strolls around gaily, as Pengejukan (Sidha Karya)
characters commonly do. Returning the child to the floor, he gives
him five *rupiah*, walks to his baskets unceremoniously, and removes
his long white horsehair wig and mask.

Pak Sija and all *dalang*s I know feel that when dancers or musicians learn
to perform, they can do it without change for the rest of their life; but a
dalang or *panasar* can never repeat a story, at least in the same neighbor-
hood. One must be learning and developing new stories as long as one
lives. The audience's aesthetic concern not to hear the same story twice

from the same *dalang* goes hand in hand with the principle of *désa kala patra*, which insists upon every performance reflecting the particular context at hand. And this in turn goes hand in hand with the aesthetic concept of *perkembangan* 'flowering', which sees art as a living form, ever-changing.

Candri speaks of the audience reflecting the feeling and intentions of the dancer. What she conceives in terms of emotion, motivation, and plot, Sija conceives additionally in terms of story choice and *désa kala patra*, and Pak Rajeg, the *dalang* of Tunjuk, as a *tali* 'cord' of sympathy. But all these conceptions involve drawing the audience in, in order that they can reflect out, into their own lives and those of other times and realms.

Back in the United States, a friend criticized a production of Peter Schumann's Bread and Puppet Theatre, "the story of one who went out to study fear," for being propaganda and of a lower artistic level than he would have expected. I answered that we cannot have one set of criteria to measure "level of artistry," but that other aspects, which we might think of as nonaesthetic, such as emotional or social impact, must enter into our appreciation of what we are seeing as art. I happened to have truly appreciated this Bread and Puppet piece aesthetically, and certainly much of their work is visionary and of an exemplary artistic level. But certain performances might be thought of as Bread and Puppets's version of Balinese *wayang lemah*, the ritual form of puppetry often required for ceremonies. It is uncommon indeed to hear Balinese saying "That was a great (or terrible) *wayang lemah*," because people do not judge it by common artistic standards. It is cherished because it fulfills an aspect of the religious ceremony. Of course, if a *dalang* is particularly good, people might so comment, and children might gravitate toward the *dalang* as he performs. But the principal audience for *wayang lemah* is of a divine nature, visiting gods and ancestors; few, if any, adult people actually attend such a performance. Many Balinese feel that such ceremonial genres are important not just as aspects of religious ritual, but as the heart of all Balinese art. It is such forms that keep the overall artistic tradition focused and profound. This is the concrete reminder that performance is most essentially a spiritual and social necessity, *sajiwani* 'food for the spirit'. This collective vision of art being as essential to life as is food, is the fuel by which all aesthetic energy and sensibility are powered. It is one key to why Balinese art is so reflective of time, place, context, and spirit, and a key motivation for artists to be inspired to spontaneity, creativity, and variation.

And this is the relationship of bread to the theater of Bread and Puppet. Director Peter Schumann (1970: 35) writes, "The bread shall remind you of the sacrament of eating. We want you to understand that theatre is not yet an established form, not the place of commerce that you think it is, where you pay and get something. Theatre is different. It is more like bread, more like a necessity. Theatre is a form of religion. It is fun. It preaches sermons and it builds up a self-sufficient ritual where the actors try to raise their lives to the purity and ecstasy of the actions in which they participate."

All of their pieces focus on the essentials, life and death, good and evil, humanity and nature, presenting their world view in the form of a total theater sermon. Some pieces are more subtle, transcendent, or lighthearted than others, still pointing a finger at the issue, in the Brechtian tradition, but with a less heavy hand. But the occasional piece that appears to some as too blatant or message-oriented can be appreciated as a direct, raw expression of the essentials, as with Balinese ceremonials, where the role of art as bread, as food, arises for a time to assert its claim to prominence.

Perkembangan

spontaneity and the flower of *désa kala patra*

❀

Balinese artists initially consider the *désa kala patra* of an event or situation in terms of the larger context of performance; including the people, histories, and environment at hand. This may determine the genre chosen or the particular story or scenario. But performers also continually refer to *désa kala patra* within performance aesthetics, and here the terms have additional connotations.

A sense of place and context apply to the process of plot construction in literature and performance. Pak Tempo uses the word *lambang*,[1] which is also the architectural term for the cross-beams of a house. With *kala*, other techniques of plot development and improvisation come into play, relying on an improvisational facility with literature and poetics. *Kala* may refer to the degree or quality of transcendence within the flow of dance, drama, and music, and may involve going into another state or possession by a spirit or deity. In this sense the artist's self-image is not as "the creator" but as the vehicle of a "process of nature" much larger than him or herself. In this sense, *kala* is referred to as the mood, tone, and flow of energy between performers and audience.

The use of colloquial dialogue and physical humor, which can go on for hours in a *topéng* or *arja* performance, creates a particular sense of time. A king or minister can make an entrance and come right to the point of his mission, or can spend forty-five minutes sensing out his surroundings, while storytellers describe him and speak for him in the poetic language of classical

---

1. *Lampahan* is the most common *Kawi* term for storyline, or plot structure, in *wayang* and other dramatic forms. "The root *lampah* in both Kawi and modern Balinese means 'to move, go forward' and carries the sense of directional progression . . . A synonymous word, *laku*, forms the base of the word used in Javanese shadow theater and Sundanese rod-puppet theater for the 'story' component of the performance: *lakon*" (Zurbuchen 1987: 207).

Kawi. Some storytellers in *wayang* or dance drama take circuitous routes along a well-known story line. *Carangan* denotes a deviation from the standard story, a subplot, which can consist of an extra three-hour intrigue or merely two lines from Middle Javanese *Malat* or Old Javanese *kakawin* poetry, creating just a subtle shading of the mood of a scene. The point here is that Balinese theater is generally improvised, using countless shared devices and sources, as well as standardized characterization techniques.

For instance, when *mantri manis* is walking in the woods with a female companion, he may say, "Oh, look at the beautiful flowers." But if there is time and inspiration, he may sing an entire *tembang— Sinom Cecantungan* or *Basung*, for instance—describing the natural surroundings with romantic and/or mystical nuances.

Or in *topéng*, a *panasar* may base his *tandak* for *Dalem*'s entrance on all of the particular movements of the king, "small fingers on his hands, gentle, graceful arms, a swaying walk to left and right, like a peacock ready to fly off . . . " Or he may choose not to follow the choreography of *Dalem*, and sing relatively simple standard phrases of homage.

In and out of the Balinese arts academies, a common theme in discussions about dance concerns how the styles of different regions place a different emphasis on choreographic posture (*agem*), movement phrases (*tandang*) and movement transitions (*tangkis*). In itself, this triad is sometimes said to reflect *désa kala patra*, with a fourth term, *tangkep*, referring to specific aspects of elaboration with hands, eyes, and head movement. Placing an emphasis on posture, stance, a character's way of holding the body, reflects *désa* 'place,' often articulating character in stylyzed, fixed positions. The aspect of movement flow and phrasing, *tandang*, is related to *kala*, the flow of time. Transitional phrases, *tangkis*, are seen as reflecting *patra*, context. Nothing is inflexible, though, and each style has its own ways of creating a transcendent sense of time through expansion and contraction.

One morning, Candri mentions that she has been invited to participate in a *Calonarang* performance that evening for an *odalan* festival at a *pura dalem* 'temple of the dead' in distant Mengwi. I ask who else will be performing in the group, but she has no idea. Someone from the village of Mengwi had invited her and she had not asked who else would be dancing.[2] She invites us to join her in

2. This is a loose variety of the *Arja Bon* ensemble, in which individual accomplished performers are invited and assembled by the host. Some of these performers have also belonged

the *bémo* passenger truck for the two-hour ride over the mountains.

So, early that evening we arrive at her house just before the *bémo* from Mengwi. When I ask, she still does not know who is in the cast. The *bémo* takes off down the dirt road and stops at a gateway to the *puri* 'palace, house compound of *Satria* caste'. "Oh, Cok. Istri will be dancing tonight," Candri exclaims. Cokorde Rai Partini, a female dancer specializing in *mantri* roles, comes out and joins us. The *bémo* takes off and stops at a little food stall where Pak Retug, Pak Regep, and Pak Rangkus are waiting. The *panasar* and *bondrés* performers hop into the back of the truck with us, exchanging greetings and mild surprise, "Oh, great, you'll be joining us, too." We make several more stops in their village before stopping by the main road where Pak Bertong is waiting. "Oh, you're coming, too," several people call out as he squeezes in.

Finally the *bémo* heads off toward Mengwi, everyone crowded in with their large baskets containing masks, headpieces, and costumes. The two intimate hours of travel are spent in chatting and joking among these friends.

If they had been on their way to perform *topéng* and I had asked who will play which roles, someone would have explained that that would be decided later in the evening, once they decide on a story. But for *Calonarang*, the role assignments and plot are obvious to everyone.

We arrive at the village's temple of the dead, the ceremony already in progress one day and night. Throngs of people are moving in and out of the temple, carrying new, elaborately designed offerings of fruit and rice for that evening's rituals. The village's *gambelan gong* is playing in the outer courtyard of the temple. Our troupe is escorted to an inner courtyard of the temple, where we sit down on raised bamboo platforms to relax and meet some of the locals. After an hour or so of snacks, some betel nut chewing, and chatting, dinner is served.[3] After this, some performers stretch out on the same platform and doze off, while others continue to chat quietly. Within the course of the next hour, everyone begins to get into costume. It is often at this time that nuances of plot and poetic or philosophical themes for that particular night get discussed. If *topéng*

---

to more organized *bon* "All-Star" groups, which have existed since the late 1960s. This contrasts with the traditional and more formally structured *sebunan* ensemble, made up of "neighbors living in close proximity, or relatives belonging to the same family or clan; and they may be members of a congregation of the three main temples (*kahyangan tiga*) of the village" (Dibia 1992: 111).

3. I have also seen a television set in this area, tuned to a sports event, though no one appeared to be watching.

I Wayan Retug as *bondrés* and Anak Agung Putu Laksmi as *mantri manis* in *prémbon* (1980).

were being performed, even role assignments and decisions concerning which story to perform and in what narrative sequence could wait until this point.

Once the ensemble is about ready to begin, the host village may precede them with locals performing any of a number of introductory dances, such as *barong, jauk, baris, péndét*, and so on.

Tempo asserts that to get to the essence of a performing style you have to have an overall sense of the materials the artist has to work with, how they're internalized, and then how those materials are shaped to be in harmony with his/her conceptions and the situation. Since an important aspect of Balinese performance is that of group improvisation and recombining, keeping in tune with *désa kala patra*, one must approach it as a process of growth, not as constituent parts. Using a script is described as "machine-like." The performance becomes dead, because when performers cannot apply *kala*, the fluid sense of time that allows transcendence, there is no "flowering."

It may be the fact that *gambuh* Singapadu has not been performed or rehearsed for a few years, and some of those performing in Sibang have never danced their present roles before.[4] But still, their preparation indicates something in the tradition, though more so of *topéng* and *arja*. Over coffee and cakes, the group decides who is to dance each role. "You'll be Panji." "Who, me?" "Yeah, you can do it." They discuss the basic plot sequence of the *Copét* story and break off into groups. Each group of two to five gathers in a different place and prepares its course of action, with *aryas* here, *prabu* here, Panji and *panasar* there.

So, in a sense, the actual way in which one group will interact with another is not determined except within performance. The *panasars* and *prabus* discuss the philosophical and spiritual themes and prepare a few specific lines of *tandak* song. They discuss the literal meaning of the aphorism *sama dana béda danda*, and how it could be applied to the story at hand. "Whoever loves their king will not go afoul of the law."

Many performers sing to themselves, going over the particular *tandak* they need. After eating, dressing, and making up, as they are about to go out to the performance space with the musicians, Bertong calls to Rangkus, "Sure you still remember how that *tandak* verse goes?"

Nyoman Candri is saying how little there really is to *arja*: there's a very limited vocabulary of dance movements, the *gambelan* varies little, and it's very easy to understand. When I protest, she elaborates that, in fact, *arja* is terribly difficult "in practice." The performer, also called *arja*, must lead the *gambelan* as with masked *topéng* and *jauk*, but also connect her singing with every nuance of gesture and dance in creating story, emotion, and character. Playing off of the lively, complex drums and colotomic gongs creates expectation and drama. Signals to the musicians for sudden or gradual *angsel* phrases, sudden turns, fast or slow walks, staccato shifts of gaze, *seledét*, are what bring the form alive. Facial expression and eyes are synchronized with the dance, song, and instrumental music. The character's

4. The only really active village *gambuh* ensembles are in Batuan, where there are two prominent groups (and recently a third). The village of Pedungan has been reviving the tradition as well. However, *gambuh* is still considered the major source of Balinese choreography, dance characterization, and musical tuning systems. Most highly formalized, the scenes depict the costumes, language, and gesture of the fourteenth-century East Javanese courts. Themes are mostly derived from *Malat*, the Balinese version of the *Panji* cycle.

expression during an opening dance may be stylized to the degree that it does not necessarily follow the literal meaning of the *tembang*, but catches hold of the melody, gesturing and signaling to the *gambelan*.

After the *mantri manis* sings the lyrics *ngamar taning* with a smile and sinuous figure-eight head-shifting, there is a slight, only momentary glance of anger with an almost unnoticeable flick of the head. This signals the *gambelan* to speed up, initiated by a patter of five light *ping* strokes from the *kendang*. Candri describes the angry glances as indicating to musicians, "Now you'd better catch my signal and change into the next musical section." A characteristic balance of playfulness and tension is created by this alienation effect, as the expression half transforms the face out of character, as actor to musicians, rather than dramatic character in transcendent time. A jolt of recognition is given to audience and other performers, as the wheels of place, time, and context are allowed to spin in midair momentarily, before the performer slips back from actor to character.

Eyes and expression are very stylized and tied into the *tembang* and dance, yet the dancer has great freedom to use the style to suit her creative instinct and feeling, as long as clear signals are sent to the *gambelan*. In this sense, *arja* music is not monotonous at all, if one perceives the signals and interplay between dance and music, which all lead to shifting shadings. Traditional *arja* drumming is considered to be the most complex and subtle, relying upon spontaneity and nuance between the two interlocked but fluid drummers and the dancer.

Candri compares *arja* with *légong*, in which the music-dance relationship is so structurally set. Here is a dichotomy between what is complex in formal structure versus complex in temporal dynamics. "Easy theoretically" but difficult in practice brings up an interesting issue of process and material, sometimes discussed in terms of "primitive tools and skills."[5] The lack of structural complexity in one's tools requires a special sophistication in the practitioner, an ability to commune with the material in a corporeal manner, acutely sensing the "present."

5. Speaking of primitive hunters, the poet Gary Snyder asks, "Why, then, does there seem to be a weakness in their hunting technology? The answer is simple: they didn't hunt with tools, they hunted with their minds. They did things—learning an animal's behavior—that rendered elaborate tools unnecessary. You learn animal behavior by becoming an acute observer—by entering the mind—of animals" (1980:107).

Kala

❋

Déwasa *and the arrangement of time*

In discussing the mystical and pedagogical implications of *nusup* 'penetration' and the *désa kala patra* of experience, a friend offers the analogy of Bali being a small boat and Jakarta a big boat. For circumnavigating a harbor, being small gives freedom of movement and diverse possibilities. A Balinese cultural trait found in all aspects of life and art involves breaking everything down into smaller units, allowing detachability of parts and flexibility.

In a complex rendering of *kinds of time* according to an elaborate calendrical system, each day has different inherent qualities and character traits, appropriate for some activities and not others. Wayan Diya likens the interpreter of *wariga* 'reckoning of time' to a chemist, mixing together aspects of *kala* 'time'. There is a balancing of *inside and outside* experience of time, viewing it both as qualities and as visible social and cosmological (lunar) forms. There are days, *déwasa*, auspicious for every conceivable activity, from cutting a baby's hair or starting construction of a new house, to holding a cremation, wedding, or tooth-filing ceremony. And every temple, from an individual family's *pura sanggah* to large community temples, has its own birthday, or commemoration festival, generally once in the Balinese 210-day yearly cycle.

Many performance genres are associated with specific days and places: *barong* with *Tumpek Landep*, the day honoring sharp objects ranging from farm tools to the sacred *kris* 'dagger' and *landep* 'ceremonial lances'; *wayang wong* with *Galungan*, the ten-day festival of ancestors; *gambuh* with *odalan* 'temple anniversary festivals' at the *pura désa* 'community temples' of a *Brahmana* 'high caste' village or at a great celebration or cremation of a *raja*; and *Calonarang* with a *pura dalem* 'temple of the dead'.

Barong landung in Ubud (1972). Photo by Beth Skinner.

There is a collective experience, shared by performers and their fellow villagers, as a date approaches and the *gambelan* is rehearsed each evening in the open air in a public area, and costumes and masks are brought out by day and repaired as needed.

In order to schedule another study session, Pak Tempo consults the calendar studiously, to find a day during which all, or almost all, aspects are favorable. The next day, already chosen for the premiere performance of his *séndratari* group, is very favorable, but he says that one aspect favors anger, which could affect the propitiousness of the day. As it turns out, while they are setting up that next evening, one of the performers gets angry at some guys playing volleyball near the *balé* 'performance area'. They argue, as he insists they are hampering and obstructing the performers' preparations. Then, just as the performance is about to begin and everyone is in costume, rain comes pouring down, and the audience is much smaller than expected. The younger dancers are disappointed and do not consider the performance a success, because of the light turnout. The next morning, while we are there, Tempo explains to the performer who had gotten into the argument how he had predicted that the one obstacle that could affect the *déwasa* was that of anger, and that was the cause of the rain, the subsequent small audience, and the subsequent artistic disappointment.

Pak Tempo explains that *kala* also refers to the character of a *yuga* 'era' or 'epoch', as each dynasty has varied throughout history. The first of four in the rotating cycle of *yuga*s is a time of peace, union, openness; second, the beginning of jealousy, likes, and dislikes; third, an era of stealing and transgressions; and fourth, our own era of war, jealousy, coveting of materials, destruction.

Another aspect of time is that of the seasons, moons, and agricultural cycles. And yet another aspect of time can reflect the character of a very specific place and context.

The people of Manukaya have a sacred stone enshrined at the holy watering place, Tirtha Mpul, (an eleventh-century Shivaite cave-hermitage) in the mountains near Tampaksiring, along the Pakrisan River. The stone is carried "on the full-moon day of the fourth month of the year to be ritually bathed in the holy waters of Tirtha Mpul. The content of the stone's weathered inscription was unknown to the villagers. Upon deciphering it, Stutterheim found that it was the charter of Tirtha Mpul's foundation, in the fourth month, on the day of the full moon of the year A.D. 962. For 1000 years the observance of the precise day had been preserved by tradition."[1]

Sitting at a food stall, I mention that I've heard of a local elder who teaches the Balinese language. The proprietress answers that it's her husband's uncle, Déwa Putu Dani, and asks if we'd like to meet him. I say yes, sometime we would. Within five minutes, he is there, greeting us. Because he begins by speaking Balinese with me, somehow (bizarre as it seems) I forget completely that he speaks Indonesian, English, and possibly Dutch, and that the whole point of our meeting is for him to help me translate songs and texts. Somehow,

1. Claire Holt (1967: 169).

his look of age and initial use of Balinese language (many of his generation still speak little Indonesian), as well as his long white hair (uncommon then, except in remote mountain communities—this was before the 1980s revival of long hairstyles) leads me to forget. He suggests that we find a *déwasa* appropriate for beginning the study of texts by consulting a friend of his, a *balian wariga* 'specialist in the reckoning of time'. I should come back in a couple of days and he will let me know his friend's suggestion. It turns out that his friend is none other than Anak Agung Aji, whom we had consulted on the timing of our move to a new house in Bedaulu. But as we sit and talk, the elderly Anak Agung Aji comes strolling down the road, leaning on his cane. Pak Dani excuses himself to speak with his friend, who suggests we go over to his house immediately. We all walk over and he brings out his *lontar wariga*. As we sit down on the porch he begins to study the text.

Fifteen minutes pass and I grow apprehensive that he'll give the same sort of advice he had given concerning our move to Bedaulu: "yes, there's a good day three months from now." When I had asked if there was a closer day not quite as auspicious but still suitable, he had thought for a few minutes and suggested a day six weeks off. So, in this case, I am thinking his long consultation with the *lontar* 'palm leaf' calendar must indicate a week by week search for an appropriate *déwasa*. But after fifteen minutes, he discusses and re-counts with Pak Dani, and pronounces *buin telun* 'in three days'. Pak Dani explains that the long search was required in order to approach that particular day from every angle, not to scour over the days and weeks; a vertical rather than horizontal perspective on time.[2] After I thank Agung Aji very politely, Pak Dani suggests I offer fifty-five *rupiah*, not a payment but a ceremonial gesture. Agung Aji accepts it to pay for some modest ritual offerings, perhaps some flowers, and wishes us well with our studies. I part with Pak Dani, agreeing to meet in three days at seven in the morning. As I ride my bicycle across the hills to Bedaulu, dark rain clouds hang all across the sky, leaving room, though, for beams of the setting sun's light and a reddish glow in the western sky.

2. Balinese calendrical notions—their machinery for demarcating temporal units—"are largely used not to measure the elapse of time, nor yet to accent the uniqueness and irrecoverability of the passing moment, but to mark and classify the qualitative modalities in terms of which time manifests itself in human experience. The Balinese calendar (or rather calendars; as we shall see, there are two of them) cuts time up into bounded units not in order to count and total them but to describe and characterize them, to formulate their differential social, intellectual and religious significance" (Geertz 1973: 391).

Trikala, wanara, *and the* dalang

Pak Rinda discusses one version of *Kala tiga* and the origins of *barong* and *wanara*. Kala is the name of a wrathful emanation of Siwa (Shiva), a dangerous supernatural presence in many stories because of his need to devour humans to satisfy his insatiable appetite. *Trikala* or *Kala tiga* (*trisemaya* in Sanskrit, according to Pak Rinda) are "three aspects, or manifestations, of Kala." *Barong*s are sacred beings in the form of tigers, elephants, boars, dogs, goats, or horses, performed by one or two people in costume and mask. Not only does the mask, costume, and choreography "represent" a supernatural mythical entity, but the manifestation in performance is sacred in itself. Most prominent and magnificent is *barong kékét*, resembling the Chinese lion, and often referred to as Banaspati Raja 'Lord of the Woods'.[3] *Wanara* most often refers to the monkey army of Anoman in the *Ramayana*, but really includes a full range of semidivine animals.

When the gods Wisnu and Déwi Sri were making love, his semen spilled into a river, and many animals of the forest—tigers, monkeys, lions, and so on, came forth and drank some of it. The females became pregnant and their offspring were born *wanara*s, some of them taking on part of the form of the human body, with an animal head. With the *taksu* 'divine power' aquired through Wisnu, they were then able to drive away the forms of Kala from the world. In a later era, Wisnu manifested as Rama, and the *wanara*s came as the monkey army to aid him in the battle against the demonic king *Rawana*. The tiger *wanara* is here manifested as Sempati. According to Pak Rinda, the threefold manifestation of Kala, *trikala* or *Kala tiga*, was manifested in the *Ramayana* as Rawana, Méganada, and Kumbakarna (Madé Bandem says it is Surpanaka).

Galungan is the most significant sequence of events on the religious calendar, when the spirits of the ancestors arrive to visit the homes of their descendants. During the Galungan festival, according to Pak Rinda, *trikala* is

---

3. The monstrous head of Kirttimukha is another source of the *barong* form. "In ancient Indian myth, it was the name of an emanation of Shiva's wrath, sprung from between the god's eyebrows, a monster of insatiable hunger, created to devour the demonic Rauh, an emissary of the Lord of Titans. When Rauh secured Shiva's mercy, Kirttimukha was, by Shiva's order, to consume his own body. He fed upon it until nothing was left but his leonine head, the "Visage of Glory" (Kirttimukha). Shiva then ordained, perhaps as compensation, that Kirttimukha live in honor above the god's portals. Thus it came to be that the monster's head appears above temple portals and niches in Java and Bali as a venerated guardian" (Claire Holt 1967: 107). See also Emigh 1984.

Despite its demonic aspects, *barong kékét* is most often presented as playful and spiritually benevolent. In magic dramas, he is generally a manifestation of the power that subdues, or at least battles with, destructive magic, *pangiwa* 'science of the left', in the form of Rangda. He protects and restores his human charge with his own *panengen* 'healing magic' or 'science of the right'.

actually manifested as a time period of three days. The first day is *Penyeke-ban* (from *sekeb* 'to cover up', referring to the accelerated process of ripening bananas—required as offerings—by heating them in covered clay urns). Next is *Panyajaan* (from *jaja* 'rice cakes'), the day for preparing these many-colored, decorative offerings. The following day, *Panampahan* (from *nampah* 'to slaughter an animal', is when pigs, turtles, or ducks are butchered for the festival feasts. It is particularly important for the *barong*s and *wanara*s to be out at this time to subdue *trikala*. Forces of destruction are present and are subdued by powers of nature that have been nourished, transformed, given energy, sacralized, by life's source, by life, by the water of life, *amerta*.

Accompanied by a portable *gambelan*, *barong*s *nglawang* 'stroll' along paths throughout the hamlet and along roads from village to village to ward off the malevolent spirits. *Wayang wong* is performed within the temples of many villages, enacting episodes of the *Ramayana*, highlighting a huge cast of *wanara*s. *Barong* and *jauk* dramas may be performed out on the village paths. *Jauk* is a semidemonic, semihuman mask character associated with *barong* magic dramas. Elaborately costumed, *jauk*s wear elaborate gold pagoda-shaped headpieces and long water buffalo–horn fingernails. *Sandaran* or *jauk luh* are female *jauk*s, with delicately shaped lips, rather than the normal wide row of mother-of-pearl teeth; *jauk dandan* may be a group of males and females. Some *jauk* masks are part male, part female. In traditional contexts, *jauk*s may either have an adversarial relationship with the *barong* or be on his side. In the course of a ritual drama, they may be the malevolent, destructive ones, and *barong* the hero—or vice versa.

Pak Rinda gives one old scenario in which four *jauk dandan* come out to confront the *barong* but are soon subdued and enchanted. They then begin to move in unison as *oyod padi* 'swaying rice plants', arms outstretched and hands joining one *jauk* to another. As they dance, they sing *kidung wireg wilet manyura*, a song of realization and repentance, *nyanyian sadar* (*masandaran*), with several male *jauk*s.[4]

All the *bahan-bahan* 'ingredients' of artistic process come together here for Pak Rinda; the movement of wind and earth in *oyod padi*, song, conflict, pleasure, intoxication, and spirit. And then, a historical sense of the past,

---

4. Up until the early part of this century, there was a great variety of *jauk*s, from coarse to refined, and entire episodes from the *Mahabharata* were enacted solely by *jauk*s and *panasar* narrators. The refined male *jauk* has not altogether vanished, the red-faced and strong *jauk* Durga is still performed occasionally, and there is a recent revival of female *jauk sandaran*, instigated at the STSI arts academy. But most popular since the 1940s has been an often comical *jauk*, somewhere in between the *manis* 'sweet' and *keras* 'strong' types. He may precede a *topéng* performance, and is invariably included in the standard tourist revue of Balinese dances.

kerta yuga, joins with both transcendent time and the present as he encounters directly unseen but immediate forces. Pak Rinda's way of "telling" suggests an intrinsic conceptualization of the artistic process. He explains that for anything to have beauty, to bind, to elicit empathy, it must flower and grow. To flower and grow, life must be within it. To have life means to have unique existence and yet be immersed in the world.

Pak Rinda's etymology of *wanara* has *wana* meaning "forest," *ara* meaning "life, *amerta.*" Water of life is what the *wanara* drink, granting deep revelation of the experience of life and the power to survive and replenish. It is the source of artistic expression, in its actual transformation of animals into different *wanara* and *barong*. Pak Rinda's *kirta basa* interprets the *Kawi* word *wanara* as *baruang* ("of the forest" in Balinese), manifested as *barong* to subdue *Kala tiga*.

In my own exercise with playful *kirta basa* etymology I find there may just conceivably be some connection with the Tibetan *'Brong* 'wild yak':

The yak . . . is characteristically shown as a fierce, raging beast that charges around graveyards with lions, tigers, vultures, and equally ferocious black deer . . . The "Dance of the Wild Yak" recorded by Jest is probably a descendant of the "Ritual of the Yak" performed by Bon priests at the tomb of the Tibetan King 1200 year ago. (Ellingson 1973: 25)

The interaction between artistic and demonic forms is also played out within *wayang*. The *dalang*, in this context referred to as Kama 'god of love, pleasure', takes on and subdues Kala by means of manifesting deep emotions and senses. In the *dalang*'s function as Kama, it is the source of *kawi suara* 'the voice,' which manifests life's qualities and powers. The *Dharma Pawayangan* text includes many invocations such as this:

May men be stimulated, may women be stimulated, hermaphrodites be stimulated; collected in front of me, excited when listening to my voice. I am the embodiment of the God of Love; may they be gratified on seeing me, may their tender feelings be aroused immediately. (*Kama and Kala*, C. Hooykaas 1973: 39)

Another image used for the *dalang* is that of sweeping out negative, destructive energies. Art is born from water of life, and the binding strength of love, compassion, in order to vanquish *kala* 'time', which is liminality and illusion.[5]

5. In the historically related Tibetan Tantric Buddhist practice, Kala is a deity of comparable qualities with the Balinese Kala, as well as being a manifestation of Time. One important aspect of Tibetan Tantric ritual similarly involves vanquishing Time, in the sense of impermanence and illusion.

Judith Becker has another take on the destructiveness of *kala* 'Time' as cultural "forgetfulness," which can be overcome by a combination of traditionally "speaking the past" and cre-

In all of these contexts, the process is not one of representation but of life being breathed into transcendent qualities that are manifested corporeally. Specific form reflects and grows out of the immediate environs and moment, and a particular vision, situation, and activity.

---

atively "speaking the present" (1993: 167). She also discusses the role of the Javanese *dalang* to "exorcise" Kala (165).

On the subject of Javanese *wayang kulit*, René Lysloff (1993: 69–71) writes: "The entire performance, like ritual, is a time out of time . . . Its three divisions have an eerie similarity to Turner's 'phases' of the rites of passage: they can quite easily be likened to what is now widely known as 'separation,' 'liminality,' and reaggregation (see Turner 1969: 94) . . . As a meta-discourse on ritual time, *wayang* dramatizes the process of transformation that ritual participants undergo."

Désa kala patra
of the arts in contemporary Bali

❁

Like everyone else around them, Balinese and other Indonesian artists are observing and discussing the rapid changes taking place in their culture.[1] While everyone "values" the arts, and Indonesian performing arts are certainly a popular commodity in the world arena, shifting contexts and subsequent new perspectives are causing some artists to ask, "What *is* Indonesian theater, dance, and music?" People are still doing dances as the culture changes over to mass media, bureaucratization, commercialization, and "modern-educated" youth. Old cultural processes that have produced amazingly diverse and varied forms are undergoing fundamental changes. And as the culture shifts away from certain life-styles, the sources of creative expression and the factors that make something sacred, or spontaneous, or even alive, become less clear.

We see the flowers on a tree and think, "Oh, how beautiful, delicate, and colorful they are, moving in the breeze." While the branches and trunk of the tree are brown, heavy, and immobile, its roots not even visible, we know that the beauty of the flower comes from below, and after the flowers fade and drop, the tree still stands and continues to produce new flowers. The flowers of human culture are even more prone to dominate our attention, obfuscating their roots.

There are a great many aspects of the arts in Bali that elicit in foreigners interest, enjoyment, and the desire to study and incorporate elements into their own artistic forms. But underlying these myriad aspects we can see a

1. This chapter is based on a lecture presented in 1980 at ASTI-Bali, since renamed Sekolah Tinggi Seni Indonesia (STSI), the Indonesian College of the Arts. As part of a lecture series on art and culture, I was invited to discuss what it is about Balinese arts that interests Westerners. The paper was originally presented in Indonesian, and later translated into English and revised.

few deeper, simple truths that give rise to this great variety of artistic forms. Before touching on these aspects, we can begin by looking at some of the more obvious qualities of Balinese performing arts that attract many Europeans and Americans, and at how cultural differences are often perceived in their broadest and most general outlines.

In much Euro-American performance training, great emphasis is placed on individual discipline and the personal attainment of skill. This has led to refined technique that often lacks the particular kind of kinetic ensemble dynamic we see in Balinese performance. The basic training process in Balinese music involves learning by actual ensemble experience; so from the earliest stages, one's sense of performance involves sharing and group identity. In Euro-American societies, which have long held ideals cultivating the strong individual, growing numbers of people are trying to feel a part of something larger than themselves. A different kind of sensitivity is required to perform in a Balinese ensemble, an intense precision without becoming machine-like, combined with encouragment of the life and imagination of the individual performer. Euro-American traditions have fostered many forms of group dynamics, but much can be learned from other kinds of group sensibilities and organization, including notions of fluidity within structure.

These sensibilities can be seen with just a few examples, ranging from the finer details of melodic and rhythmic interplay to the social dynamics of ensemble organization. The technique by which a single melodic line is produced by two interlocking parts played by musicians on separate instruments is called *kotékan*. *Polos* 'simple, direct' plays the more basic part of the melody while *sangsih* 'differing' fills in to create the two-part figuration. The interdependency inherent in this means of melodic expression is intensified in many ways, such as gradual or sudden dynamic shifts between soft and loud, fast and slow, or even more obvious coordinated *angsel* 'cadences' that accompany an improvising dramatic character. Melody takes on a particularly spatial characteristic when being departmentalized in this fashion. Interlocking drum rhythms reflect a similar sensibility, joining *lanang* 'male', the smaller and higher-pitched in a pair of drums or gongs, with *wadon* 'female', larger and deeper-pitched. Complex drum phrases consist of a dynamic intertwining of rhythms and tones from the two instruments. For some dance genres the interlocking parts are set precisely with the choreography, while others involve a spontaneous and somewhat improvised interplay between the two drummers and the dancer, maintaining a very formalized and precise, though at the same time fluid form.

A social form exhibiting a related sensibility is the *seka* 'to be as one', a traditional Balinese organized group put together for a specific kind of activity. It is common for a Balinese villager to belong to three or four different *seka*. Beyond the more formal, obligatory *seka* organized around village, temple, and irrigation affiliations, there is a wide range of "noncoordinate, components of 'pluralistic collectivism' . . . " (Clifford Geertz 1980: 53).[2] A performing *seka* includes musicians, dancers, and nonplaying members who help with maintainance, religious offerings, and so on. It is said that the sense of equality within the *seka* transcends one's role and responsibilities. Most village dance troupes are organized as *seka*, except for *topéng*, which is more often a temporary aggregate of individuals.

The dynamic interrelationship between dance, drama, and music is also fascinating to European-American artists. While much Euro-American theater has been verbal and descriptive, Balinese theater is not intended as a depiction but as a corporeal manifestation of spiritual states, through a unified, stylized language of sound, gesture, word, and characterization that, even without deep study, is easy for foreigners to appreciate. Antonin Artaud, metaphysician of European theater, observed Balinese performances in 1931 at the Paris Exposition and later wrote: "The drama does not develop as a conflict of feelings but as a conflict of spiritual states, themselves ossified and transformed into gestures . . . [T]hrough the labyrinth of their gestures, attitudes and sudden cries, through the gyrations and turns which leave no portion of the stage space unutilized, the sense of a new physical language, based upon signs and no longer upon words, is liberated" (1958: 53–54).

In Balinese arts the sense of "pleasure" is so very basic to performance. Although there are artists everywhere who derive pleasure from their work, there is the common cliché in Europe, the United States, and elsewhere that the artist should suffer to attain inspiration and success.[3] Practice of technique is often accepted as boring and "work," a means to an

2. Clifford Geertz also (1980: 158) refers to the "*seka* principle" as "the equality of members in the context of the group of which they are members, the irrelevance of that membership with respect to other groups to which they may belong . . . " This kind of group dynamic is significant in this otherwise stratified society consisting of kinship groups of various levels of status and function. Within the *seka*, it is said, all are equal, whether they be gentry or commoners.

There are voluntary *seka* "for housebuilding, for various kinds of agricultural work, for transporting goods to market, for music, dance and drama performances, for weaving mats, moulding pottery, or making bricks, for singing and interpreting Balinese poetry, for erecting and maintaining a temple at a given waterfall or a particular sacred grove, for buying and selling food, textiles or cigarettes, and for literally dozens of other tasks" (Geertz 1959: 999).

3. Susan Sontag writes of "The artist as exemplary sufferer," making the contrast and generalization broader still, to include "the ancient Hebrews, Greeks and the Orientals . . . Suffering was not the hallmark of seriousness; rather, seriousness was measured by one's ability to evade or transcend the penalty of suffering, by one's ability to achieve tranquility and equilibrium. In contrast, the sensibility we have inherited identifies spirituality and seriousness with turbulence, suffering, passion. For two thousand years, among Christians and Jews, it has been spiritually fashionable to be in pain" (1961: 47).

end, but not nececessarily something to enjoy in itself. A foreign observer immediately picks up on that Balinese sense of pleasure in rehearsal and performance, joy in the physical sensations of resonance and rhythm as well as the kinesthetic feeling of ensemble.

In much of our contemporary world, art is more often confined to specific halls, schools, museums; art rarely enters into other aspects of life. Specific people designated as professionals are brought into a place to entertain other individuals who pay to experience art.[4] As the concept of "art for art's sake" has tended to dominate, our understanding of the usefuness and necessity of art for community and society has remained amorphous. This is evidenced by contemporary educational priorities and cultural debate in the United States. Balinese art is usually part of a larger community activity in which the art is needed to facilitate life's transitions and activities. You don't have to go to a specific place to experience art. It happens where a social or religious activity is happening: in your house, in the middle of the road, at the community hall or temples.[5]

Performance has also been closer to people's lives, as neighbors can perform for their own community's needs—familiar faces of friends or family providing the music or dance for the situation. Even if outside performers are invited in, it is still considered a village event, for extraperformative reasons. For many foreign artists, who often feel apart from their community and may even cultivate and champion the isolation of their personal imaginative world, the strong Balinese sense of bonds, interconnections, and sharing is a refreshing inspiration.

This is changing somewhat in contemporary Bali, as audiences travel from their villages and buy tickets to attend performance events. The "business" of performance, though present in the tourist industry for a good part of this century, has developed most rapidly in the 1980s and 1990s, for both tourist and general Balinese audiences. Referring to performers involved in the business, Dibia reports, "the latest fee for an *arja* dancer, from the *Bon Bali* group, was 25,000 *rupiah* [approximately 12 American dollars]. When they are invited to a religious ceremony, however, the artists may receive less than their standard fee. It is common that the artists who are associated with, or are members of the temple congregation or the village, may take only a small portion of their fee and return the rest to the host as a donation. In some cases, these artists take no

4. Contemporary innovations, spearheaded by the government-run Art Centre and STSI Arts Academy in Denpasar, have created a new context of indoor concert halls, outdoor arenas, box office, and, it is intended, a "professional" status for performers.

5. Wayan Dibia (1992: 80) reports that 25 percent of *arja* performances today, just as one example, "are for modern events not associated with Hindu-Balinese religious ceremonies."

money at all since the artists regard their performance as part of their spiritual obligation" (1992: 99).

Another interesting aspect is how Bali has valued its older artists. As a dancer, actor, or *dalang* grows old, he or she is said to grow in subtlety, knowledge, and experience and offers a depth that the young have not yet developed. Often, the older performers are most interesting, because of their spirit and dramatic power, as well as refined technique. In the West, a dancer, whether ballet or modern, usually stops performing at a relatively early age, with some exceptions.

Balinese performance is intended to teach as well as entertain and propitiate. To be interesting and humorous to children and adults while at the same time teaching important issues of an ethical, spiritual, literary, and historical nature is something rarely found in Western art. In the United States, we have regular theater and childrens' theater companies specializing in entertaining that particular audience. This genre is usually on a very simple level, based on the intrinsic assumption that children must learn about life in very small doses and cannot appreciate, in fact must be protected from, deeper aesthetic experience.

There is a remarkable variety of artistic and cultural forms in Bali, and endless varieties within a form, from village to village. Geertz touches on this in his "Form and Variation in Balinese Village Structure" (1959). There is an ability in Balinese culture, in many ways unique, to maintain very formal structures, while allowing for great variety, as each person, group, or situation breathes life into that form. Within the very small area of this island is a dense, complex cultural ecosystem. If we compare any two sets of *gendér wayang*[6] from two different *banjar*s 'hamlets', or even within the same *banjar*, we will surely hear two distinctly different sets of pitches, creating differing intervallic relationships. *Topéng* still varies from place to place, with an emphasis put on story here, masks there, postures here, and spirit there, sometimes as entertainment, other times as sacred rite. Each region is thought to have a distinct character in terms of land, people, customs, history, and arts heritage. As we see in other cultures as well, each form varies from another (such as *gambuh* from *arja* or *topéng* from *wayang*) partly because of its unique role in the social and spiritual life of the community. But in Bali it is striking how each form varies endlessly from village to village, reflecting the variety of character from place to place. Why is it that Balinese culture has given rise to such unusual artistic variety in comparison with many other societies, to become what James Boon (1977: xi) has described as "anthropology's 'Shakespeare'"?

6. *Gendér wayang* is the quartet of ten-keyed metallophones that accompanies the *wayang* shadow puppet theater.

One answer to this, which I hear from many older Balinese performers, is that the approach they learned when they were young requires them to always be studying, growing, taking in experience. Not thought of as a profession (until very recently), art has not been so much a product to be sold as a continual process of development to be shared for spiritual and social needs, and performers have had the time to learn the wide range of knowledge necessary to be a great *panasar*, *dalang*, or other artist.[7] When people are looking for results, products, they tend to reproduce, or at least work superficially. When they are involved in a continual process, they grow in a unique direction, dictated by place, time and situation. Another characteristic of Balinese performing arts that gives rise to variety is the great tradition of combining improvisation with a store of knowledge to produce something alive, relevant, and deep. If a great performer of *topéng*, *arja*, *wayang*, and so on, combines, as he should, spontaneous composition with traditional techniques and forms, the results will vary from place to place and situation to situation.

I often think of music, dance, and theater in terms of ecological dynamics, and cultures as human ecologies. In our present times, people throughout the world are becoming increasingly concerned with the balance of nature. Because of man-made changes in the environment, life is becoming less rich; the air, water, and soil are polluted and unhealthy. And now scientists, artists, and the general public want to understand more about our role in the balance of nature, which has long been ignored. The scientist Marston Bates wrote:

The trend of human modification of the biological community is toward simplification. The object of agriculture is to grow pure stands of crops, single species of plants that can be eaten directly by man . . . efficient, perhaps; dismal, certainly; and also dangerous. A general principle is gradually emerging from ecological study to the effect that the more complex the biological community, the more stable. The intricate checks and balances among the different populations in a forest or sea look inefficient and hampering, but they insure the continuity and stability of the system as a whole and thus, however indirectly, contribute to the survival of particular populations.[8]

Growers generally breed crops to produce varieties that are more commercially useful, sweet, easier to transport and sell without getting dam-

---

7. A clear, *sakala* 'manifested in the physical world' aspect of time has to do with the duration of performances. Up until recently, *wayang*, *topéng prémbon*, or *arja* performances would be open-ended, ordinarily beginning at ten or eleven o'clock at night and continuing for anywhere from three or four hours until dawn. Since the late 1980s, the encroaching nine-to-five work day necessitates audience and artists rising early for their day jobs (traditionally, early-rising farmers had more flexibility to catch up on their sleep with midday naps). This has influenced performances of all kinds to beginning at nine and ending by eleven or twelve o'clock.

8. Marston Bates (1964: 254).

aged, or more uniformly red or yellow. But often each variety is weaker than the previous one, susceptible to insects and disease. So, they have to use machinery, pesticides, and sprays to protect the crops from their environment, killing many other plants and animals, as well as the pests, unintentionally. Life is becoming less complex, less rich, and less strong.

The variety of species on the planet is decreasing every year because of human misuse of the environment. One response has been to develop "seed banks," keeping a vast collection of seeds from all the existing plant life, so that the genetic material does not disappear forever. Even though it may disappear from its place of origin, samples remain in the seed bank, and if individuals or the government want to develop a strain again, the possibility will still be there. It is a storehouse of genetic information.

Just as American agriculturalists have been undeliberately destroying the variety of plant life to develop products, in Bali, modern, centralized influences such as television, radio, and newspapers tend to encourage certain varieties of art and leave others to decay. Instead of locally grown varieties of performance, people begin to listen to, or want for their local festivals, the select group from outside their community that has been developed to a high quality. Or the desire to produce a product for tourist consumption may limit the range of expression. Just one example of a form unique to a particular village (and still passing in and out of existence) is from Peliatan, which traditionally had a *légong Calonarang*, all parts being played by the three young female *légong* dancers, *condong* as the old witch. In the period around World War II, they revived it, with the *condong* using a mask for Rangda, walking cane for Matah Gedé, the old widow (before her magical transformation). In recent years this genre has not been seen. Several other thematic and choreographic varieties of *legong* do exist. But in recent decades, more and more *légong* have followed a single choreographic model and theme, *Lasem*. Similarly, local *arja* groups have become fewer and fewer partly as a result of being devalued when held up against the superstardom of Radio Républik Indonesia's ensemble, bolstered by broadcasts and tours throughout Bali. In a related issue, some Javanese physicists and acousticians from Gaja Mada University have proposed a single, uniform tuning for all *gamelan*s in Java, set by electronic devices.[9] The very quality that artists and anthropologists have called distinctly Balinese, the great variety from place to place, seems to be undergoing change.

One interesting role that arts, educational, and media institutions, such

9. Wasisto Suryodiningrat, et al. (1968).

as STSI might play within the present cultural framework would be to think of themselves, in a sense, as "seed banks." Instead of using its resources to develop a "*super seka*" in competition with the villages, each institution could be a storehouse of artistic ideas, information, skill, and research, studying the great varieties of artistic seeds that still exist, and helping to distribute those seeds throughout the island, in communities, *seka*, and schools. Researching old teachers and styles, analyzing what are essential aesthetic qualities unique to the culture, and sharing that knowledge and skill within the community could promote diversity.

What foreigners appreciate most in Balinese art is in fact born from the life within the arts, which depends upon the principle of variation, which in turn depends upon the fact that art is still part of the life of the people, reflecting time, place and context. The great pressures to produce that people and communities experience today leaves them with less time to study and grow artistically or to maintain diversity. The greatest role that I, as an outsider, can see for educational, arts, and media institutions in Indonesia would be that of resource managers—to experience, learn, and collect from the culture and then distribute artistic resources where needed. This might establish a healthy balance between a central institution and the diverse communities and arts traditions. In terms of actual presentations of performance, another important and inevitable direction for such institutions is to support the creation and development of new work that reflects a younger generation of internationally oriented artists. This need not be seen as a *super seka* or a direct threat to village ensembles if it is conceptualized and presented as coming from and working within a new cultural context.

But, as we differentiate between "traditional" and "new" contexts, and before we begin looking for the "seeds" of Balinese performing arts, we must know what exactly is being sought. In the reality of contemporary Balinese culture, this process is difficult. It is obvious that classic forms such as *gambuh* must be considered as "seeds," but we can also focus more on attitudes and creative processes than on forms and particular genres. We very well might find Balinese experimental artists working within new forms that utilize those deep, essential qualities of Balinese art: creation from within a group, spiritual, environmental, or community context; incorporation of *désa kala patra*, spontaneity, improvisational skill, and enjoyment. Certain new performance styles may, in this sense, be more traditional than older styles performed without inspiration, sense of context, nature, or "flowering."

Baris tumbak and *banten* 'offerings' at Sukawana (1972). Photo by Beth Skinner.

Of the many varieties of rice in Bali, we prefer a traditional pre–Green Revolution brown rice with high protein and the sweet smell of Basmati. This is only grown in a few places, since the government gives very few licenses to grow any traditional varieties, white or brown, insisting on plentiful but pesticide-dependent Green Revolution strains. Our brown rice is only available in the main city market of Denpasar.

As soon as my teacher and friend Madé Gerindem sees that we have set up our own kitchen, he insists that we never buy rice. We are no longer "visitors" or "foreigners," and to him that means that as village locals we should either grow it ourselves or have it provided by family. For him, once we are "of the area," the thought of not having noncommercial access to the staple of life is alienating, unacceptable, and actually repugnant. So this musician in his mid-sixties regularly bicycles over the hills with large sacks filled with rice he has cultivated himself. The problem is that we love the traditional brown rice best, and his rice is not being consumed rapidly enough.

Whenever he pays a visit, we hide the brown rice before he inspects the rice urn to see if we need more. Though he knows that we love Balinese rice, he finally concludes that we must still be bread eaters, since no one could live on so little rice.

After his three-hour performance of solo *topéng pajegan*, we return home with sixty-seven year-old Pak Kakul, riding bicycles along roads, dirt paths, and through ricefields for an hour and a half. Finally arriving at four in the morning, we all go to sleep. But at dawn, an hour later, I hear noise from the porch and see him grabbing his pitchfork and heading out toward the ricefields.

I call out to him, "Aren't you exhausted?" and he answers, "This is what keeps me from going crazy."

Intrinsic aesthetics
désa kala patra within performance, continued

❀

Some contemporary Indonesian artists and scholars have been finding themselves in the position, not just of trying to understand and react as individuals, but of having to legislate and respond in a systematic manner to the effects of intense societal transformation upon traditional arts and religion.[1] In a few recent attempts to grapple with these issues, people often suggest clear delineations between such concepts as sacred and secular/profane, form and function, or aesthetics and efficacy, in order to clarify shifts in cultural priorities. Often these delineations prove limited in scope, and tend to diminish rather than enhance our perspective on the rich ambiguities of a complex tradition. I shall try to clarify the nature of some of these ambiguous issues of aesthetics in performance, ritual, and everyday life.

Ethnomusicologist Judith Becker (1980: 103) has written, with particular reference to Javanese *gamelan* music: "In a traditional society in which music is closely linked to religion and ritual, in which the music system supports the entire edifice of belief, the question of beauty is always subordinate to the question of efficacy." This kind of analysis reflects an anthropological perspective arising from a desire to avoid seeing all human cultures in terms of ethnocentric Euro-American aesthetics. Art is more than something intellectually and sensually pleasing; it "does something" quite different in every culture (and subculture, as well). Art, in this performative sense, can effect change by reordering and redefining the spiritual and social environment. But this implication—that a greater significance is to be found in the results of having done something ritualistic than in the

---

1. An early draft of this chapter was first presented at the New England regional meeting of the Association for Asian Studies, October 1981. It was then published in *Asian Music* (1981: 43).

participants' appreciation of the actual process—relies upon a distinction that does not exist in practice.

Beauty is defined by the *Oxford English Dictionary* as "that quality or combination of qualities which affords keen pleasure to the senses, or which charms the intellectual or moral faculties, through inherent grace, or fitness to a desired end." Two different interpretations of the word *aesthetic* define it as "of or pertaining to sensuous perception, received by the senses," and "of or pertaining to the appreciation or criticism of the beautiful." P. J. Zoetmulder (1974: 173) defines the *Kawi* 'Old Javanese' word *langö*: "*Alangö* means both 'enraptured' and 'enrapturing'. It can be said of a beautiful view as well as of the person affected by its beauty. It has what we might call a 'subjective' and an 'objective' aspect, for there is a common element—the Indians would say a common *rasa*—in both subject and object, which makes them connatural and fit to become one. Objectively *langö* is the quality by which an object appeals to the aesthetic sense." J. Stephen Lansing (1983: 79–82) discusses this concept of *langö*, ultimately leading to the suggestion that "*wayang* reveals the power of language and the imagination to go beyond 'illumination,' to construct an order in the world which exists both in the mind and, potentially, in the outer world as well."

In Bali, beauty within ritual is a basic ingredient of efficacy and, in a sense, of any social activity at all. Not only are the Balinese gods and deities notorious connoisseurs of the arts, appreciating both embellishment and minute aesthetic detail, but also, physical interaction or activity within any environment or space seeks a flow and balanced ordering, an equilibrium that is appreciated as an aesthetic property, sensually, formally, and psychologically. The *Tripramana* threefold unity, "Three Ways of Knowing" or "Three Powers," expressed in *Kawi* as *bayu sabda idep*, is a source of much philosophical discussion but is concerned with, and often applied, at least in principle, to everyday life. *Bayu* is wind, breath, energy, activity; *sabda* is vocalized expression; and *idep* is thought, perception.[2] Basically, this Balinese conception aims at integrating these three levels and balancing them within any activity that may initially tend to favor one or another. If someone is engaged in a physical activity, he or she should meditate (consciously focus his or her mental faculties) on the situation at hand, and also find

2. Zurbuchen (1987: 129) offers additional interpretations. "In a general sense they refer to action or results (*bayu*), the form in which these occur (*sabda*), and the motives or meanings (*idep*) that underlie them." She also suggests linguistic and aesthetic aspects of the terms and the role they might play in *wayang* performance: "In language, *bayu* = the act of uttering; *sabda* = speech forms; and *idep* = semantic and symbolic force. In performance, *bayu* = movement, action; *sabda* = verbal/vocal artistry; and *idep* = conceptualizing the *lampahan* (plot)."

ways to express the experience vocally, for example by explaining or singing. On the other hand, if one is involved in some intellectual or spiritual considerations, he or she should activate or demonstrate the ideas as well as vocalizing them. And Balinese religion is very much concerned with manifestation, as we see in its elaborate forms of worship. This threefold principle indicates to me an intrinsic aesthetic concept and idea of beauty, in that it incorporates emotional-intellectual content with action and expression. Even though this may be viewed as a rationalized Hindu terminology and may not always be taken into consideration by everyone, it does express a common sensibility and reference point.

Clifford Geertz (1973: 171), drawing from the sociologist Max Weber, likens Balinese religion to an ideal of "traditional religions" in which every aspect of the world has spiritual, magical meaning and life, and sacredness exists in all phenomena. Although this perspective on "animist" religion is far from absolute, it still gives us some insights into beauty and efficacy. As proposed earlier, there is a general Balinese concern with maintaining a standard of beauty (*bayu sabda idep*) in all aspects of life. Now we find a spiritual orientation in which one is regularly concerned with maintaining a psychic harmony with all worldly objects and attributes (forces of nature), directing one's daily actions or thoughts in a way that will be most efficacious in showing respect to both natural and supernatural elements of their environment. In a sense, the means for achieving an efficacious relationship with the world is to maintain a standard of beauty (balance, harmony). I would doubt whether efficacy could be brought about without beauty; in a sense, they are one and the same. Beauty here is not a static attribute but a way of ordering one's experience and world.

It is true that Balinese will say there are certain elements essential for a given ritual or ceremony and that anything additional is a matter of choice or circumstance. However, this does not alter the basic point that the essential must be enacted in a state of balance or beauty. There is also an attitude toward *patra*: if one has minimal resources, certain essential elements may suffice, but the greater the resources, the more is expected or required for efficacy to be achieved. Again, this indicates an emphasis on attitude, on spiritual disposition in relation to ceremony, rather than on static material criteria for efficacy. One begins with beauty, does the best one can, drawing from available resources (as long as essentials are met), and creates an efficacious climate. At the same time and from a somewhat contrary perspective, there is public debate over whether the costs of those ritual essentials are still excessive for common people with more "worldly" economic constraints.

I would like to introduce three specific performance situations that demonstrate the ambiguity of the beauty/efficacy distinction. The first deals with the role of efficacy within the learning process. Children in Bali are encouraged (and expected) to perform for ceremonial events as soon as they have attained a basic level of proficiency. One obvious reason is that the experience of performing publicly is the only way to learn to relax in that situation. *Bayun kalangan* 'the energy of the performance space' implies a performer's "ability to spontaneously respond to other artists and audience,"[3] something that comes through the lessons and experience of public exposure. But to Balinese, the importance of a student's first, and seemingly premature, public display (*melaspasin*) is that they receive a certain *taksu* and blessing from having been part of an offering to the deities. This is considered a necessity for remembering the dance as well as for strengthening the dancer's spirit. A special *mawintén* ritual during which a student receives blessings via a *padanda* 'Brahmana priest' is considered particularly beneficial to the learning process. A *mapasupati* ritual is performed to spiritually purify performers' headdresses, costumes, and *gambelan* instruments. And performance within the context of ceremony (*ngayah*) is often intended as a religious offering, contributing to the efficacy of the event. At the same time, the efficacious climate of ceremonial offerings (*bantén*) and the presence of deities conveys *taksu* to the performer, which is necessary for the attainment of specific aesthetic goals. Efficacy is in this sense a means to an aesthetic end.

Ceremonial group dances such as *rejang* are performed during many temple festivals and in at least one village throughout the rainy season. In Batuan, the village with which I am most familiar, every family belonging to a particular temple is expected, really required, to send female household members ranging from adolescent girls to old women. They perform *rejang*, accompanied by the temple's *gambelan*, just outside the temple walls. Although this ritual dance is performed throughout the rainy season, special ceremonial clothing is worn only on the evenings of dark or full moons, leaving the other nights' dancers wearing normal dress, embellished only with the compulsory ceremonial waist scarf. One rationale for this nightly ritual performance is that the dance diverts the attention of a dangerous fanged demon, Jero Gedé Mecaling, from the neighboring island of Nusa Penida, who flies over Bali spreading disease and killing people throughout the rainy, and most unhealthy, season. As he passes over their village, he sees the beautiful dance and is so enamored and enchanted that he forgets his malevolent mission. Another explanation I have heard in Batuan concerns the presence of Jero Gedé Mecaling in the distant past. As the demon was victimizing and terrifying the village, someone suggested

3. I Wayan Dibia (1992: 124).

Rejang in Batuan (1972). Photo by Beth Skinner.

that one way to protect themselves might be to dance *rejang* as a form of meditation. As long as one is able to calmly concentrate on life-giving energies, and overcome inner weakness by means of inner serenity, one can be insulated from malevolent forces. The community effort worked, and the practice continues as a general antidote to seasonal illness and sorcery.[4]

Now, by what standards are we to characterize the dance as beautiful (the key to efficacy, in this case) if all females are expected to participate from time to time, young and old, "skilled" and "unskilled," and even in everyday attire? The adolescent girls seem to be appreciated for their physical beauty and innocence, while they simultaneously engage in the dance and pose self-consciously, as much, possibly, for their male companions on the sidelines as for supernatural beings. The older women give greater attention to the meditative state to be achieved within the dance, and exude a feeling of tranquillity and a beauty of balance. One may be quick to draw a

4. Lansing (1983: 140) writes: "All Balinese 'demons' may take form either in the outer world (*buana agung*) or the world of the self, the microcosmos (*buana alit*). Demons (*buta*) may be viewed from many perspectives. A strong Buddhist element in Balinese religion suggests that demons are essentially psychological projections, but differs from Western psychology in insisting that 'demonic' forces are part of the intrinsic constitution of inner and outer reality. The demons, according to this interpretation, are simply the raw elements from which the higher realities of consciousness and the world are created. *Buta*, which is usually glossed as 'demon', actually means 'element.'"

conclusion in favor of functionalism and efficacy because of the range of aesthetic values and "informality," not seeing one overall standard of beauty. But even here, some criteria for balance and beauty is present, however ambiguous. People of that village cite the beauty of the dance form itself as affecting the critical spiritual situation, and they clearly refer to a multiplicity of criteria for beauty.

The more visible manifestations of both beauty and efficacy may sometimes be subordinated to a performer's own internal, psychic experience. *Topéng pajegan*[5] involves a single performer enacting an entire dance drama singlehandedly, taking on all of the characters by utilizing numerous masks. Once the story is concluded, a dance of the special Pengejukan mask follows. The character tosses a bunch of old Chinese coins toward the surrounding children as good-luck tokens and will often charge upon the children and take one up in his arms. Only certain performers are inclined or spiritually prepared (or as they say, "brave") to use this mask dance to enact a ritual, which involves blessing the congregants (audience) with a series of offerings and *mantra*s; the actor-dancer functions as a kind of priest, *pamangku topéng*. Especially in this context, the same Pengejukan mask is referred to as Sidha Karya 'completer of the work'.

During one particular ceremonial event, namely a section of *ngabén* 'death rituals', Bapak Nyoman Kakul, a *pamangku topéng*, was invited to perform *topéng pajegan*. Although he was well accustomed to this role, the hosts had invited another actor to share the performance with him, creating a situation of two performers, for which he was not prepared. The play proceeded, with *gambelan* playing, as actors went through dance, story, comedy, and finally (*pajegan* performer alone), ritual offering. The audience was entertained and pleased, and the ritual had fulfilled its function, according to hosts and audience, adding to the efficacy of the overall ceremony. However, as Pak Kakul left for home, he commented to me that the distraction of a second performer had reduced his ability to build up his customary spiritual, meditative power during the course of the play, which was necessary for him to perform the final offering effectively. Although the general aesthetic form came across, and the overall ritual need was fulfilled, his own psychic relationship to the "ritual process" was left in midair. Upon returning home at about two o'clock in the morning, Pak Kakul sat out on his porch for an hour and carefully proceeded to go through all of the *mantra*s and *mudra*s 'ritual hand gestures' again in order to complete, not the ceremony itself, but the personal, psychic, internal ritual process.

5. In the traditional Balinese economic sphere, *pajeg* is taxation (Geertz 1980: 68). The performance of this genre is often thought of as a ritual requirement. However, another common meaning of *pajeg* is "to do an entire job."

I Nyoman Kakul performing ritual *topéng Sidha Karya* (1972).

We can see the problems inherent in trying to demarcate borders between aesthetics and religious concerns within a culture such as Bali. The
inclination to determine factors specific to the realm of the sacred, as distinguished from the realm of aesthetics, is actually one aspect of an issue
that has received a good deal of attention recently among Indonesian
artists, scholars, and some government arts officials. The main impetus for
this discussion was a growing concern over the effect that tourism and
commercialism were having on Balinese arts and religion. Many were concerned with the use of "sacred" masks or *gambelan* for commercial performances, the regularly scheduled trance dances for tourists, and the multi-
plying hybrids of sacred-commercial forms, combining aspects of both for
"nonaesthetic, nonspiritual" reasons. Ritual performances involving trance
and magical activity were being performed on a nightly basis not for the
deities or supernatural forces but for foreigners with money. The initial
intent of the alarmed artists and intellectuals was to arrive at some set of
religious-aesthetic criteria that could delineate sacred from secular so as to
advise the government in setting rules and guidelines for commercial performance practices.

When a conference was held by the Balinese Arts Council, Listibiya, in
1971, it soon became clear that not only were the gradations from sacred
to secular numerous, but the very criteria for sacredness were always

shifting according to context. They eventually came to an agreement, but one that is limited and tentative and will surely have to evolve in the near future. In trying to legislate spiritual-aesthetic values in a magical-animist-multilayered Hindu culture of the twentieth century, which could apply directly to performance practice, they were confronted by the ambiguous nature of the "sacred context." I shall try to explain some of the particular issues here, as I feel that the present necessity for Balinese to apply broad concepts to living spiritual-aesthetic practices, in a direct and active way (from within the same cultural context), forces those involved to deal with values as they really exist and are embodied. It is not just an intellectual exercise.

The Listibiya conference participants arrived at a three-tiered model of the spiritual contexts of performance in which spatial and functional considerations were prominent.[6] The first category, *wali*, is the most sacred and is generally distinguished by taking place within the *jeroan pura* 'inner courtyard of a temple'. In keeping with this spatial characteristic, such performances are considered to be a part of a ritual; they fulfill an aspect of the ceremonial process in its most formal sense. They are especially considered as offerings to deities or ancestors, manifesting as a women's dance such as *méndét* and *rejang*, *pamangku*'s dance, *wayang lemah* 'ritual shadow-puppet play', and so on. In fact, one further criterion is that actual ritual offerings such as flowers, holy water, and incense may be made within the actual performance. Another criterion often applied to *wali* is that there be no narrative element within performance. But as we shall see, this, as other criteria, applies irregularly to actual contexts. *Wali* means "sacred," but the literal meaning of the word is *bantén* 'offering', referring to that which sets up a direct link to deities or other supernatural forces; not just as entertainment for the deities but as a formal exchange of energies. One nonspatial, nonfunctional factor that always deserves the designation *wali* 'sacred' is the entering into a trance-state. Whether it be a *kerauhan* trance created by a deity entering into a young *Sang Hyang* dancer, or a *nadi* trance caused by any of a number of spirits entering into a *balian* doctor-shaman, dancer, or ritual congregation, the appearance of the trance-state qualifies the entire activity as *wali*. In this sense, perhaps, state of consciousness provides the clearest, most consistent definition of the sacred. However, although trance is *wali*, certainly not all *wali* is trance.

The second category, *bebali*, comprises performances that take place in connection with *yadnya* 'religious ceremony' but that are not an aspect of

6. This model was based on traditional Balinese terms and conceptions, but also involved much interpretive application to contemporary contexts. In terms of the *désa kala patra* of this classification itself, it could be suggested that aspects of the terminology and ordering involve a contemporary process of "rationalization," referring back to Geertz (1973: 171).

the ritual. They are considered more as entertainment for the deities than as a direct means of contact. The word *bebali* is derived from the word *wewalén*, which roughly means "that which can be performed." Such forms as *wayang*, *topéng*, *arja*, *wayang wong*, *parwa*, *baris*, all dance dramas, and many more may be included here. *Bebali* performances may take place in the outer courtyard of a temple, or in any other appropriate location.

The third category, *balih-balihan*, is made up of performances that are not related to ceremony and take place solely for the entertainment of people, as opposed to deities. The term is derived from *mabalih* 'to watch'. Most of the *bebali* genres could also fall within the contextual framework of *balih-balihan*, while others seem to be firmly entrenched in this "secular" category. Oft-cited examples are the *Cupak* dance drama, *jogéd*, a sort of popular, social dance, and *drama gong*, a modern (popular in the 1960s and '70s), relatively naturalistic theatrical genre.

This *wali–bebali–balih-balihan* system, proposed during the 1971 Listibiya conference by the noted Balinese scholar I Gusti Bagus Sugriwa, helps to make useful distinctions but leaves almost as many questions as before. It generally defines sacredness spatially and functionally and not in terms of the process itself, leaving the scholars and officials to judge each situation by different criteria and somewhat arbitrarily. A description of several performance situations may suggest the range of ambiguity.

Baris gedé is a ritual martial dance genre performed by groups of men, considered "very *wali*," and central to certain ceremonies in some villages. Recently, a European ethnomusicologist proposed a tour of Europe and America, including this particular sacred dance form. The Balinese authorities agreed to allow the dance to be taken out of the country on this commercial venture, along with its accompanying "sacred heirloom *gambelan*," as long as the troupe did not use some of the especially sacred martial equipment such as spears and daggers. As it turned out, the village performers brought some of the sacred props anyway, perhaps not being interested or facile in sorting out this contemporary issue of sacred and secular. In any case, the council's criteria extended to the sacred weapons and the use of ritual offerings within the dance, but not to the dance form or the *gambelan*, otherwise considered *pusaka* 'sacred'.

Rangda and *barong* are included in the ritual play *Calonarang*, a dance drama of great magical and spiritual power, involving masks that are always considered sacred and *tenget* 'magically charged'. Another aspect of this ritual is a group trance during which men attack the witch Rangda and then, because of her magical spell, turn their *kris* 'daggers' upon themselves, entranced. Their trance presumably keeps the strongly pressed *kris* from penetrating their bodies. For obvious dramatic reasons, this ritual became a very popular tourist attraction, and it is now enacted nightly in several villages commercially. There is a much lower incidence of real trance in these contexts, and the men merely "act" their roles, but still it is not uncommon for some to enter the trance state. What can we call sacred here? The context is not sacred since it is not being done for the temple, as an offering or an exorcism. The masks are sacred, as is the trance-state, when it occurs. Can we say that it is a sacred genre at some times and not at others, according to the performers' states and the religious context? So we cannot necessarily refer to the dramatic "form" as sacred.

Jangér is a popular dance-music form created in the early twentieth century. Considered strictly secular in theme, its origins are linked to the *Sang Hyang* trance ceremonies and their *cak* choral accompaniment. Sometimes narrative, sometimes not, performed outside of temples, it often precedes an evening program of other dance dramas. It is generally considered as purely human entertainment. However, recently the young boys and girls performing *jangér* in some villages have been going into *nadi* trance, becoming possessed by various spirits. When this happens, in whatever context, *bebali* or *balih-balihan*, without sacred objects or location within a temple, the performance is again considered sacred, though no one would refer to *jangér* as a sacred form. As a matter of fact, government officials became so embarrassed at these repeated "unscheduled" trances that they prohibited the group's *jangér* performances.

To take yet another example, the village of Tenganan in the mountains of Karangasem possesses an extremely sacred *gambelan selonding* that dates back to the twelfth century. It is played only on ceremonial occasions and even then only with many strict and unique regulations to insure ritual form. Visiting that village for a week in 1972, during the course of their yearly *Abuang* ceremony, I was allowed to record that *gambelan*. However, there were just a few pieces, *gagurun*, the recording of which was prohibited because of their connection with a particular series of rituals within the larger ceremony. The explanation was that these pieces were too sacred to be allowed out of the ritual context (or the village). Once, when an outsider secretly recorded the *gagurun* pieces, the village petitioned the Indonesian government, which ordered the man to return his tapes to them. Thus, played on the same instruments, in the same location, during a different ritual within the same ceremony, certain melodies are considered to be in a different class of sacredness.[7]

My last example concerns *Cupak*, a drama that is most often considered to be "secular," *balih-balihan*. Yet one well-known performer of this comic

---

7. It should be mentioned that Tenganan, a *Bali Aga* 'Original Balinese' village, is atypical in many important ways. Balinese think of *Bali Aga* social and religious practices as archaic, and apart from the mainstream influence of Hindu-Javanese Majapahit culture.

dance drama describes often entering a trance-state during which, as the glutton Cupak, he is able to consume seemingly endless quantities of food and water. In a different village, one does not even dare discuss this popular story within the vicinity of a ceremony because of its spiritual connotations. My friends in this village have related to me how local lore has it that a *dalang*, returning home after having performed a *wayang* version of *Cupak* for a temple festival, was struck and killed by a falling tree. While in some locales this story is performed as lighthearted entertainment, others consider any presentations to be spiritually charged and potentially dangerous.

After having touched upon numerous gradations and ambiguities along the path from "sacred" to "secular," we might take a more extreme view, challenging the very distinction between these terms. As Dr. Madé Bandem has observed,[8] there are really only phenomena that are "very *wali*, *wali*, and less *wali*" (very sacred, sacred, and less sacred), for nothing is ever taken entirely out of a spiritual context. Now, in addition to the previously discussed spiritual-magical daily orientation, we can speak directly to the realm of performance. As suggested earlier, state of consciousness may be the surest guide to sacredness. The aspect of the sacred that involves direct contact with the supernatural, through trance-states, is sometimes said by Balinese to be an indigenous feature of Indonesian traditional religion rather than the result of Hindu or Buddhist influences. In this view, active participation with the sacred is the older and culturally deeper value and the most fundamental criterion for sacredness, touching a place in the Balinese soul that has remained central to its religion through two thousand years of Buddhist, Hindu, and European influence.

Religious worship permeates all contexts of music and dance, at least to the extent that any performance, whether it be in the inner courtyard of a temple or on a hotel stage before tourists, will be preceded by ceremonial *bantén* 'offerings' for the deities and *caru segehan* for troublesome spirits, as well as a prayer for inspiration and spiritual power, *sanggah taksu*. Since a basic criterion for *wali* is that contact be established with a deity or supernatural force, even this most simple sequence seems to fulfill that description. For the offering is thought to be received by the spiritual entity, as is the prayer, which presumably leads to a response from the deity, granting the inspiration.

In keeping with the Balinese cosmological concern for proper orientation with regard to the cardinal directions, a performance space, *kalangan*, should be arranged with regard to the direction of the sacred mountain Gunung Agung, which is northeast of central Bali. A general ideal is for

8. Personal communication (1979).

performers to be facing *kaja* (toward the mountain, which usually means north) or *kangin* 'east'. This is no rationalized religion's edict, but a deep psychic and physical sense, finding its place in daily life as well as formal ritual. In practice, there is much flexibility in arranging a *kalangan*, especially for more secular performance events. And there is variation in practice from village to village, and among performance genres. A *kalangan* may have performers facing *kelod* 'toward the sea' or *kauh* 'west', but they most definitely take this orientation into account in a conscious way. There is a psychological confusion and nausea, *paling*, that Balinese people describe feeling (and I have witnessed) upon losing their sense of *kaja/kelod* 'toward the mountain/toward the sea'. Restoration of health is quickly achieved by spatial reorientation. The performance space is a ritualized parameter for spatial orientation, but no more so than is the standard architectural layout of a Balinese family compound, with the *sanggah*, or *pemrajan* 'family shrine' in the northeast corner, toward the mountain, and the kitchen in the southwest corner, toward the sea. The physical arrangement of the Balinese family household is not an ornamental or arbitrary arrangement arising out of an intention to suggest or "symbolize" some detached "spiritual reality." In is, in fact, one particular manner in which Balinese actively participate in a cosmic arrangement; they are acting in accord with the macrocosmos by making their own domain as beautiful as possible, with "inherent grace and fitness to a desired end."

Perhaps I can carry this idea a bit further by bringing in the perspective of Madé Sija, *dalang* and authority on ritual offerings, their preparation, arrangement, and significance. He explains that there is only one divinity, Sang Hyang Widi Wasa, and that is the world, nature, the universe. All other divinities are aspects of the whole, seen from different contexts or vantage points. If people need this, or have an abundance of that, they will focus on that particular aspect. But this unity of nature and cosmos is all there is; it is complete.

However, Pak Sija continues, the human body is coarse, forever incomplete and unbalanced because we are tied to desires and wants. We can see the body of the world manifested in us as follows: the blood is water, stone is bones, coral is legs, mountain is head, grasses are hair, wind is breath, fire is liver, right eye is sun, left eye is moon, heart is lime, calcium. Just as we cannot isolate one component of our organism, eye or breath, for instance, from the whole, we must extend our perspective from *buana alit* 'small body' to *buana agung* 'large body'. If our rivers are dirty and polluted, our blood is sick and weak. If a mountain is desecrated, our head is beaten or amputated. One is not symbolic of another; we are kindred entities and share the same qualities. We have within us the *panca maha buta* 'five great elements' or 'forces' of the physical world: earth, light (fire), wind (air), sky (space), and liquid (water).

Part of human *dharma* is that we have the ability to move, to have compassion, to help others, to make and change things. This gives us a special relationship with nature, a responsibility to help maintain balance. There is really no distinction between great and small except (and this is ultimately unreal) that of magnitude.

Everything in the world of nature has its own spirit and significance, he explains, and we must develop the awareness to identify with everything, great and small. However, we cannot spend all of our time meditating on every aspect of creation, so we single out an aspect, such as "the mountain," not to separate it from all else as a symbol, but to unify the activity of attention by incorporating other aspects into the aspect of the mountain, the quality of "highness." Yet one cannot go to *Besakih*, the mother temple of Bali located by the side of the great volcanic mountain, Gunung Agung, every day. So Balinese have the *kahyangan tiga*, every locality's basic three temples: of origins, of the local dead, and the "great council temple," focused primarily upon the contemporary village community. Again, *kahyangan tiga* is meant not as a representation of greater forces but as an incorporation of those forces into a more compact form. Every *pura sanggah* 'family's temple' is a further step, as are all sorts of offerings, *bantén*, *sajén*, in every context. The oft heard Sanskrit *mantra*, *Ong bhur bhuwah swah* (earth air [atmosphere] heavens),[9] in a compact trinity, takes it all into account. Offerings are miniature manifestations of the "greater" aspects, no less complete or alive because of their "smallness." They possess all the inherent qualities of the macrocosm and so are one with them.

Spiritual activity, then, is relative to and dependent upon the area of collective or individual focus, which in turn is relative to context. Such activities as the performing arts possess an orientation in harmony with the essential spiritual-aesthetic order, an order within which the question of efficacy is a matter of aesthetics. From the human sphere, what is essential is the orientation inherent in *bayu sabda idep*, the aesthetic unity of energy, thought, and expression.

9. This is Pak Sija's interpretation, as well as that of Zoetmulder (1982) and Wallis (1980: 110). However, Eiseman (1989: 5) suggests another meaning as "underworld-earthly realm-heavens."

Bali—no longer—unplugged
electronic technology, amplification, and the marginalization of presence

❀

When I returned to Bali in 1992, I was struck by how loudspeakers, tape recorders, radio, and television are rapidly transforming kinesthetic, kinetic, and spiritual realities. Performance of *gambelan*, dance drama, *wayang*, and ritual religious activity is mediated nowadays through electronics in one way or another. This affects not only realms of perception, spirit, and the idea of artistic process, but also the equilibrium between traditional artistic/cultural communities and contemporary governmental and private instititions.

Esoteric aesthetic issues have become objectified and standardized. On page 21 (Aji nusup) I describe how direct transmission of subtle kinesthetic qualities is altered when tape recorders are introduced into the pedagogic process. Amplification systems alter the physical and spiritual relationship between performers, expressed through characterization, acoustics, and the relationship between voices, musical instruments, and dance. As many aspects of music are becoming objectified and re- if not de-contextualized, the agrarian, ecologically balanced culture from which they are derived is growing marginalized and quaintified—that is, depicted as quaint—and objectified for commercial reasons. As "modern Indonesia" seeks to distance itself from "the past," government and business simultaneously write a scenario for tourism in Bali that self-consciously asserts "traditional Balineseness" as a valuable but ambiguous commodity.

Most *dalang*s use microphones and loudspeakers in *wayang* performances now, and it is interesting that it has been so long in coming. In 1972, I attended an *odalan* temple festival at a *pura désa* 'community temple', one of many varieties of temples, which are large outdoor areas of inner and outer courtyards with stone, wood, and bamboo platforms and thatched roofs. I was attending a performance of *gambuh*, a classic, by Balinese standards, and quiet dance drama without bronze-keyed *gambelan* accompaniment—the music, described earlier, characterized by long bamboo flutes playing in subtly shifting modes or tunings, with an overall ethereal quality, accompanied by comparatively delicate percussion. But as the *gambuh* performance was beginning, the overwhelming sound heard was that of someone singing *kakawin* poetry—a blaring noise, so it seemed to all around, coming from a loudspeaker somewhere—making it quite impossible to hear the *gambelan* or the actors. Some visiting dignitaries had come expressly for the purpose of seeing and hearing the *gambuh*, even then an uncommon, special occasion. Disturbed by the intruding amplified chanting, one of the dignitaries circled the many temple courtyards before finding the loudspeaker, and then began to trace the path of the cable to find the source of the sound. It was a little old man in the *jeroan pura*, inner courtyard of the temple, intoning the *kawi* verses, as he had no doubt done countless times before, in that same place, but then only heard by a few nearby friends and passersby bringing their offerings. We learned that some kind of power play was being enacted and that whoever was in control of the microphone was not willing to delimit his newly acquired technology. The visiting dignitary could not convince the possessors of the amplifier to turn down the volume. Now, it turns out that intravillage rivalries had been going on since colonial times, in which performance forms were already being incorporated into the struggle for power and social order. The amp and speaker happened to be a new instrument of power and dominance in this dynamic between several kinship groups and political persuasions. As it turned out, the loudspeakers did stop soon after, for a performance of *wayang wong*, a different dance drama genre depicting Ramayana episodes, but the amplification resumed again later in the day. Perhaps those *wanara*, the monkeys that make up the monkey general Anoman's army, had influence on the powers that be, in more sense than one.

We may speak of the role of these electronic instruments as one of amplification, by which we mean the oscillations of the particles of a sounding body are magnified, much as we believe we are seeing the cells of a sample of skin or onion being magnified by a microscope. We may think of increasing amplitude as getting more of something, but the reality is quite different—we are, of course, getting a different sound with a different contextual meaning. Marshall McLuhan's ideas concerning the medium being, in many ways, the massage, or message are relevant to the present discussion. (In traditional Balinese performance practice, the medium is also the message, and not just in the sense that a *dalang* can be a kind of spiritual medium. There is mediation of a certain order inherent in the use of language, masks, and puppets.) The message within amplified *gambelan* or chanting may be a statement of power or it may signify a certain resonance or sympathetic vibration with the overall environment, which, in Bali, is growing rapidly into modernity, with modernism's inherent characteristics—air pollution from automobiles and motorcycles, degradation of the environment, loss of trees that had provided shade and animal habitat, hence loss of birds, destruction of coral reefs from industrial pollution and the digging up of reefs for limestone to build new roads, vast quantities of garbage without sufficient landfills or any alternative, and noise pollution from automobiles as well as from such sources as loudspeakers in stores and public events. Art forms are thus reflecting the Balinese philosophical concept of *désa kala patra* in this sense also.

When performing artists employ amplification, or at least allow their local sponsors to, it may be, some tell me, less a statement of power than intended as a deterrent—reaching a sufficient volume to compete against the other loudspeakers at a ceremonial event, which are saturating the air with sound waves from recorded chanting or *gambelan*. Or the motivation may just be a means of changing aesthetic priorities, by shifting the balance of performative elements, such as the relativity of time and spirit that inhabit Balinese performance.

Someone could argue that technological innovations in amplification could advance the live performance medium by making subtle aspects of Balinese vocal music more audible, but I have yet to hear such sophisticated systems anywhere. The most immediate issue is whether transferring the sound source out of the performer's body is compatable with such a psychokinesthetic aesthetic. As the singer is supposed to be perceiving the inner flow of vibrations and inner-outer spatial and acoustical correlations, one is hearing a substantially altered sound coming loudly from loudspeakers.

In the 1960s, *séndratari* already had the *dalang* sitting away from the action with a microphone, either to the side of the dance drama with the *gambelan*, or backstage. Now *wayang* itself has caught up. While several *dalang*s have expressed to me their feelings of a need to keep the interest of their less-focused contemporary audience, many recognize a difficult trade-off with the sound blaring from a loudspeaker, rather than the body of the *dalang*, changing the corporeal and spiritual nature of performance. In my recent discussions with *dalang*s, several have pondered whether the *dalang* is losing his real voice, and whether *kawi suara* (the transcendent, spiritual voice of the *dalang*) can exist in such a disembodied, detached form. In a discussion I had in 1992 with two prominent *dalang*s, one even went so far as to say that loudspeakers could be the death of *kawi suara*.

One village I know has a general agreement among its members that amplification will not be used for any *wayang* performances. They will only commission *dalang*s who will perform without a mike.

At one *wayang* performance I attended in 1992, a youngish *dalang* had set up with his four musicians and assistants, checking the mike and loudspeakers. The *gambelan* progressed through their introductory pieces, the *dalang* very quietly intoned his opening mantra and then began the *Panyacah Parwa* prologue to the story. No sound came from the speakers, and he started looking around to his assistants as he continued to sing. They scurried around to find someone who knew about the sound system, but returned without results. By then the *dalang* was very upset, and he scolded the assistants in between lines of *kawi suara*. He got to the point of introducing the evening's story and was so upset that, as he took a long breath between vocal phrases, he started slapping one of the assistants for not being motivated enough to solve the dilemma. There was a loudspeaker in another area of the temple playing taped *gambelan* music, and he could not imagine how he could keep performing. Interestingly, he was not projecting his natural voice as most *dalang*s would—he must have been already used to performing with an amplification system—so he was at a double disadvantage. People were walking by the screen without sitting down, or even stopping momentarily to watch. Luckily for him, after about thirty minutes the sound system was resuscitated and he was finally able to gather a crowd.

Today, microphones and loudspeakers are widespread for dance theater performances such as *arja* and *topéng*, especially the more popular version of *prémbon* and the repopularized magic drama *Calonarang*. With a couple of microphones hanging from a permanent or makeshift bamboo roof or roof frame, vocalizing dancers come in and out of the mikes' range, making the sound surge into distortion and then subside into unrecognizable utterances, as another mike picks up another performer's surge. Besides masking all the physio-acoustic properties of the singing, it also affects aspects of the vocal style that are specifically geared toward spatial considerations, removing their kinetic meaning and purpose within live performance environs and reducing them to mere decorative play. More subtle aspects of the vocal style become irrelevant to the new context.

As mentioned earlier, mikes and loudspeakers were being used in the 1970s for the *dalang* in *séndratari*, to balance his sound with the full *gambelan*. But in more recent times, the *gambelan* is often also miked, perhaps, in turn, to match the newly acquired volume of the *dalang*. So, now you have distortion from both. Balinese *gambelan* is true outdoor music, crafted with precision and acoustical insight to create crystal clear audibility in a large spatial environment, through forging the bronze instruments and tuning them in *ombak* 'acoustical beats'. This is an intrinsic kinetic ingredient of Balinese *gambelan*. When the sound passes through microphones, you are hearing acoustical beats merely as pulsations in time, but the kinetic element of carefully placed vibrations in motion is eliminated, as is, my own experience tells me, the sensual pleasure derived from those dancing acoustical beats.

Sometimes accompanying audio mediation is what I would call spatial mediation—the increasing use of proscenium stages, promulgated by the larger arts institutions, with many villages following suit. The intimacy of traditional staging, with 270 or 360 degrees of audience seating is lost, bamboo chairs are arranged in rows, and audiences are stationary, in contrast with the fluid audience, which would take in the performance as part of a larger ceremonial environment. Choreographic ideas are adapted to become more frontal and presentational. New staging formats often create an extreme distance between performers and audience. This has also already changed the nature of Balinese choreography, since flicks of the hands and fingers, eyes, and facial expression are not seen, while a larger space must be filled. Group dances are replacing intricate characterization, with more elaborate, expensive costumes to catch the distanced eye. Evolving along with this presentational style involving distance and frontal view is the creation of dance forms in which there is a necessity to *show*, in a more pantomimic manner, more than subtly to suggest or imply unseen forces, as has been the style in the past. A dualistic dynamic takes hold, of performers at one extreme and audience at the other. The performance is also framed in, as a clearly delimited phenomenon—another new aspect of mediation. This contrasts with the preproscenium setting in which the performers are surrounded by other activities and visual information that is part of their everyday lives and their environment, and of interest even in the course of the performance, and through which the dancers manifest another reality that exists within the larger, present-tense, shared reality rather than as a discrete and separate entity, a commodity.

Performers are trying to adjust to a new, growing urban audience that has less patience with subtle elements and is geared toward pure entertainment—whistling at female performers, reflecting the stereotype of "sexy" seen on television, and interrupting performances with derisive calls. At the same time, economic mediation is much more common, with tickets being sold for events, sometimes even for those associated with a religious occasion.

Another path of recontextualization has been the use of indoor buildings with prosceniums; here, the dance becomes further objectified and delimited. By any standard, the audibility is affected adversely by these indoor halls, *kendang* suffering the most. Verifying the pain and confusion my own ears tell me, I have heard from the director of one prominent Balinese performing ensemble that medical doctors have recently been reporting loss of hearing amongst many *gambelan* academy musicians. Even in small village performances for an *odalan* temple festival, amplification is often set at full volume, with accompanying distortion and often incredible feedback. I have not observed great resistance amongst Balinese audiences to the volume or feedback, which is fascinating in itself, but I did not pursue this question of audience while I was there, except in the one village that eschews amplification. In the midst of a dance performance, a great electric hum of feedback will swell over the sound of the music itself, maintaining its dominance for a minute or so. People are not holding their ears or expressing bother, but seem to be accepting the manifest destiny of coming into the new age of modernity.

At another village's *odalan*, I was standing in the outer courtyard, but still within the temple, as people were carrying in offerings of fruit and lavishly decorated rice cakes piled high on their heads, and an enormous gale of feedback overcame the sound system, which had been playing *gambelan* music. The feedback took on varied melodic inflections, swooping tonal contours of which Jimi Hendrix, I dare say, would have been envious. This blaring unintentional electronic piece continued for twenty minutes, a new variety of processional music, as people bearing offerings issued in and out. I know that John Cage would have savored the experience. If we allow for a broader concept of discrete music (which often implies more a delimited product of organized sound), this *odalan* phenomenon begins to sound different. First of all, when we speak of sound distortion from amplifiers and speakers, we can, if we choose, do so as rock musicians do—as an attribute of timbre rather than as a pejorative. If someone in a position of influence has turned the amplification system on, and for at least twenty minutes no one is turning it off, we should really think of that sound as meaningful and, in the John Cage sense, interesting as nonintentional music. This enters into a large body of twentieth-century nonintentional process music derived from Cage's ideas. Even if the Balinese examples are somewhat less self-conscious, they are not any less meaningful or audible, even more so when we think of them as "soundscapes," an idea developed by Canadian composer R. Murray Schafer: "the general acoustic environment of a society can be read as an indicator of social conditions which produce it and may tell us much about the trending and evolution of that society" (1977: 7).

The anecdote I relate in *Aji nusup* 'lessons in penetration' regards one set of problems arising from the appropriation and recontextualization of *tembang* songs by means of audio recording. But there is also an obvious

I Madé Pasek Tempo with the author in an informal recording session (1981). Photo by Beth Skinner.

benefit of tape recording. A few of my older Balinese mentors and teachers, the generation born around the turn of the century, did not have their own children among their most dedicated students. As in many societies, children may choose to find their own path or creative direction as an alternative to following in an illustrious parent's path. On my 1992 visit to Bali, I happened to hear a similar story from three different close friends, children of these illustrious but now deceased artists. The parent would appear in their dreams at night and teach them. With water welling up in their eyes on each occasion, each of these friends said they regretted not showing an interest in their parent's art before the older generation had passed away. But the dreams were a redemptive source of education. This inspired me to use an audio tape player with dubbing capacity to duplicate some of my research recordings, not of polished performances, but of process level rendering in an informal style, potentially of great value to them. I made this a bit of a project—discussing with children or grandchildren of my teachers whether they were interested, and then duplicating my recordings specifically to meet their perceived needs. The results elicited deep emotional responses from these aspiring masters and gave them much pleasure but they also raised a question for me. One of these old masters had on numerous occasions in 1980 mentioned to me how pointless and bogus it was for the younger generation to come to him, a repository of music and dance tradition, only when they had a specific project for public display. He would say that in the old days learning was a continuous process and that people would practice not just to show something but as part of a collective way of life. He would always eventually let them persuade him to go along for the rehearsals and performance, but with a touch of cynicism. So even now I can hear him chuckling, suggesting that a grandson may prize a recording of his music and dance teaching, but that the message was of such a kinesthetic nature, transmitted from the tone of one's body to the tone of another's body, that the message was the medium, and he was it. However, to balance this out, another of my mentors arranged a special recording session with me in 1980 to document for his descendants his particular vocal style so that they could learn from the tapes. I am sure they have had some of the desired result.

On my most recent visit, I was being driven in a van by the grandson of a *dalang* friend, when he asked me how much things had changed since my last visit. I told him that Bali had become smaller. Once he realized I was not putting him on, he found this to be an interesting and peculiar concept. I explained how performers used to have a two- or three-hour walk home from a performance, often just as the day was breaking, but now it took only twenty minutes by minivan. Distances had shrunk. At the same time, though, the experience of the distance from place to place had also shrunk, and the perceptions, the personal experience of nature, which many a *dalang* and *panasar* have told me are basic to their creative process, is reduced in turn. Now, of course, the minds of people in any situation are going to be active, and some artists will create new work reflecting their new mediated environment, more distanced from nature, but still reflecting changing contexts of human life. But nonetheless, presence in a place is marginalized by the form of transportation. Ivan Illich has dealt with related issues of transportation in socioeconomic terms in *Energy and Equity* (1974). After several months of getting used to 1990s Balinese automobile traffic, I realized that distances were increasing again, but in a different way: the island Bali seemed in a sense to be growing in size, as road congestion showed its temporal effects. But as the space-time continuum plays games with us in the form of bumper-to-bumper traffic, confusing the issue a bit, the context and experience of sitting in traffic remains different from that of bicycling or walking. Now, I am not interested in reinventing some idyllic "spice islands" or a static "beautiful Bali," but rather in bringing up and being aware of issues that frame aesthetic realities during this period of rapid transition that I have witnessed and experienced in the past twenty-five years. Indeed, these are issues being discussed by Indonesian artists with whom I associate.

Further penetration
"branching out of Bali"
into other interpretive modes

❀

As we consider the human organism in its musical ecology, the nature and manifestation of sound, we can distinguish three spheres of articulation.[1] State of consciousness is intrinsic to the first sphere. Form is intrinsic to the second sphere, as it deals with differentiation of emanations from distinct states; it is in this sphere that the element of time appears. Instrumentation is intrinsic to the third sphere, in which emanations are manifested through a physical vehicle; this sphere introduces the element of space, as a distinct entity. Each of these spheres is, in turn, made up of three aspects.

State of consciousness is the intrinsic aspect of the first sphere (I), permeating all other aspects, yet distinct in its pure sense. This aspect represents personal orientation and is composed of spiritual (finer) vibrations. The next aspect is that of shape-form visualization, a conceptual level composed of intellectual (less fine) vibrations. Here, phenomena take on form, and shape is considered as a dynamic quality, in a time-space sense, manifested as neume, gesture, color, and so on. The third aspect is that

---

1. This discussion reintroduces aspects of cognition and manifestation in a more abstract form in order to cross over disciplines to the realm of religious hermeneutics and, obliquely, Tantric Buddhist discourse. The Tantric Buddhist historic period in Indonesia very much influenced Bali, though centered in the kingdom of Sriwijaya, which ruled from the seventh until the fourteenth century in Palembang, South Sumatra, and in Central Java from the late seventh until the tenth century (Wolters 1970: 133–35). Over the centuries, monks from India and China traveled to Sumatra to study Buddhism (Coomaraswamy 1965: 200; and Holt 1967: 36). This strong influence remains in contemporary Bali's syncretic culture. Although my discussion does not deal directly with explicit Balinese categories, it reflects much consultation with Balinese philosophers as well as scholars of Tibetan Buddhism, in an attempt to distinguish some of these ontological issues outside of culture-bound contexts. For religio-cultural studies, see Stephan Beyer (1978) and Judith Becker (1993).

of physical atoms (vibrations), which includes the realm of sound. There cannot be physical vibrations without both "visualization" and "state," nor can there be visualization without state. This is the sense in which we say that state is intrinsic to this sphere.

The aspects of this and other spheres are thought of as an ordering of qualities, and not necessarily of sequence. In certain practices, we may observe that physical qualities lead to visualization and then to state, or visualization to physical to state, and so on. The aspects are not completely distinct from one another in practice, but rather in origin and quality.

Each aspect may offer a frame of reference to any other aspect of any sphere. However, it seems most appropriate to apply aspects of the state sphere to either the form or instrumentation sphere, and the form sphere to that of instrumentation. For instance, the visualization (conceptual) of a given stylization (II); or the form, context, or stylization (all II) of a given vocal phenomenon. Three of the many ways in which context (II) could be applied are cultural context (within II), performance context (within III), and ideational context (within I).

As we move on to the next sphere (II), the intrinsic aspect is form. This may be thought of as a conceptual articulation of ordering, or the differentiation of emanations from a state (I). As the element of time is stressed here, of concern is the articulation and quality of any given moment, whether that moment include an inflection, a gesture, or an entire ritual event (which may still be considered a moment in itself).

The second aspect of this sphere is context: the circumstances and interrelationships of a given state, concept, or phenomenon. For example, this may apply to a particular melody, as it changes from one set of lyrics to another, or to recognizing a multicontextual temporal event (involving many simultaneous conceptual levels). Stylization, the third aspect, has to do with the form of presentation of any given emanations, referring to "how" rather than "what." Stylization uses selective limitation to focus on essential qualities, leaving other qualities for each individual perceiver to supply on his or her own.

We might approach the third sphere by way of instrumentation, which could be aligned with stylization in sphere (II) and physicalization in sphere (I). In this regard, our concern is with the means by which things become physically manifested. Modes of stylization are realized through instrumentation, the physical properties of which affect, as they are affected by, the other aspects and spheres.

The next aspect, text, refers to actual sound properties of a language, as well as to the "meanings" of words, and could, in certain senses, be aligned with context (II) and state (I). The shapes of vowels and consonants provide the space in which a given phenomenon takes place. Text may determine the particular usage (context) of a musical entity, by means of color, rhythm, mood, character, action, story, genre.

In the next aspect of this sphere, the vocal, our focus is on the actual manifestation (in time and space) of emanations from distinct states. Vocal may be aligned with form in sphere (II) and shape-form visualization in sphere (I). It is through the vehicle of the human body that all states, forms, and colors may become audible. Unique to this aspect is the context in which instrument is one and the same as both conceiver and perceiver.

Penetrating what, where, and how

❀

what is happening, where is it happening, and how is it happening?[1]

tone is how, form (overall shape of sounds and silences) is where,
and in the hearing is "what" (even the Earth hears)

wherever one enters, one feels how whatever is happening, happens

"When" is perceived in the small dimension of time (the body and its immediate relations), and is really a temporal aspect of "where," which is
sensed in time and space, at once. The greater dimension of time has to do
with relativity and energy—reflected in qualities, ways, and overall tones
and vibrations—and concerns "how."

The path of masolah

My initial approach to any phenomenon is to see how it is generated
rather than how it is organized. The two often go hand in hand, but each
of us may place greater weight on one or another of these questions. Structure tells "where it happens" as distinguished from "how it happens." Art
may be leading the way along a certain path by paying the least attention
to "what happens." Edmund Leach (1972: 239) asserts that it is the "structural patterns embedded in mythology rather than the superficial content
that conveys the significant message." I still maintain that structure is static
and cannot actively "convey" (transport) anything anywhere. We still want
to know how a message gets from here to there, or from the myth to the
"culture-carrier."

1. Elements of this chapter were presented in a paper entitled "What, Where and How is
Gambelan in Bali" at the First International *Gamelan* Festival, at Expo '86, Vancouver, B.C.,
Canada. Throughout this chapter, explicitly Balinese ideas are identified as such; otherwise,
they are broader concepts coming out of my own ideas and speculative process, derived in
part from, and applicable to, much Balinese aesthetic theory and practice.

Edmund Leach also says that, "myth is a charter for ritual performance . . . we understand what is symbolized by what is being 'said' in mythology." In the same way, belief systems, myth, and shared sense of time-space orientation inform all activities, but are particularly necessary as a complement to stylized aesthetic forms (related directly to Leach's rituals). This is precisely why the Japanese $N\bar{o}$ actor may dare to feel successful when his audience dozes off into sleep during a performance. An explanation given by one Balinese actor is that audience members already have a sense of the story, so they can afford to tune into the performance for a while, pick up some of its depth, state, form, and style, and then supply the rest of the experience with their own imaginations. It is taken for granted by the performer that the audience has sufficient reference points, and it is taken for granted by the audience that the performer will remain true to the style, so they can land safely and then take off again.

It is in this sense that stylized performance bears a resemblance to Ndembu concepts and terminology (Zambia, Africa) regarding ritual, as described by Victor Turner (1969: 15). The Ndembu liken the ritual process to the "blazing of trails" in the forest. The ritual actions, *chijiki-jilu*, are "landmarks" or "blazes," the marked trees along the way, that keep the participants on the right path. Stylized aesthetics also function in a way that allows such a path to be marked, along which the intuitive (as Turner and Arnold van Gennep's "liminal") flows.

However, as we look into the generative process of such forms, stylization seems a mere reflection of the internal continuum. It is as if a light were reflected from one mirror to another, the light following a continuous path, and the mirrors being located in such a way as to let the light cover the desired area. Myth is the desired area to be covered, light is the internal process, and the image in each mirror is the stylized form (or ritual element). Ideally, we see both reflector and image, because that is the aspect of stylization that gives freedom to the perceiver. The clarity the image can present allows it to cry out, "it's not me that you are watching: I'm a reflection." (A South Indian *Bharata natyam* dancer fixing her hair in between verses is unabashedly the performer surfacing momentarily from the character.) Stylized aesthetics offer a more direct cognitive process, allowing the mind to deflect the rational process.

A corollary to this notion of deflection may be seen in the use of an object or image of focus (visualization) in meditation practices, and with *T'ai-chi*. By putting weight or concentration on one point, the energy (*chi, prana*) is allowed to flow through other areas freely. The object of focus (landmark, blaze) does not become the area of activity, but serves to stimulate a dynamic internal process elsewhere. A stylized form is such a pressure point.

What state-specific criteria apply to phenomena of musical, dramatic, and ritual content? One aspect lies in the sphere of explicit systems, revealing what Lévi-Strauss and Turner refer to as "isomorphic" relationships between biological, structural, and cultural processes (the ancient theme of macro and microcosmos). Another aspect has to do with artists' and others' verbal statements concerning purposes, values, motivations, and feelings about performance activity. Yet another level involves context, materials, forms, and states as described in terms of *wali, bebali,* and *balih-balihan.*

But the best source of knowledge concerning state-specific factors has to be personal experience, through the actual process of learning and interacting. It is through this experience that the many methods and values of reflection, stylization, and state are transmitted directly. Without working from the inside outward, I would not trust my own "organizing principles" to be anything but arbitrary and subjective. Perhaps it would be helpful to reverse the isomorphic (macro/microcosmos) concentricities common in much social science, and indicate a progression from biological, phenomenological structures to cultural and social morphologies. What I mean is that in order to integrate certain aspects, or kinds of knowledge, it may be necessary to swallow that knowledge whole, as a psychic, biological isomorphic entity, and then come to know something about the world by knowing something about one's self.

Another désa kala patra *within performance*

... with particular reference to what ... I termed "structure" and "method." By "structure" was meant the division of the whole into parts; by "method," the note-to-note procedure. Both structure and method (and also "material"—the sounds and silences of a composition) were, it seemed to me then, the proper concern of the mind (as opposed to the heart) (one's ideas of order as opposed to one's spontaneous actions); whereas the two last of these, namely method and material, together with form (the morphology of a continuity) were equally the proper concern of the heart.[2]

To begin in concord with John Cage, linking the idea of continuity to the realm of the heart is suggestive on more that one level. According to spiritual traditions throughout the world, the rational mind may be said to work in delimiting and differentiating ways (nowadays generally associated with the left hemisphere of the brain), while the heart works by seeking affinities ("atom attracts like atom"). The ultimate aim of the heart is to form a "chord of sympathy" with its surroundings, a melting of the I-Thou distinction and a unity of qualities. The means to that end is to extend a

2. John Cage (1973: 18).

cord of sympathy that joins previously disparate energies into a common flow. The heart establishes sympathy with phenomena by seeing those phenomena reflected in itself.

Within a Balinese *Sang Hyang* trance-inducing song there is a poetic image likening a metaphorical boatman's spirit to *kué*, a sticky paste, that encourages phenomena and experiences to stick to the spirit: possession. There is no discontinuity or interference in matters of the heart, for any gap would short-circuit the bonding current.

Another aspect of continuity is in the temporal, which also relates to the nature of the heart. Both meditation and performance technique teach us the importance of sustained attention, of not "dropping character," as the cord of energy and belief disintegrates as soon as a pause, or gap, occurs. Needless to say, silence can be as sustained a factor in the continuity as sound.

I have some difficulty, though, with Cage's notion of a "morphology of a continuity," for that seems somehow a contradiction in terms. If we are speaking of morphology, we are involved with reflections of a continuity, which do not share the unique one-ness referred to earlier. What are cited as defining features of morphology are in fact incidental features of a continuously varying process.

With "Heisenberg's Principle" in mind, we may be equipped only to speak of morphology or continuity as discrete factors. Perhaps we would be closer to the truth if we described form as an echo, or a shadow, of a continuity, each of these requiring an outside surface to bring it into existence, as morphology exists on a different level from continuity. Morphology is the itinerary of a continuity and is, in that sense, similar to form, especially if we think of form's basic nature as that of time-space.

Perhaps we have circled back to Cage's intended meaning and may tentatively accept his definition of form, although I do think that the term *morphology* asserts an unwarranted dominance over continuity, partly because of our materialist orientation. However, it is still most likely that Cage's basic concept of continuity differs greatly from ours. Later in that particular lecture, Cage indicates that all he is interested in using to fulfill his continuities is the arbitrary. Whatever he wishes to be illogical or spontaneous is left "out of his hands" compositionally; rather than integrating the intuitive and rational, he insists on keeping them apart (this dialectic is intrinsic to his aesthetic). In this case, the potential for change exists only outside the composer and does not allow for an inner process of revelation or development. Whatever is "of the composer" is logical, and whatever we call illogical is the result of forces "outside the composer." The dichotomy is noticeable in the disparity between Cage's conceptions of some of his pieces and the performers' and audiences' perspectives.

Directly following the section quoted earlier for discussion, Cage refers to "the opposites, the rational and the irrational." The notion of opposites is itself an intellectual concept (the heart seeks a unity of opposites), so even though Cage is interested in integrating the two, his basic definition tends to push the intuitive into a corner. Ambiguity between structure and continuity is a necessary component of art, the balance shifting back and forth, with each throwing a shadow on the other. As the Sun's light crosses Earth's sky, shadows change shape and dimension, just as the relationship between structure and intuition is always in transition. In order to insure the nonrational, Cage tries to legislate its place, but in doing so he almost rationalizes it away.

Continuing with Cage's approach in which the mind (through structure, method, and materials) and heart (through method, material and form) complement each other, let me extend this idea into the area of pitch relationships. Structure (mind) implies a static, fixed set of pitch levels that function as a phonemic (defining) characteristic of melody. Pitch contour (the shape of a melody) is an implicit function here. On the other hand, form (heart) implies a dynamic function, with pitch levels functioning as a phonetic (incidental) feature of melody; pitches can be viewed here as isolated points along a continuously varying melodic contour (to borrow two phrases from Ter Ellingson [1979]). The (implicit) "inner melody" discussed by Sumarsam (1976) is a continuous function, and the (explicit) "outer melody" is a set of discrete functions adding up to constitute structure. Cage states this in similar terms. However, other musical traditions treat pitch values in different ways.

For instance, Ellingson describes how in some Tibetan chants (*dbyangs*), continuously varying melodic contours are treated as explicit features (stylized gestures) and the "inner melody" takes on a different relationship to the "outer" (refer to my discussion of stylization and *masolah* above). When the explicit melodic features of a music are presented as time-space contours (as opposed to discrete variables), they take on the characteristics of gesture, of intrinsic form (as opposed to elements adding up to form). Balinese vocal music contains many similar explicit features of continuous melodic contour, but this aspect has not been systematized in the sense that Tibetan chant has.

Perhaps the threefold unity of performance theory, *désa kala patra*, can be compared with Cage's compositional format. Hearkening back (coincidentally) to my interpretation of structure as "a place for something to happen," *désa* 'place, location' can accommodate Cage's use of the term *structure*. Cage's "dividing the whole into parts," is the equivalent of establishing a location for each of the parts, viewing them as subject to organizing principles. It is this organizational feature that applies to *désa*, which can refer to the map of an event, locality, social and spiritual orientation, which all combine to determine the story, "message and meaning." Message and meaning are evident in this category in both senses in which Edmund Leach uses the terms: that is, both in the sense that "structural patterns embedded in the mythology . . . convey the message," and as "superficial content."

Both of Cage's factors, method (note-to-note procedure) and material (the sounds and silences of a composition), can fall within the range of the Balinese concept *patra*. This word designates activity in the sense of context (method) and movement, and the physicality of performance (material). The procedures are conceived of as *jalan* 'steps' as well as postures, stances. The argument among structuralists and functionalists concerning "what" is happening in performance (ritual or other) is relevant to our distinction between *désa* and *patra*. Is it the structural organization or the practice and physicality that tell us "what" is going on, or even "where" it is going on? What I have been calling a "where" Leach calls a "what" (structure). Structure (*désa*) and practice, physicality (*patra*) are both "whats" and "wheres," depending upon your structuralist or functionalist point of view (neither of which satisfies my question of "what").

Now we can move on to what Victor Turner (1969) and Arnold van Gennep (1960) call "liminality," Cage calls form (morphology of a continuity), and I call the source of stimulation for dynamic internal processes leading to the "what"—related perspectives beautifully suiting the Balinese application of *kala* to their threefold performance theory. *Kala* is time, sense of timing, and here refers to the flow of events within the performance. Within the Balinese theatrical context, this involves bringing into the drama a flow of elements from outside the story (song, extemporaneous poetry, dance, improvised dialogue), creating a different sense of time for the drama and audience alike. This new sense of time allows each audience member his/her own time frame, to drift in and out of attentiveness, *kalangén* 'rapture', into sleep, dreams, or other activities (ceremonial, relaxing). The audience's ability to complement the performance with their own imaginations actually serves an important function of *kala*, completing the performance process. This suits Cage's linking of form to concerns of the heart.

The method of attaining this sense of time, of course, is stylization, gestural language (in a broad sense), a body of continuities, or as Turner refers to it in ritual, "a conspicuous feature of the landscape." What this sense of *kala*, time or continuity, tells us is "how" things happen.

What, where, and how is gambelan?

The *Oxford English Dictionary* defines contemporary as "living, existing, or occurring together in time." Tradition is defined by *Webster*'s as "the handing down of information, customs, beliefs" or "an inherited pattern of thought or action." Since all arts practices reflect characteristics of both terms, we can view each phenomenon as a process of continuity and change. There is certainly a tendency in industrial societies around the world to think of tradition as static and the contemporary as creative and dynamic. Just after President and Mrs. Reagan's visit to Bali, the *Los Angeles Times* published a photograph of some friends of mine in Batuan, Ketut Kantor and some children. In the caption, they were identified as performing an "ancient ritual frog dance." Now, really it was a lesson in *godogan*, a pure entertainment genre created and performed for tourists. The masks were conceived by Kantor's next-door neighbor, Déwa Putu Bebes.

"Contemporary" might really refer to anything existing at the present time, and any living, creative phenomenon requires continual inspiration, reinterpretation, and change. There are examples of new performance genres in twentieth-century Bali: *arja, Calonarang, cak, kebiar, séndratari*, and so on. But our concern here is more with the creativity, *perkembangan*, within any genre; the dynamic interplay between the soul of a *gambelan* (or divine, sacred presence in a space) and the performers; improvisation between instrumentalists and singers, dancers or *dalang*. We may sense more inventiveness in a spirited "traditional" *gambelan* than we do in some of what is specifically called contemporary, which may tend to put too high a premium on a more superficial idea of inventiveness. On the other hand, new forms—with or without standard instrumentation—might sometimes reflect the kinetic energy, transcendence, and spontaneity of the tradition more than something called *gambelan*, which looks and sounds like "the real thing." So, continuity and change (Claire Holt's term) are aspects of both the traditional and nontraditional. We are in both cases dealing with artistic processes, some of which possess the vitality of a living phenomenon.

So what is *gambelan*? Is it a collection of metal objects, a set of principles, or a complex and diverse living confluence of spiritual experience and physical, corporeal experience, transcendent expression of cosmic order with down-to-earth expression of human community and group affiliation? *Gambelan* "music" lives amidst, rather is composed of, a vast web of connections: with dance, shadow puppetry, theater, with ceremony, recreation, and spiritual reflection.

Playing from notation is a very modern phenomenon in Indonesia, a result of European influence.[3] The aural learning process is by nature kinesthetic, and involves a physical interaction among musical materials, teacher, and student. In aural music, the only physical manifestation occurs in performance, and the music itself (at least the actual production of sound in time and space) is conceived as a corporeal entity, a being with its own life. In notated music cultures, written notation is considered to be a manifestation of the music (in fact, we generally refer to notation as "the music," as in, "Did you bring your music?").

Aural learning has its parallels with notated musical practices, in particular sight-reading. The more obvious point is that when one has relied upon listening to learn all that he knows, his auditory sense and aural reflexes are bound to be relatively highly attuned. What that means is that the "inner hearing" is sensitive and responsive enough to perceive the aspect of form immediately, expending less energy on the assimilation of the physical or state aspects.[4]

But less obvious is that the internal sphere has assimilated structural forms, which cannot be recalled arbitrarily (consciously) at will, but can respond intuitively to the beckoning of another impulse bearing structural affinity. This is similar to the phenomenon of sight-reading, where, presumably, the musician may never have "seen the music" before but is able to make sense out of the notation with fluency. He or she does not have to begin at the simplest level, reading note for note, but can intuitively sense the phrasing and form by previous experience with similar structures. The intuitive sense characteristically makes faster and more complex analogies among structural affinities than does the rational, analytic sense (at least in the context of music).

This question of the memory of structural forms lends itself readily to the issue of "formulas" and standard patterns in Indonesian music. Dynamic processes may be interpreted as formulas and standardized patterning for the purpose of getting a "handle" on the internal dynamics of subtle aesthetic systems. But we must ultimately look beyond grammatical forms and come back to the question of how aural traditions utilize their deep-structural forms in practice.

The aural learning process I underwent in the study of the instrumental

3. See Sumarsam (1995: 106) for a discussion of European influence and changing musical conceptions in late-nineteenth-century Java.

4. Some of these ideas regarding the relationship between "inner hearing" and the assimilation of musical form were stimulated by a discussion the author had with Charles Seeger in 1977.

Iron-keyed *gambelan
selonding* in Tenganan (1972).

music of *gendér wayang* in Bali was of a thoroughly different character from anything I had previously encountered. One aspect of the perceptual process is that the student often integrates a musical phrase or sequence before it is conceptually realized. Although, obviously, some cognitive process is necessary before one can play a musical phrase, a substantial area of consciousness is bypassed. Often, it is like a room without windows: one must enter the room before knowing what furniture is inside. At times, one must enter the music—be playing it—before integrating or even recognizing the form; physical precedes form. During my own study of *gendér wayang*, this stage of learning seemed to involve letting my hands play a phrase on their own, while my conscious mind watched, one step behind. This pedagogical process is referred to as *maguru panggul* 'the mallets doing the teaching'. Whenever I tried to imagine the next phrase, my mind would not respond until the next phrase was already unfolding. Actually, a stage of form cognition precedes this physical stage and involves taking in smaller, less continuous units. The process is perhaps best described as the solving of a musical and physical riddle, most blatant in the specific technique of studying the *gendér*, which involves the two hands often playing contrapuntal rhythms. One must approach a phrase from different angles, as if peeking into a room from various windows, before succeeding in taking the first step into the room.

Perceptions seem to vary between seeing a room without windows and then with windows, but the two views complement each other. Even if they did not, it wouldn't matter, because it's not a room anyway; it's a musical phrase. Or is it a room?[5] The process of solving the riddle, approaching it from various angles by successive repetition, is more kinesthetic and intuitive than it is analytic, since it involves coming to grips with a dynamic entity, always unfolding, changing (especially as my teacher, Madé Gerindem, usually refused to break a phrase down into small units, playing it in its entirety before repeating it). Once such a small phrase is grasped, it is added to a larger melodic form. It is at this moment that the mind realizes the melody is known on a relatively unconscious level, forcing the student to rely on kinesthetic memory. The next stage usually involves performing the rote-learned forms while the process of change, the unfolding of variation, and the state of the music are fully incorporated into the player. It is by entering the state (mood, space-time flow) of the music that one comes to know it; as distinctions of physicality, form, and state dissolve, one is left with the music itself. "Getting" a phrase, or even the totality of a piece, is only the initial step of the learning process.

Similarly, both Balinese and Javanese dancers have related to me how learning a dance, in the sense of acquiring the ability to perform the movements and choreography, is only the first stage of study. Once the dance form and technique are internalized, the longer, more important and subtle, process begins: that of attaining the state wherein the spirit of the dance can enter the performer. This point may seem obvious, and is indeed applicable in some degree to any musical or dance tradition, but I maintain that there is an aesthetic priority quite specific to Bali and Java in this kinesthetic learning context, requiring and emphasizing a particular process of "settling into a state."

Perhaps it would be more accurate at this point to say that a dancer begins by preparing his/her own energy field (rather than state), gradually learns the dance (space-time formula), and those two combined factors result in the attainment of a specific state. Once mentally prepared and receptive, the dancer comes to know specific sequences of gestures or musical accompaniment as elements of the state's environment. The formal patterns and physical sensations gradually fall into place as part of a composite

5. Indeed, Gilbert Rouget sees music as "an architecture of time" (1980: 179).

Gambelan musicians and children at ceremonial *rejang* outside the *pura désa*, Batuan (1972).

kinesthetic process occurring within a focused and/or meditative state. In that sense, successful performance implies the attainment of a particular state, the result of those combined factors, while the student's (or performer's) initial task is the preparation of an energy field. In learning Balinese and Javanese dance, the aspect of form may often seem to follow physicality and energy field.

In an aural tradition, music exists on its own terms, which is either in performance or within one's own imagination; but not as a separate musical entity such as notation. Therefore, in order to learn, one must go to the musical experience itself and enter into it. Since the intrinsic nature of Indonesian music is collective and social, a single musical instrument cannot be taken out of the collective context anyway; one cannot come to know the music by practicing at home. Although this principle can also apply to ensemble musics of other cultures, the fact remains that most Balinese musicians do not own their own instruments: they have little or no opportunity to practice in the privacy of their homes. And so, the dictates of both collectivity and aural learning direct the aspiring musician toward direct participation in a musical totality—ensemble activity.

Another important ingredient of the aural learning process is the cumulative effect of casual listening, important in any culture, but of particular significance in the lives of young, rural Balinese and Javanese. Before a person has begun to think of himself as a musician, he has been repeatedly exposed to a good deal of the repertoire he will need to know, and the musical forms, instrumental relationships and roles, and total ensemble effect will have filtered into his inner ear. Young Balinese children, and even babies, most often sit among the musicians as they rehearse, and often as they perform, where they are bound to receive at least a deep kinesthetic sense of the music, experiencing the spatial and temporal dynamics in a relaxed, often unconscious fashion. The cumulative and aural process is dramatized by the kind of Balinese scene where boys carry the *gambelan* instruments from the storage area (in a temple, village meeting hall, etc.) to the rehearsal or performance space and begin playing together, to be gradually replaced, one by one, as the adult musicians arrive, the music continuing through the shift of personnel. The boys make room, in time, for the adults, but still they have had the temporary sense of being included in the ensemble, as well as a lasting sense of aural and physical participation. One major social factor contributing to the aural learning process is that rehearsals are open events, just as much as performances are; they are held in public and are open to any interested listeners.

So, *gambelan* is a phenomenon, an event, rather than a discrete, objectifiable entity. One can enter a "where" that permits the connections of place-time-context intrinsic to *gambelan*. We must not think of *gambelan* only as a window when the point is what can be seen through it. Thus with *gambelan* and all the phenomena related to it we can ask: What is happening, where is it happening, and how is it happening?

Form (the overall shape of sounds and silences) is where it happens. Tone is how it happens. Sensations of tone are perceived in ambience, mood, sound, color, muscles, and reflect tension, gravity, density, and atmospheric conditions. Only within the actual experience of hearing do we get to "what" is happening. "What" is found in a quality of stillness, nonaction in the midst of motion, when something is being moved by a force with greater momentum than itself. What is happening in *gambelan* is a confluence of temporal, spatial, and spiritual dimensions reflecting a specific space, time, and context.

Everything in nature is in some state of motion (if only that of the planet or of subatomic particles). The still lake's water is constantly evaporating or condensing, or even flowing up or in from springs or streams. We see the still lake changing as it reflects changing light and the motion of wind, swimmers, boats, ducks. So, we are not speaking of stillness as an absolute measurement; we are interested in the quality of stillness or nonaction.

Water flows into any path open to it. Stillness, transported by momentum, takes on the character and qualities of the motion and of the force generating the motion. This characteristic is evident in puppets and masks: in themselves they are still, but they change as a force clearly other than their own moves them. Because it is still, it is open, and because it is open, it is translucent; the stillness allows one to focus directly in the midst of motion, while the translucence allows one to perceive through it, into it. For instance, one is able to listen not "to" a sound, but into or through the sound, as through a window, into a realm of other, more subtle qualities that are not "heard" in the same way. This stillness in motion leads directly to the heart, because of focus, clarity, and translucence, and the qualities of the momentum. It is simple, not complex; there is nothing extraneous to or outside the momentum. The life breathed into these forms is not of our own devising; we devise the river bed, and nature and intuition provide the flow.

> A reflection of the moon is there on the path
> in that clear pool of water
> it is like that with you, when you meditate,
> if you make yourself clear and pure,
> a reflection of divinity will be reflected[6]

Where do we see? In the pond. How? By the pond being still and clear and us looking in the right direction. What do we see? A reflection of something. The image of moon further suggests something transcendent and transitory. Form that possesses the quality of fluidity is receptive to being acted upon by gravity's momentum. The mind can be clear and fluid (in this focused state of realization, achieved by meditator or performer) while allowing for motion, not differentiating a-b-c-d-e, but rather a single articulatory gesture.

In a sense, with naturalistic art forms, we are supposed to "make believe" that what is happening is "real"; illusion is a process of stimulating imagination. It is made to seem as if the "what" is explicit; the "where" (form, sounds, and silences) is kept vague, unspontaneous, or even lifeless, in order to keep the bound-up imagination and concentration intact. With gestural form, as most often found in stylized genres, the "where" is explicit, allowing whatever is happening to exist on its own. One knows that a puppet play is not about puppets, a masked drama not about people with wooden heads. One does not confuse the form with what is happening—it is where it is happening. The "what," which does not manifest visibly, is

6. Wayan Diya's free quotation and translation from *Arjuna Wiwaha* (personal communication, 1979). Zoetmulder's literary version (1974: 234–37) has the moon reflected in a vessel of water.

approached by means of a gesture that contains a quality, stimulating observers. Imagination, through illusion, also exists here and provides an impulse that induces involvement, or in the Balinese shadow puppeteer's terms, seduction. But this other perceptual process I speak of also comes into play, offering a process of sympathetic resonance with physiospiritual qualities.

In the flow between great and small, gesture allows you (microcosmos) to enter great (macrocosmos); a clear mind allows qualities (macrocosmos) to enter you.

> amid stillness
> a gesture flowers,
> inhales the air around it,
> and exhaling, shapes the surrounding air,
> forming a unity and direct flow between great and small

The flow is what is happening, the form or gesture is where, and the stillness (clear mind) is how.

Hearkening back to *buana alit* as a process of "letting them (qualities) enter into you," and *buana agung* as "to be able to enter into things," state of consciousness is one's relative interfacing with the flow between great and small. One *way* is that of undifferentiated attention, a state of openness in which the mind does not obstruct direct perception. It is open to a unified field of present phenomena. Here, one does not objectify any given thing by one's attention—things are allowed to remain themselves. One is not listening to anything in particular, but rather to everything. Instead of imposing upon an energy or phenomenon the force of objectification, it is as if one takes a step back (as with *T'ai-chi* and some martial arts). One does not obstruct the process of receptivity, but rather allows that energy the space to flow into one's own. This is the late-night state, the *Nō* state, the *wayang* state, and that of some meditative disciplines.

This is the realm of penetration. If we see a chair and think, "chair," that puts a lid on the matter and ends the process of perception. Penetration is the ability to enter into things, to focus without objectifying and delimiting, to see things as qualities in a process of change. In penetrating, one resonates sympathetically and reflects the quality that is "outside." One receives the quality as a reflection, which is in reality all that qualities are; and one becomes one with that "outside" thing, as one more reflector of that light which travels from one point to another. Again, the *Sang Hyang* trance-inducing song likening the boatman's spirit to *kué* 'sticky paste'—receptivity.

That state of undifferentiated attention is a way of letting things enter you. We do our most subtle feats of physical and mental coordination when the operating factors are not conscious. When we are objectifying, seeing things as *other*, we are less perceptive, less open.

> Being similar to the tree
> bending in the wind
> the state of undifferentiated attention (open heart) allows
> for a receptivity to qualities, essences

We see a tree swaying in the wind. But the tree is not doing the swaying. Though its branches are moving, the tree is still, while the unseen wind is bending and swaying.

At the other end of the equation is gestural form, the leaning point, concentration of energy, which is a singular impulse expressing the intrinsic, natural form of particular qualities. Gesture is undifferentiated internally, in that diverse qualities become submerged in a singularity of character, impulse.

We see the moon reflected on water. We are seeing the moon, and yet what we are looking at is the water, which is where we see the reflection. Form is where qualities are reflected. One can enter into a "where," but not a "what." When forms are perceived as where we see, not what we see, they are penetrable.

The process of stylization brings together these two approaches, penetration and receptivity. Although it is implicitly reached in other contexts, gestural form is most explicit within stylized performance and ritual. When gestural form derives from a stylized refinement of a shared, known cultural entity or action (language of the seen), the focal approaches of penetration and receptivity together manifest as the greatest kind of performance-audience context. When the gesture is derived from an esoteric language or discrete spiritual discipline, the two foci manifest as ritual phenomenon. Both contexts intermediate between penetration and receptivity with the aim of short-circuiting the dialectic of the differentiating mind, by the concentration of energy within a gesture, mask, or puppet, and receptivity to qualities.

> While the state of undifferentiated attention (open mind)
> allows for a receptivity to qualities, essences,
> gestural, stylized (undifferentiated) form
> focuses without objectifying
> proclaiming itself "where," not "what"
> making it penetrable

Perkembangan: *spontaneity and another flower of* désa kala patra

As I read the classic fourteenth-century treatise on Japanese *Nō*, Zeami's *Kadensho*,[7] I am struck by a clear similarity to Balinese aesthetics.

---

7. Chuichi Sakurai, et al. (1968: 6).

I Nyoman Antat, I Nyoman Kelub, and I Madé Ruju make up for *gambuh* performance in Batuan (1972).

Ze-ami says, "*Hana* is mind, technique is the seed." What I read from this now is that *hana* is *perkembangan*, the inner process of growth and flowering, within the feeling of *désa kala patra* ("whatever is suitable to the occasion is *hana*"). *Hana* is a state of openness to the mood of the audience and situation, the environment, and to the sense and spirit of the performance process, the work at hand. This heightened sensitivity to influences from within and without is attained by a performer's state of mind as that state comes to reflect the world view embedded in the form. The reason it is said by the translators of Ze-ami that "*hana* is the very essence of variety" is that, if one is truly reflecting *désa kala patra* within the mood of the piece, each performance will vary. When mind is in a state of fluidity, variety will be a reflection of the different qualities of place, time, and context.

Now, as to "technique is the seed": what an audience is aware of is not the *hana*, the "rarity," the profound particularity, uniqueness of the moment. *Hana* is the "secret flower" that affects, involves, and moves them, but technique is the seed that is nurtured into a perceptible flower; it is "what is seen." Technique within either a given formal style or a more experimental discipline involves the skill of working from within the state of *hana*: working with visible, external forms while being moved, initiated by, and becoming one with the inner state of fluidity and openness, thus becoming one with creation. The visible form grows from technique, the seed, conceived and nourished by *hana*. What an audience is aware of is the feeling of freshness, of life, but *hana* is "the *essence* of variety," the spirit within the expression. As Ze-ami says about why the "secrets" are secret: "Rarity is the flower. If the audience knows this secret they will always expect that some 'rarity' will occur. If the audience is expecting it there will be no freshness in the impression that he makes" (1968: 91). They will never see it or be moved by it as they would without presuppositions. One cannot watch a plant growing—bamboo being the closest to the realm of visual perception—it is too slow and subtle. One can observe the signs of growth and feel the internal energy of growing.

"*Hana* is spirit, and the seed is technique." The image of a flower is apt because, "as every kind of plant and flower blooms at its proper time in the four seasons, people think it is beautiful because they feel its blooming as something fresh and rare."

Mun, mun, mun [8] 'well, well, well', how does all this come about? How do these processes unfold, interact, come in and go out? Nature is never stagnant. Things are always unfolding, growing, decaying, responding to and interacting with their ecology. In the same sense, any sound, movement, experience, expressive gesture should, from its inception, be in a state of transformation and growth. A quality of energy has a certain chromosome makeup from the genetic pool, and contains within it the potential for growth. But the crucial aspect is an organic development, so that the identity of a quality remains, though it grows into what we perceive as new forms. In reality, there is no "seed" but rather a flow of energy seen as seed, sprout, tree, leaves, fire, ash, and earth. Qualities are generated that flow, within themselves, and into others. A "world view" involves perception of diverse qualities interacting.

So, structure tells us "where it happens," as distinguished from what or how. It is possible that all we can do in a creative, transformational process is to create a space for something to happen. Structure demarcates the space. But we should not mistake the empty urn, gebah, for an urn full of wine or amerta, the water of life. We create a space and let nature (or supernature) run its course. My interest is in filling and emptying the urn (inspiration and sharing) and in between those stages, tasting the amerta. But this urn is always made of fragile materials, bound in time and space by

8. Rhyming with *fun*, the actual Balinese spelling of the word is *men*, and this expression is used by *panasar*s in pensive moments.

the power of belief and concentration, and is extremely difficult to transport. And really, the binding of time and space prevents its detachment and transport anyway. So, we cannot move fragments of the urn out of a specific time-space and reconstruct them into a useful vessel (to carry liquid and not leak, rather than just appearing intact). But the process of wine or amerta flowing into and out of the vessel is an experience of a continuum with a life of its own (nature running its course), and the taste of the liquid is both a personal and a transcendent experience. As inner processes, they can be taken anywhere (smuggled across the border), and one can build a new urn out of indigenous time-space materials.

Afterword

René T. A. Lysloff

❁

[The] realization, that to study an art form is to explore a sensibility, that such a sensibility is essentially a collective formation, and that the foundations of such a formation are as wide as social existence and as deep, leads away not only from the view that aesthetic power is a grandiloquence for the pleasures of craft. It leads away also from the so-called functionalist view that has most often been opposed to it: that is, that works of art are elaborate mechanisms for defining social relationships, sustaining social rules and strengthening social values.
—Clifford Geertz

Locating Performance

Almost fifteen years ago, Clifford Geertz wrote the passage above in his now well-known essay "Art as a Cultural System" (Geertz 1983: 99). When I first read it as a graduate student, it brought about what seemed like an epiphany of understanding and insight, and defined for me what the field of ethnomusicology should be in the study of music. Ethnomusicology straddles both the social sciences and the humanities because, while scholars may employ anthropological methodology and address larger social issues, they are also concerned with matters of musical creativity and aesthetics. They understand, too, that music is embedded in and fully saturated with culture, inseparable from social context. Indeed, most ethnomusicologists now are familiar with the Geertzian claim (from the same essay) that "Art and the equipment to grasp it are made in the same shop" (Geertz 1983: 118).

While social and/or musical analysis may be a significant aspect of ethnomusicology, a large part of what ethnomusicologists do is interpretive work. By interpretive work, I mean a discursive rendering—or, perhaps better termed, representation—of a music and the people that make and enjoy it. This work might be done through careful and detailed exegesis of knowledge, practices, or values related to music or by writing broad ethnographic narratives that illustrate the musical life of a given people. Good interpretive work not only explicates a musical tradition (or culture) but demonstrates a relevance to broader interests outside the field of study. Scholars like Steven Feld, Anthony Seeger, John Chernoff, and Marina Roseman (to name only a few) have shown that interpretive study leads to a profound understanding not only of a particular music but also of the people that create, listen to, or otherwise participate in it. Edward Herbst, I believe, has accomplished such a goal in his study of the aesthetics of Balinese vocal music.

Herbst's book is about meaning in Balinese music: what *gambelan* and related vocal music mean to Balinese practitioners and listeners. It is about getting at that meaning as a foreign scholar, about understanding Balinese music in both senses of comprehension and sympathy (or empathy)—and conveying that understanding to others. Its importance goes beyond the details of describing what Balinese music is (or is not) because it reminds us why we should learn about it in the first place. The book is a study of Balinese vocal music and aesthetics based largely on the indigenous philosophical principle of *désa kala patra* 'place-time-context'. To put it crudely, learning *what* Balinese music *is* means learning *where*, *when*, and *how* it has come to be. In this way, the book is reminiscent of Steven Feld's study of Kaluli muscial aesthetics. Like Feld, Herbst provides insights into indigenous understandings of the world while focusing on music and music-related aesthetic values. The book, however, is unique in many ways (in its unusual and compelling writing style, for example) and reflects a profound understanding of Balinese language and culture.

In his introduction, Herbst has made an important argument: "I suggest that what we generally think of as our object of study is actually 'where' it is happening (within the musical or social structures)." Indeed, a musical event is not an objectifiable articulation of an "inner" model or system that, in turn, reflects a kind of abstract formal reality (as many Western music theorists and structuralist anthropologists might have it). Ethnomusicologists only recently have begun to recognize that such cognitive models are the products of theorists and pedagogues and the musical practices arise out of the particularities of prior experience. In other words, conceptual models are inferred; they are not pre-existent realities. Thus, in Herbst's discussion, performance (specifically, music performance) is an experienced *process* taking place within a particular social context. His approach is to determine local understandings of cultural ideals by stressing the particularities of the performative act over broadly defined classifications and conceptual models. More specifically, Herbst describes the internal relationships and variations of Balinese musical performance within the particularities of social context. He examines a Balinese exegesis of music, interpreting what musicians and dancers say about musical performance according to their terms rather than his own. The ideas of these artists are replete with the particularities of prior experience. Completing the hermeneutic circle, Herbst also reflexively describes his own role, and the insights he gains, within this scheme of things.

Modern Versus Traditional Music

Herbst has raised some important issues about our understandings of modern (what he refers to as "contemporary") and traditional music. Western (read: American) modern, or contemporary, music is rooted in the present time, dynamic, and innovative, while traditional music (particularly that of the Other) is ancient, static, even obsolete. Yet categorical designations of modern and traditonal are misleading, especially when applied cross-culturally. Taking a global view, we might argue that the Western obsession with textualizing music, whether through notation or by means of audio recording, fixes each composition in time and place, archiving it like a library book and removing it from the immediate concerns of day-to-day life. One might also argue that Western Modernist art music is not necessarily innovative but perhaps reactive (even reactionary) toward earlier forms—one simply does not compose "in the style of" past composers but *against* them. Modernist views of the composer as individualist, breaking away from the past (perhaps even the present), buttress such reactionary understandings of musical change. Individualism, prized so much in the West, also fixes a piece of music in time and place, attaching it to a composer and historicizing both. Any lover of Western art music will know not only the name of the composer of a canonized piece but also the approximate year when that piece was composed. Even in popular music, listeners are sensitive to the historical place of each piece of music, to a large extent making aesthetic judgments based on how old or new a particular piece is.

On the other hand, many musical traditions, like Balinese *kebiar* or *kecak*, are hardly older than certain American popular musics like swing or rockabilly. The term "traditional" implies that they are ancient musics, yet they are not. Indeed, what then makes them traditional? They are not frozen in time, like flies in amber. Rather, traditional music, perhaps any living tradition, is contemporary but informed by past sensitivities, knowledge, and practices. Traditional music performance is not an attempt to recreate past performances (as it might be in Western art music) but a synthesis of past and present. The past is evoked in the present circumstances of performance yet, because of its ephemerality, each performance is a unique and innovative act of creativity.

Evoking the past lends authority to performance, particularly ritual performance, but a music tradition, perhaps any tradition, can only survive as long as it has relevance in present-day life. Indeed, traditional music performance involves a kind of "reading" of the past, but past meanings can only be conveyed in the *immediacy* of the present performance. Thus, by understanding music performance as an ephemeral process rather than an objectifiable product, we can perhaps get a better understanding of the meaning and aesthetics of a particular musical tradition. As Zurbuchen (1987: 112) argues for Balinese language arts, "the object (or text) from the past is incomplete without its recapitulation (or paraphrase) in language or behavior of the present."

The Pleasure of Musical Performance

As Herbst has pointed out, the pleasure of performing music in Bali lies in the communal activity of making music, in music's relevance to other aspects of life (especially religion), and in the view that music is central to the lives of all people. Pleasure in performance also lies in the music's power to transport performers and listeners alike. Such an understanding of aesthetic pleasure in the arts is centuries old. The term *langö* is found in Old Javanese epic literature (*kakawin*), describing both the state of rapture that arises out of the aesthetic experience and that which gives rise to the state of rapture.[1] P. J. Zoetmulder describes the term as follows:

. . . a kind of swooning sensation, in which the subject is completely absorbed by and becomes lost in its object, the appeal of which is so overwhelming that everything else sinks into nothingness and oblivion. All intellectual activity ceases; the perception of the object itself becomes vague, and in an experience of oneness that blurs the distinction between subject and object, consciousness of the self vanishes, too. (Zoetmulder 1974: 172)

Herbst has suggested that the subjective (the aesthetic experience) and objective (that which gives rise to the aesthetic experience) in *langö* are two aspects of a single reality; they are, as Zoetmulder says, connatural. This makes sense in light of Herbst's futher discusssion of the Balinese threefold concept of *bayu sabda idep* (breath, sound or utterance, and thought) as metaphors for action, form, and meaning. The pleasure of musical performance thus lies in the ordering of one's experience and world through expressive acts, collapsing religious efficacy and aesthetic beauty. Ideally,

1. See also Zoetmulder 1982 under *langö*.

then, performance both transforms its audience spiritually and transports them sensuously.

Pleasure of performance might also have to do with music's relevance to the particularities of time and place. The cultural ideology of *désa kala patra* lies behind the enormous variety of expressive forms in Bali. Herbst describes Bali as possessing a dense and complex cultural ecology. He points out that relatively few formal structures allow for an astounding diversity of musical forms, and for individual, regional, and situational variation of each form. As a communal and spiritual activity, as an experiential process, musical performance is a social necessity in the everyday lives of Balinese. Pleasure and the idea of beauty are closely tied to place, time, and situation. Hosts of performances and performers make the most out of the limitations of circumstance—aesthetic pleasure and spiritual efficacy are as much based on the realities of situation as on pre-existing standards of beauty.

The Embodiment of Music and Musical Bodies

Finally, Herbst's work has led me to consider questions related to the anthropology of the body and to embodiment.[2] What can we learn about the bodily experience of making and listening to music?[3] How is musical embodiment related to identity, aesthetics, learning, and communal action? As Herbst points out, vocal training is a matter of disciplining the body, of pushing voice and throat to their limits, of controlling the body's energies. To develop their voices, young *dalangs* sing into the crashing waves of the sea while others swallow concoctions of chili peppers soaked in oil. Studying music is perhaps like undergoing the rigors of spiritual—or even military—training. The body is disciplined, even punished (in extreme cases) to focus and shape sound.

Herbst has touched on this theme of embodiment throughout his book. In his discussion of learning Balinese instrumental music, he described the experience as kinesthetic and intuitive: "One aspect of the perceptual process is that the student often integrates a musical phrase or sequence before it is conceptually realized." In other words, bodily experience of movement and bodily memory precede intellectual and analytical understanding.

A particularly interesting form of musical embodiment is perhaps what one experiences with (either through listening to or participating in) Balinese ensemble performance. By this, I mean the cooperative enterprise of closely integrated, interlocking melodic and rhythmic parts in Balinese

2. See for example, Csordas 1994.
3. One of the few studies that directly addresses Western art music and embodiment (as opposed to music and the mind) is McClary 1995.

gambelan. Herbst describes the melody of Balinese *kotékan* playing as having a particularly *spatial* characteristic, stressing the interdependency of interlocking parts that combine to form a seamless whole. His reference to space in *kotékan* is significant since it suggests the notion of a melodic line created by different musical bodies (or bodies making music) in particular (interdependent) relation to one another. Clearly, the bodily experience of performing in such as ensemble where a single melody arises out of joint effort is radically different than, say, participating in a Western orchestra or band. Consider this description of the band by Katherine Bergeron, using Bentham's Panopticon (as described by Foucault), a prison design allowing constant and centralized surveillance of inmates:[4]

Like any large instrumental ensemble, the band relies on the same sort of panoptical arrangement: players are seated (out of convenience, we say) in curved rows around a central podium, completely visible to the conductor who stands above. Yet the discipline of the band is not so much visual as aural: the conductor *listens*. Here the player is entrapped by an acoustic constraint; he cannot escape his own audibility. And, as with the Panopticon, he never knows precisely the moment the conductor—this master of acoustic surveillance—may be listening to *him*, picking out his instrument from the dense ensemble of musical sounds. The effect, as we all know, is to cause players to assume more and more responsibilty for their own performance: to play in tune, at tempo, on cue, controlling their part both individually and in relation to the whole. Inmate-players learn to conduct *themselves*, so to speak, according to the canons of performance they share. As a field of audibility, a type of acoustic enclosure, the band thus implicates the musician in a network where acts of mutual surveillance serve to maintain the musical standard. (Bergeron 1992: 4)

To use Foucaultian discourse, the orchestra thus represents a social body in which power is centralized in the individual body of the conductor. He (and I use the pronoun "he" intentionally) has complete control over his inmate-musicians, maintaining discipline and order through (aural) surveillance. In the Balinese *gambelan*, on the other hand, power and control are dispersed among the performers. Players are *interdependent* musical bodies. The music is a result of cooperative effort and, because of its situational revlevance, performance becomes community action.[5]

Conclusion

What may be controversial about this book is Herbst's unique style of writing. While he presents an astute study of Balinese vocal music, his narrative is also deeply personal. The writing style (inspired by the essays of

4. For a detailed discussion of "panopticism" see Foucault 1995: 195–228.

5. This is not to say that *gambelan* playing is necessarily egalitarian. Indeed, the musical organization of the *gambelan* may reflect the highly complex traditional social hierarchy of the Balinese, upon which is imposed the political stratification of the modern Indonesian state (with power distributed through increasingly localized leadership, ranging from governor to regency all the way down to village headman).

John Cage), mixed as it is with personal anecdotes, the stories of his teachers, Herbst's own insights, and his solid scholarship, not only makes for engaging reading but also challenges us to think about representing the music of the Other discursively. The book reflects a profound respect for the Balinese artists with whom Herbst worked. His writing is filled with the voices of his teachers—*their* ideas, *their* experiences, and, perhaps most important, *their* understandings of music-making. Herbst's own voice comes through as well, and is both interpretive (explicating what his teachers have taught him) and reflexive (narrating his own experiences as researcher and student).

Recently, some anthropologists have begun to examine how the poetics of ethnography are deeply embedded in the politics of representation. In past works, the Other is clearly distinguishable from the Self—sometimes in colonial and racist terms. The politics of such writings are reflected in the narrative practices and strategies of the writer. From the privileged perspective as authoritative but neutral observer, the writer "speaks" for natives who, as discursive objects, are rendered mute and unable to speak for themselves. These narrative strategies are also reinforced by an absolute faith in the neutrality of descriptive writing and the belief that there can (and must) be a separation between author and his/her object of study. As Clifford and Marcus (1986: 13) point out, "the subjectivity of the author is separated from the objective referent of the text."

More recently, however, the author himself/herself is written into the narrative but without the privileged perspective that he/she once may have been able to enjoy. The author thus becomes just another actor in the ethnographic drama. As Clifford and Marcus put it (ibid.: 23): "Now ethnography encounters others in relation to itself, while seeing itself as other." Yet, if ethnography is now understood as a set of discursive practices in which selves and others are constructed, and in which the Other is encountered in relation to the Self, then these constructions and relationships, too, must be explored.[6]

We might argue that all ethnographies and narratives (whether descriptive, interpretive, or reflexive), are influenced by contingencies such as rhetoric, power, gender, and history (Clifford and Marcus 1986: 25). Ultimately, ethnographic "truth" can only be found in the relationship that is forged between the reader and the world created by the ethnographer. In this way, the personal and reflexive style in which Herbst wrote *Voices in Bali: Energies and Perceptions in Vocal Music and Dance Theater* represents an important experiment in musical ethnography.

6. See further Marcus and Fischer 1986.

Notes to Companion Compact Disc

❁

All recordings were made by Edward Herbst in 1980 and 1981 on a Sony TCD-5 stereo cassette recorder, except selections 12 and 19, which were recorded by Herbst in 1972 on a Tandberg II mono reel-to-reel recorder, and selection 4, recorded by I Madé Bandem in 1977 with a Nagra stereo reel-to-reel. The recordings have been digitally processed to reduce noise, however some tape hiss was left in order not to alter the quality of the voices. Playing time: 73:36

1. *Tembang Pucung pélog lebeng*　　　　　　　　　　　1:23
   sung by Ni Nyoman Candri
   lyrics and translation on page 5.

2. *Tembang Pucung sléndro*　　　　　　　　　　　　　1:20
   sung by Ni Nyoman Candri
   same lyrics and translation as selection 1 on page 5.

3. *Tembang Durma manis*　　　　　　　　　　　　　　3:19
   (from the story *Sampik*, as sung by the *mantri manis* 'refined prince' to the *galuh* 'princess' in *arja*)
   sung by Ni Nyoman Candri

   Nunas ica sasambaté ngelad prana,
   Dong padalem ké beli,
   Nguda manampokang
   tresnan beliné manyama,
   Titiang mula subakti,
   Daging titiang
   nunas iwang ipun sami

   I ask you to talk with me heart to heart,
   Please have pity on me,
   Why do you push me away
   while I have such feelings of affection for you?
   I worship you,

These are indeed my true sentiments
and please forgive me for all of them

4. *Tembang Adri*   9:47
   (as sung by the *galuh* 'princess' in *arja*)
   performed by Ni Nyoman Candri, accompanied by *gaguntangan* ensemble
   under the direction of I Madé Kredek, Singapadu

   Tan pendah ratih wawu metu,
   mélok san warnané,
   sasat Sang Hyang Saraswati,
   kenyung manis madu jurug,
   Kudiang jani nudut kayun,
   Lakiné gawok tumingal,
   Katon kadi gunung santun,
   kadi arca né kanaka,
   sinarin ban ratna mulia

   Like the moon just appearing,
   her appearance very pretty,
   like Sang Hyang Saraswati,
   her smile sweet as honey,
   What can we do now that she pulls at our heart?
   Young men just stand around and stare,
   She looks so beautiful, like a mountain (of flowers),
   like a statue bedecked in jewels,
   all kinds of jewels shining like the sun

5. *Tembang Durma*   2:25
   (as sung by *arja*'s Punta)
   sung by I Madé Pasek Tempo; lyrics and translation on page 76

6. *Sendon* for *topéng*'s *panasar*   1:28
   sung by I Madé Pasek Tempo; lyrics and translation on pages 73–74

7. *Gambelan mulut*   5:18
   "mouth gambelan" for *jauk* dance (excerpt)
   sung by *Pandé* Madé Kenyir, Banjar Sungguhan, Singapadu

8. Music for *jauk* dance (excerpt)   5:39
   performed by *gambelan bebarongan* of Banjar Sungguhan, Singapadu

9. *Tembang Sinom Wug Payangan*   5:00
   sung by Ni Nyoman Candri

   Yan Sang Nata puniyéng wadua,
   punia ring Brahmana resi,
   Beberatan yang Indra manggo,
   ngamertaning jagat sami,
   Wenang tan wanining kapti
   ring wadua dalidré lemuh,
   Pitegas yang Yama brata,
   wenang sepat sikun gumi,

kanti sadu,
malung maling patiananya

If the venerable king gives alms to the people,
gives alms to the Brahmana priests,
It is like the laws of the god Indra
giving life to all the populace,
So wicked people are not brave
and the populace will be safe and peaceful,
The laws of the deity Lord Yama,
like a model for the world
until they all know,
people who are malicious must be condemned

10. *Tembang Pangkur*   4:07
    (as sung by *arja's condong*)
    performed by Ni Nyoman Candri

    Makelap mangalap bunga,
    langsing lanjar pamuluné nyandat gading,
    tangané lemet maléngkung,
    (Ma)ngenah kukuné lantang pakuranang,
    luir kadi manik banyu
    yan nyuréré ia malihat
    nyaledét mekadi tatit

    Distant flickering image [of a young woman] picking a flower,
    slender and tall, forehead golden yellow,
    her swinging hands move and bend gracefully,
    You can see her fingernails, long and shiny,
    like healing water derived from the immersion of precious stones,
    when she looks with a sidelong glance
    her eyes flicker like bolts of lightning

11. *Tembang Ginada lumbrah*   3:06
    (as sung by *arja's mantri manis*)
    performed by Ni Nyoman Candri

    Bapa tiang manguningan,
    krana tiang wawu prapti
    Tiang kaduk maangguran
    kagriya malajah nutur,
    anggon bekel maring awak
    okas mati,
    anggon tiang pajimatan

    Let me tell you, father,
    as I am just arriving,
    I have been visiting
    the homes of Brahmanas to study moral teachings,
    preparing my body and soul
    from now until I die,
    as if providing me with a precious protective amulet

12. *Méong Sang Hyang* (excerpt)   1:04
    performed by the five-tone *gambelan angklung* of Sawan

13. *Tembang Sinom Cecantungan*   3:48
    (as sung by *mantri manis* to *galuh*)
    performed by Ni Nyoman Candri

    Lawutang mangalap bunga
    di taman sambilang melali,
    sambilang ngilehin tlaga
    Lawutang menek kegili,
    sampan ada kategakin,
    Anggon ngelap bungan tunjung,
    Yadin ya suba uwudan,
    gadungé masih unuhin,
    Bunga liu,
    anggon ngubah carang dosa

    Please go ahead and pick a flower
    in this garden as we go strolling,
    as we circle around the pond,
    Let's board this little boat,
    a boat we can sit in as we row all around,
    I'll pick a lotus flower,
    Though many are already wilted,
    a few flowers still remain
    There are indeed many other kinds of flowers,
    but I'm going to change my fickle thoughts [and be true to only one]

14. *Tembang Durma*   2:44
    (as sung by *arja*'s Punta)
    performed by Ni Nyoman Candri
        These lyrics were borrowed from the *mantri*'s version of *Durma manis*
    (selection 3) to illustrate the musical style of Punta's singing.

15. *Tembang Durma*   4:49
    (as sung by *arja*'s Punta)
    performed by I Wayan Purna accompanied by *gaguntangan* ensemble, in
    rehearsal with the young people's *arja* troupe of Banjar Mukti, Singapadu.
        The first line refers implicitly to the notion that in earlier, more benign,
    eras, people would live to hundreds or even thousands of years.

    Tuwuh jatma né jani tigang benang (tiban),
    Jatmané gangsar mijil,
    Wong laré (k)enggal tua,
    Wong tua (k)enggal pejah
    sesayan sebudi-budi
    Panengan punah,
    Pangiwané sakti mangendih

    Kadi tindakang miwah ditayungan,
    mangamong icetih destih,
    Ngelarang mantra manguncar,

paican Hyang Puradah miwah gadung kasturi,
ganda pudak mekar

Nowadays humans only live to about seventy-five years,
More and more souls fast being born,
Young people are too soon to grow old,
Old people are soon to die
confused and not knowing what to think,
The truth is not believed,
Sorcerers' magic ignites in flames

[Evil even in the ways they move] in every step and the sway of their bodies,
disseminating poisonous black magic,
[While others] perform the recitation of mantras,
giving Hyang Puradah [white magic practitioner] offerings of aromatic
gadung [yam] flowers
and the fragrant *pudak* flower

Ucapan 'spoken text'

Béh! Dewa ratu agung
Sing ambat-ambat
antian arenan tusta paidepan idéwék lamunin kalijani
Arah!

Hey! Great gods and kings!
Nothing can compare! (with my happiness)
with my joyful thoughts at this moment
Wow!

16. *Gambelan mulut* 'mouth *gambelan*' for Punta's *papeson* 'coming out'   3:15
    sung by I Madé Pasek Tempo

17. *Tandak Dalem*   9:41
    sung by I Madé Pasek Tempo, filling in more—for pedagogical reasons—
    than he would in performance

Panasar:
Sekar emas ngararoncé (Adorned with gold flowers in his hair)
sekarang mangigel gambuh (worn for his regal dancing)
gambuh di rejang kendran (*gambuh* and *rejang* danced as if in heaven)
gagambelan mangasih-asih (the *gambelan* music flowing in waves)
manisé ngasorang madu (sweeter than honey)
inggek-inggek sadanayog (heel step and shuffle, arms slowly sweeping down)

Dalem: *Pangaksaman ing ulun ring pada hyang mami* (I kneel in obeisance
before the one supreme divinity)

Panasar: *Ratu betara Dalem sasuhunan titiang* (Divine king Dalem, my ruler)
Ngararis-ngararis ratu ngaksama ring bukpadan Ida Sang Hyang pramakawi
(Please go ahead, your highness, give respect humbly to the god of creation)
Rawé rawé (Swaying [like tassels])

Dalem: *Sang ginelaran sarining ongkara ratna mantra* (Who already embodies
the essence of the holy Vedic scriptures)

Panasar: *Inggih-inggih dwaning paduka betara sampun-sampun maraga tunggil* (Yes, yes, just like the one supreme divinity)
satmaka mangga amertaning jagat (your very existence an embodiment of protection and care of the populace)
Inggek inggek sadanayog (Heel step and shuffle, arms slowly sweeping down)
kemikan bibihé manis (his lips form a sweet smile)
raga lempung magoléran (body relaxed and swaying)

Dalem: *Wreda, mawas ri sapa wijil i kanang ika tuwanta mangké* (Old one, pay attention now as your ruler comes out)

Panasar: *Inggih-inggih, ha-ha-ha ratu betara Dalem pidaging-daging ngarasis mangu* (Yes, yes, your royal highness, please, please arise)
Ratu, deresatsat kasiratan amerta waluya manah titiang, (Your highness, it's as if you are spreading the water of life, I feel in my heart,)
Rarisang maungu palungguh Dalem, ha-ha-ha-ha-ha (Please, go ahead, your highness)
Simsim alit mungwing tuding (Little rings on his fingers)
Kelap-kelap dedari makebeh ida mekeber (Like a heavenly peacock about to take flight)
nyerégség tur nyaliog (feet making fast side steps, head tipping side to side)
tatanyeké nolih-nolih (footsteps and glancing eyes moving together)

Dalem: *Wreda, adan kita pomo kawinkingga* (Old one, please, you may follow, behind)
Aptin ulun mangké ang lumaksana, wredah (I intend to go out, old one)

Panasar: *Ha-ha-ha ah inggih ngararis memarga palungguh Dalem* (Yes, please go ahead, your highness)
Dwaning sampun ratu bata mantri wandawa, sampun ébek ratu (Because all of your ministers already await you)
ring kerta pagosana kantun nyantos anggan palungguh cokoridéwa (at the meeting pavilion, your highness)
Ngararis-ngararis ratu, ngararis (Please, please, go ahead, your lordship)
Dauh kalih sampun ayas (It is already eight o'clock)
Wijil sira sri bupati (Out comes the supreme regent)
akampuh sutera né ijo (wearing green silk)
renyep maperada pakurining (with little gold decorations like stars)
Hyang Semara ngulanguling (Just like the god of beauty, so alluring and handsome)
Inggih, ratu betara Dalem kangkat purun titiang (Yes, your divine highness, I must gather my courage)
Nanginin mapunguatur ring palungguh cokoridéwa (I must have courage in addressing his highness)
Inggih mawinan kangkat padgatasemeng? (Why does the supreme regent arise so early in the morning?)
Tedun palungguh cokoridéwa wentené ring kerta pagosana (And come down to the meeting pavilion)
Napi ratu sané wénten pacang bawosang? (What very important words will the ruler be saying?)
Durus nikayang ring titiang ratu (Please inform me, your highness)

Dalem: *Wredah, yan tuning mangkana lah séng songana kene srota kalih?* (Yes, if so, then listen carefully)

Anyangga pangartikan ri kayaning mangké wreda (Two ears are ready to receive the meaning of my intentions)

Panasar: *Inggih, titiang buyuh-buyuh pacang lengah* (Yes, I will absolutely not be inattentive)
Nampa nyuwun kadi pawa canan palungguh cokoridéwa (I am indeed ready to listen respectfully to what you have to say)
Ngараris-ngararis mawacana ratu (Please speak, your highness)
Cakra angkara dén parané (The raja's power and authority extend as far as he is able)
Kukus gunung sangkan alih (Even if what he seeks is in the smoke at the top of a volcano, he still must attain it)
Tangané lemet maléngkung (His hands are graceful and pliant)
Kadi busungé amputang (The gentle swinging of his arms like the leaves of a coconut tree)
Rawé-rawé (Swaying, like tassels)

18. *Sendon panasar topéng*   1:06
    sung by I Ketut Rinda, Blahbatu; notated on page 75
    These lyrics are purposefully ambiguous and amusingly difficult to make out clearly. Several words are open to other interpretations, especially as they overlap (the last syllable of one word could be the first of the word following it). For example, *bakikuk* is pheasant, but *kukang* is a small frog; *pancak* is an adz, but the reference could also be to the pheasants numbering five, *panca*. Balinese performers will interpret these words as they wish.
    Spoken by Pak Rinda in apologia: *Seperti tiang niki, nada suara sudah habis, sudah hilang, kurang baik.* (For myself, the sounds of the pitches are gone, already lost, not so good.)

    Méh rahina waspada
    patingkahin kayu
    risaréng ikang gaga
    pancak ikuk ing bakikuk ang lawang ikakung
    ipinggiring jurang

    See the very early morning,
    the swaying of the trees
    on top of a hill,
    and the sound of an adz (tapping against sandstone), calls of pheasants and croaking frogs
    by the river in a ravine

19. *Sendon panasar topéng*   3:11
    performed by I Nyoman Kakul, accompanied by the *gambelan gong* of the village of Jelaika; a few unclear words are omitted.

    Lumihat kalangen ikang negara,
    di sobo awirya
    Indra buana nurun
    wédang pakuana nitip

    pada kabinawa sarwa pendah
    Pangurupukang (cari)

Méh rahina waspada, patingkahin kayu
risaréng ikang gunung mageng
pancaking bakikukang lawang ngiagung ingping ngiring jurang
gumerancang ata ri banyunika
katkat luklak likalika lulut warwaning wiwalik pupuk paksa ngupéksa
Déwa ratu agung! Déwa ratu agung!

Pragat legan paidepan buka kalijani
Cen ké mangranayang, cen ké makawanan?
Titiang mamarakang iriki ring Wilatikta
ngiring palungguh ida
palungguh Dalem,
ané mapeséngan singgih Dalem, Sri Kalagemet

Mimpin jagaté iriki ring Majapahit

See the incredible beauty of our kingdom
its greatness known everywhere
As if the god Indra had come down to rule
these spacious environs

Everything is beautiful in its own unique way
and exciting
See the very early morning, the swaying of the trees
on top of a great mountain
and the sound of an adz [tapping against sandstone], calls of pheasants and
croaking frogs
the river water gushing and spraying
cockatoos and other birds, the proud *kelik* (crow) enjoying the pleasing
company of others, the energetic fluttering of wings
Great gods and kings! Great gods and kings!

I am always as content and happy as I am now
What is the reason?
Because I am a servant here in the kingdom of Wilatikta
following the royal raja
with the royal title Dalem
the ruler referred to as regent and raja, Sri Kalagemet

The leader of this land having come from the kingdom of Majapahit

Glossary

❀

amerta water of eternal life

angsel instrumental and dance rhythmic phrasing break, often used as a cue to begin a new vocal phrase, mood, or dance sequence

arja operatic dance drama genre, the term derived from Old Javanese (*Kawi*) *reja* 'beautiful', according to Zoetmulder (1982)

balih-balihan performances that are not related to ceremony and are intended for the sole entertainment of people; from *mabalih* 'to watch'

baris male warrior dance, performed solo as entertainment genre, but in groups as ritual *baris gedé*

barong sacred animal personages, performed by one or two people in costume and mask. Most prominent is *Barong Kékét*, resembling the Chinese lion. *Barong landung* are eight-foot tall human personages, also sacred.

bayu wind, breath, energy, activity

bebali performances that take place in connection with religious ceremony, but that are not an aspect of the ritual; from *wewalén* 'that which can be performed'

bondrés comic half-mask characters, generally in *topéng* performances

buana agung macrocosmos, from *buana* 'world', *agung* 'great' or 'large'

buana alit microcosmos, from *buana* 'world', *alit* '*small*'

cak also called kecak; and "monkey dance"; a popular tourist entertainment developed in the 1930s, the *cak* chorus is derived from *Sang Hyang* trance rituals while the Ramayana serves as the theme for the dance drama.

Calonarang magic drama enacting the eleventh-century story of the Witch of Dirah, East Java

carangan branch; also signifies deviation or "branching out" from a standard story, but on a larger scale, as a dramatic subplot

cecantungan, cecelantungan from *cantung* 'branch'; poetic quotations sung in performance; offshoots or "branching out" of the dialogue or narration

cents a system devised by Alexander Ellis for measuring pitch intervals. A cent is one hundredth of one of twelve equal intervals of the equal tempered octave; hence, a tempered whole tone is 200 cents.

condong, inya maidservant to the refined *galuh* 'princess'

Cupak boastful, greedy character occupying his own dance drama genre, related to *arja* and *gambuh*, as well as a purely Balinese theme for *wayang*

dalang shadow puppet master

Dalem king; most often refers to the refined king in *topéng*

dedéleman a movement, mask, or other characteristic in the style of Délem

Délem *panakawan* 'comic attendant' to the Korawa (of Rawara's) side in *wayang*

désa village, place

déwasa spiritual qualities inherent in a particular day on the Balinese *wariga* calendar

gaguntangan traditional instrumental ensemble for *arja*, including *guntang* 'one-stringed bamboo zither' instead of bronze gongs, and only *suling* 'bamboo flute' for melody

galuh refined princess (or principal female character) in *arja* and *gambuh*

gambelan any of a variety of ensembles composed primarily of percussion instruments, including gongs, metallophones, gong-chimes, two drums, and bamboo flute

gambelan angklung a four-tone *sléndro* ensemble distinct in its bright timbres, and essential for temple festivals and cremation ceremonies. An unusual five-tone variety is mostly found in North Bali.

gambelan gong most prevalent instrumental ensemble, used mostly for ceremonial occasions, *topéng*, and *baris* performances

gambelan gong kebiar modern, streamlined version of *gambelan gong*, re-orchestrated for versatility with dance and dance drama

gambelan luang an archaic sacred ensemble of bronze and bamboo instruments employing seven tones

gambuh highly formalized dance drama form; a classical source of many choreographic and musical elements used in other genres

gedong céngkok the movement of sound through the body; the shape, jumps, and spaces within the flow of melody

geguritan poem or story set in Javanese-Balinese indigenous meter, *pupuh tembang macapat, sekar alit,* or *sekar madya*

gendér wayang quartet of ten-keyed metallophones accompanying *wayang* performances

getaran vibrations

guntang one-stringed bamboo zither, replacing the gong in *arja*'s traditional *gaguntangan* ensemble

idep thought, mind, perception

ilegan melodic shape or flow

iringan instrumental accompaniment

jauk semidemonic, semihuman mask character associated with *barong* magic dramas

juru tandak solo vocalist who sits with the *gambelan* for *gambuh, légong,* and related dances

kala time; also the name of a wrathful emanation of *Siwa*

kalangan traditional performance space that can be set up almost anywhere, often demarcated by bamboo poles and decorations

kalangén rapture; "a state [of] being carried away, emotionally moved or transported by an art object or artistic presentation" (Dibia 1992: 381)

kartala younger (*cenikan*) of the two half-mask *panasars*, comic narrator-philosophers of *topéng* and other dance dramas; referred to as Wijil in *arja* stories

Kawi Old Javanese language, also a term for "poet"

kawi suara the voice of the poet; vocal style used by *dalang* for narration and moments when not speaking as any character within the story

kempur medium-size hanging gong that articulates phrasing within the larger gong structure. In *arja*, the *kempur* is the chief phrase marker, replacing the large gong.

kendang two-headed drum, with hour-glass shape carved inside

keras strong or coarse in character

kidung song, poem in Javanese *sekar madya* meter

kirta basa etymology, discussed philosophically and playfully by *panasar* and *kartala* within performance

lagu melody

langsé curtain for performance entrances and exits

laras scale, tone series

lawang door, entranceway, curtain

lebeng cooked to proper consistency; in aesthetic discourse, something very good, fitting; also refers to a seven-tone *gambuh* and *gambelan luang* tuning and its subtle use of semitones

légong formally choreographed dance performed by three girls, intricately linked to *gambelan*

Liku *arja*'s eccentric, jealous, comic female character, usually stepsister of *galuh*, and daughter of *limbur*

limbur *arja*'s strong, older female antagonist character, stepmother, queen mother

luk "to curve" or "bend" as in a vocal slide

lumbrah common, referring to specific variations of *tembang*

macapat poetry "read in fours"; another name for *tembang, sekar alit*

manis sweet, refined

mantri buduh crazy prince, antagonist character

mantri manis refined, "sweet" prince (or principal refined male character)

masolah characterization, or "to perform"; movement of a shadow puppet; kinesthetic and spiritual *désa kala patra* of a character

mata batu style with wooden eyes on mask

mata bolong style of mask with open, cut-out eyes

menjiwai animating, or transmitting spirit, as from dancer to mask; *dalang* to shadow puppet; *panasar* to nonspeaking character

miring "slanted" tonal shadings

ncah coarse voice used by *dalang*s and strong dramatic characters

nding (1), *ndong* (2), *ndéng* (3), *ndung* (5), *ndang* (6) are the names of the five pitches in *pélog* or *sléndro* tunings. (4) and (7) are included in less common *tekeps*. The *d* is often silent. The actual names of the *gambelan* instrument pitches are often given as *ding, dong, déng, dung, dang*, but they are always sung with the *n*.

ngengkuk repeating "waves" or vibrations in a vocal melody

ngigel to dance (from the root "to bend")

nglawang performers strolling along the roads, from door to door, as with a *barong*

nyimbang to toss up (referring to a technique of vocal phrasing)

nusup penetration

nyutra nyerod style of shaping subtle vowel sounds within swirls of melody

nyutra suara subtle shaping and transforming of vowel sounds

odalan temple festival generally occurring every 210 days

pacaperiring syllabic style of reading with just the skeleton of a melody

palawakya stylized, contoured prose intoned in classical *Kawi*

pamangku "lay" priest usually associated with a particular temple

paméro semitones used in seven-tone tunings and related vocal styles

panakawan, parekan court retainers, comic attendants to royal protagonist characters in *wayang* and related dramas

panasar half-mask comic narrator/philosophers, attendants to the royal protagonist and antagonist characters of *topéng* and other dance dramas, and in *wayang*

pandangan visual gaze of a dancer, character; perspective

papeson coming out; initial vocal music used by a dance character to come through the curtain or gateway

patih prime minister

patra context, situation; leaf, foliage in visual art

pélog the seven-tone scale system from which various pentatonic scales are derived

perkembangan development; creative flowering

pragina dancer-actor

prémbon genre combining *topéng*'s male mask characters with nonmask *arja*-style characters performed by females; from *prema* 'romance'

Punta *arja*'s version of *panasar* character

pupuh melodies, poetic meters of *tembang macapat, sekar alit* and *kidung, sekar madya*

Rangda widow, witch; monstrous mask character of *Calonarang* and other magic dramas, also used for wrathful deities such as Siwa

rasa mood, feeling, range of emotion

sabda voice, speech form or expression

saih pitu the seven-tone *pélog* scale of certain classic ensembles, such as *gambelan gambuh* and *gambelan luang*, from which several five-tone variations are derived

seka to be as one; a traditional Balinese organized group put together for a specific kind of activity

sekar alit "small flower"; poetic Javanese-Balinese meters, also called *tembang, macapat*, and *pupuh*

selisir most common of the *pélog* tunings

Semar Pagulingan a *gambelan* genre featuring the *trompong* (a row of horizontally mounted gongs) as melodic lead instrument. A rare seven-tone version is its complete form, but more common is its five-tone *selisir* version. Without *trompong*, this latter version is also called *pelégongan*.

sendon poetic lines or verses sung by *dalang* or *panasar topéng* coming from behind curtain; often containing a series of brief fragments of *Kawi* poetry strung together; free of *gambelan*'s melodic contours, usually used during *batél* or *bapang* ostinato sections, and still keeping or playing off of *gambelan* pitches. Contrary definitions exist as well.

séndratari dance drama developed in the 1960s, with *gambelan gong kebiar*, mainly performing stories from the *Ramayana* epic but, occasionally, *Mahabharata* or other stories

Sidha Karya "completer of the work"; solo genre of ritual *topéng*; often the name of the final mask character, also called Pengejukan

sléndro pentatonic scale used in *gendér wayang, angklung*, and *tembang*, having no semitones in instrumental *gambelan* context, but more chromatic variation vocally

suara sound, or voice

suara ngilik a slight rise in pitch, likened to the sound of water passing from a wide to a narrow bamboo irrigation tube

suling end-blown bamboo flute with four, five, or six fingerholes

taksu spiritual inspiration and energy within a mask, puppet, character, ceremonial weapon

tandak sung poetry that follows, and plays off of, the instrumental melody in *topéng, légong, wayang*, and so on

tari dance, in the Indonesian language

tebek to stab or pierce with a sword or pin; referring to eye contact, focused visual attention of dancers

tekep to close or cover, as with fingering a *suling* or *rebab* "bowed lute"; refers to any of the various modes or tone series; also the process of silencing *gendér* 'metallophone' keys, *metekep*

tembang the verb *nembang* means simply "to sing," but *tembang* generally refers to a specific poetic form, *sekar alit , pupuh, macapat*

tenget spiritually, magically charged, as with sacred masks and weapons

topéng mask dance theater dealing with Balinese historical chronicles

Twalén or **Malén** venerable and comic *parekan, panakawan, panasar* character of *wayang*

wali sacred; performances intended as religious offerings, often taking place within the *jeroan pura* 'inner courtyard of a temple'

wanara most often refers to Anoman's monkey army in the *Ramayana*, but really includes a full range of semidivine animals

wariga calendrical-astrological-spiritual reckoning of days

wayang shadow puppetry

wayang lemah ritual *wayang* generally performed during the day, without shadows and screen

wayang wong dance drama based on the *Ramayana* literature, with many mask characters

Wijil *arja*'s version of *kartala* character

wirama kakawin classical Old Javanese sung poetry; poetic meter with its associated melody

Bibliography

❀

Anderson, Benedict R. O'G. 1965. *Mythology and the Tolerance of the Javanese*. Data Paper 27. Ithaca: Cornell University Southeast Asia Program.

Artaud, Antonin. 1958. *The Theater and Its Double*. New York: Grove Press.

Attali, Jacques. 1985. *Noise: The Political Economy of Music*. Minneapolis: University of Minnesota Press.

Bali, Studies in Life, Thought, and Ritual. 1960. Dutch Scholars: Swellengrebel, Goris, Korn, Grader. Vol. 5 of *Selected Studies on Indonesia*. The Hague and Bandung: W. van Hoeve.

Bandem, I Madé. 1972. "*Panji* Characterization in the *Gambuh* Dance Drama." M.A. thesis, UCLA.

———. 1984. "*Kehidupan Mario Dalam Seni*." Paper presented at Baliologi Conference, Denpasar.

———. 1986. *Prakempa: Sebuah Lontar Gambelan Bali*. Laporan Hasil Penelitian. Denpasar: Akademi Seni Tari Indonesia.

———. 1992. *Wimba Tembang Macapat Bali*. Denpasar: Sekolah Tinggi Seni Indonesia.

Bandem, I Madé, and Fredrik E. de Boer. 1995. *Balinese Dance in Transition: Kaja and Kelod*. Kuala Lumpur: Oxford University Press.

Bandem, N. L. N. Swasthi Wijaya. 1982. *Dramatari Calonarang Di Singapadu*. Sarjana Muda thesis. Akademi Seni Tari Indonesia, Denpasar.

Barth, Fredrik. 1993. *Balinese Worlds*. Chicago and London: University of Chicago Press.

Bates, Marston. 1964. *The Forest and the Sea*. New York: Time, Inc.

Bateson, Gregory. 1970. "An Old Temple and a New Myth." In *Traditional Balinese Culture*, edited by Jane Belo, pp. 111–36. New York: Columbia University Press.

Bateson, Gregory, and Margaret Mead. 1942. *Balinese Character: A Photographic Analysis*. New York: Special Publications of the New York Academy of Sciences, vol. 2.

Baum, Vicki. 1938. *A Tale of Bali*. New York: The Literary Guild of America, Inc.

Becker, Alton L. 1979. "Text-Building, Epistemology and Aesthetics in Javanese Shadow Theater." In *The Imagination of Reality: Essays in Southeast Asian Coherence Systems*, edited by A. Yengoyan and A. L. Becker, pp. 211–43. Norwood, N.J.: Ablex Publishing Company.

Becker, Judith. 1979. "Time and Tune in Java." In *The Imagination of Reality: Essays in Southeast Asian Coherence Systems*, edited by A. Yengoyan and A. L. Becker, pp. 197–210. Norwood, N.J.: Ablex Publishing Company.

———. 1980. *Traditional Music in Modern Jawa: Gamelan in a Changing Society.* Honolulu: University of Hawaii Press.

———. 1993. *Gamelan Stories: Tantrism, Islam, and Aesthetics in Central Java.* Arizona State University: Program for Southeast Asian Studies.

Becker, Judith, and Alan H. Feinstein, eds. 1988. *Karawitan: Source Readings in Javanese Gamelan and Vocal Music.* 3 vols. Michigan Papers on South and Southeast Asia. Ann Arbor: The University of Michigan.

Belo, Jane. 1960. *Trance in Bali.* New York: Columbia University Press.

Belo, Jane, ed. 1970. *Traditional Balinese Culture.* New York: Columbia University Press.

Bergeron, Katherine. 1992. "Prologue: Disciplining Music." In *Disciplining Music: Musicology and Its Canons,* edited by Katherine Bergeron and Philip Bohlman, pp. 1–9. Chicago: University of Chicago Press.

Beyer, Stephan. 1978. *The Cult of Tara: Magic and Ritual in Tibet.* Berkeley and Los Angeles: University of California Press.

Boon, James. 1977. *The Anthropological Romance of Bali.* Cambridge: Cambridge University Press.

———. 1982. *Other Tribes, Other Scribes.* Cambridge and New York: Cambridge University Press.

———. 1990. *Affinities and Extremes.* Chicago and London: University of Chicago Press.

Brandon, James. 1970. *On Thrones of Gold: Three Javanese Shadow Plays.* Cambridge: Harvard University Press.

Brecht, Bertolt. 1964. *Brecht on Theatre.* Translated by John Willett. New York: Hill and Wang.

Cage, John. 1973. *Silence.* Middletown: Wesleyan University Press.

———. 1990. *I–VI.* Cambridge: Harvard University Press.

Clifford, James. 1988. *The Predicament of Culture.* Cambridge: Harvard University Press.

Coomaraswamy, Ananda K. 1965. *History of Indian and Indonesian Art.* New York: Dover.

Covarrubias, Miguel. 1956. *Island of Bali.* New York: A. A. Knopf, 1937.

Csordas, Thomas J., ed. 1994. *Embodiment and Experience.* Cambridge Studies in Medical Anthropology 2. Cambridge: Cambridge University Press.

Daniel, Ana. 1981. *Bali: Behind the Mask.* New York: Alfred A. Knopf.

Dea, Alexander. 1979. "*Bawa*: A Javanese Solo Vocal Music." Ph.D. dissertation, Wesleyan University.

Denyer, Frank. 1977. "Melodies." Ph.D. dissertation, Wesleyan University.

Dibia, I Wayan. 1992. "*Arja*: A Sung Dance-Drama of Bali: A Study of Change and Transformation." Ph.D. dissertation, UCLA.

Eiseman, Fred B. 1989. *Bali: Sekala and Niskala.* Berkeley and Singapore: Periplus Editions.

Eliade, Mircea. 1972. *The Forge and the Crucible.* New York: Harper Torchbooks.

Ellingson, Ter. 1974. "Musical Flight in Tibet." *Asian Music* 5/2, 3–44.

———. 1979. " '*Don Rta Dbyangs Gsum*: Tibetan Chant and Melodic Categories." *Asian Music* 10/2, 112–56.

Emigh, John. 1979. "Playing with the Past: Ancestral Visitation in the Masked Theater of Bali." *The Drama Review* 23/2 [T82], 11–36.

———. 1984. "Dealing with the Demonic: Strategies for Containment in Hindu Iconography and Performance." *Asian Theater Journal* 1/1, 21–39.

Fabian, Johannes. 1983. *Time and the Other: How Anthropology Makes Its Object.* New York: Columbia University Press.

Feld, Steven. 1982. *Sound and Sentiment.* Philadelphia: University of Pennsylvania Press. Second edition, 1990.

———. 1994. "Aesthetics as Iconicity of Style (uptown title); or, (downtown title) 'Lift-up-over Sounding': Getting into the Kaluli Groove." In *Music Grooves*, by Charles Keil and Steven Feld, pp. 109–50. Chicago: University of Chicago.

Foucault, Michel. 1995. *Discipline and Punish: The Birth of the Prison*. Translated from the French by Alan Sheridan. New York: Vintage Books.

Geertz, Clifford. 1959. "Form and Variation in Balinese Village Structure." *American Anthropologist* 61/6, 991–1012.

———. 1963. *Agricultural Involution*. Berkeley: University of California Press.

———. 1964. "Tihingan, A Balinese Village." Bijdragen tot de Taal-, Land- en Volkenkunde 120, 1–33.

———. 1973. "'Internal Conversion' in Contemporary Bali," "Person Time and Conduct in Bali" and "Deep Play: Notes on the Balinese Cockfight." In *The Interpretation of Cultures*. New York: Basic Books.

———. 1980. *Negara, The Theatre State in Nineteenth-Century Bali*. Princeton: Princeton University Press.

———. 1983. *Local Knowledge*. New York: Basic Books.

Geertz, Hildred. 1991. "A Theatre of Cruelty: The Contexts of a Topéng Performance." In *State and Society in Bali*, edited by Hildred Geertz, pp. 165–98. Leiden: KITLV Press.

Geertz, Hildred, and Clifford Geertz. 1975. *Kinship in Bali*. Chicago: University of Chicago Press.

Gennep, Arnold L. van. 1960. *The Rites of Passage*. Chicago: University of Chicago Press.

Hanks, Lucien M. 1972. *Rice and Man: Agricultural Ecology in Southeast Asia*. Chicago: Aldine. New edition. Honolulu: University of Hawaii Press, 1992.

Hatch, Martin. 1969. "Vocal Pictures: Transcribed Songs of Central Java." M.A. thesis, Wesleyan University.

———. 1980. "Lagu, Laras, Layang: Rethinking Melody in Javanese Music." Ph.D. dissertation.

Helmholtz, Hermann. 1954. *On the Sensations of Tone*. New York: Dover Publications. Republication of the (second) 1885 edition.

Herbst, Edward. 1981. "Intrinsic Aesthetics in Balinese Artistic and Spiritual Practice." In *Asian Music* 13/1, 43–52.

———. 1986. "What, Where and How is Gambelan in Bali?" In *First International Gamelan Festival and Symposium*, edited by But Muchtar and I Madé Bandem, pp. 35–42. Vancouver, Canada: Expo '86.

———. 1997. "Baris, " "Gamelan," "Indonesia: An Overview," "Balinese Dance Traditions," "Balinese Ceremonial Dance," "Balinese Dance Theater," "Balinese Mask Dance Theater," "Kakul, I Nyoman," "Kebiar," "Légong," "Mario, I Ketut," "Sardono," "Wayang." In *International Encyclopedia of Dance*, edited by Selma Jeanne Cohen. New York: Oxford University Press and Dance Perspectives Foundation.

Hobart, Angela. 1987. *Dancing Shadows of Bali*. London and New York: KPI.

Hobart, Mark. 1978. "The Path of the Soul: The Legitimacy of Nature in Balinese Conceptions of Space." In *Natural Systems in South East Asia*, edited by G. B. Milner, pp. 5–28. London: School of Oriental and African Studies.

Holt, Claire. 1967. *Art in Indonesia, Continuities and Change*. Ithaca: Cornell University Press.

Hood, Mantle. 1954. *The Nuclear Theme as a Determinant of Patet in Javanese Music*. Groningen, Jakarta: J. B. Wolters.

———. 1966. "Sléndro and Pélog Redefined." In *Selected Reports*, pp. 28–48. Los Angeles: Institute of Ethnomusicology of UCLA.

———. 1971. *The Ethnomusicologist*. New York: McGraw-Hill.

Hooykaas, C. 1964. *Agama Tirtha: Five Studies in Hindu-Balinese Religion*. Verhandelingen der Koninklijke Nederlandse Akademie van Wetenschappen, Aft. Letterkunde. Nieuwe Reeks 70 (4).

——. 1973. *Kama and Kala*. Verhandelingen der Koninklijke Nederlandse Akademie van Wetenschappen, Aft. Letterkunde. Nieuwe Reeks 79.

Illich, Ivan. 1974. *Energy and Equity*. London: Calder and Boyars Ltd.

Kakul, I Nyoman. 1979. "Jelantik Goes to Blambangan." *The Drama Review* 23/2 (T82), 11–36.

Kartomi, Margaret J. 1973. *Macapat Song in Central and West Java*. Oriental Monograph Series No. 13. Canberra: Australian National University Press.

Keeler, Ward. 1987. *Javanese Shadow Plays, Javanese Selves*. Princeton: Princeton University Press.

Keil, Charles. 1979. *Tiv Song: The Sociology of Art in a Classless Society*. Chicago: University of Chicago Press.

——. 1994. "Participatory Discrepancies and the Power of Music." In *Music Grooves*, by Charles Keil and Steven Feld, pp. 96–108. Chicago: University of Chicago Press.

Khan, Hazrat Inayat. 1976. *The Sufi Message of Hasrat Inayat Khan, Vol. 2: The Mysticism of Sound*. Reprint of 1962 edition. The Netherlands: Barrie and Rockliff.

Kleist, Heinrich von. 1966. "On the Marionette Theater." Written 1804, translated by A. S. Wensinger in *Reflection: The Wesleyan Quarterly*, 1/1, 30–33.

Kunst, Jaap. 1968. *Hindu-Javanese Musical Instruments*. The Hague: Nijhoff.

——. 1973. *Music in Java*. 2 vols. 3d enlarged edition. Edited by E. L. Heins. The Hague: Nijhoff. (Revised English edition of *De Toonkunst van Java*, 2 vols., The Hague: Nijhoff, 1949.)

Kusumo, Sardono W. 1978. "Studi Lingkungan." In *Sewindu LPKJ*. Jakarta: LPKJ.

Lansing, J. Stephen. 1983. *The Three Worlds of Bali*. New York: Praeger.

——. 1991. *Priests and Programmers: Technologies of Power in the Engineered Landscape of Bali*. Princeton: Princeton University Press.

Leach, E. R. 1972. "The Structure of Symbolism." In *The Interpretation of Ritual*, edited by J. S. LaFontaine, pp. 239–75. London: Tavistock Publications.

Lendra, I Wayan. 1991. "Bali and Grotowski: Some Parallels in the Training Process." *The Drama Review* 35 (T129); 113–28. Cambridge: The MIT Press.

Lévi-Strauss, Claude. 1967. *Structural Anthropology*. Garden City: Anchor Books, Doubleday.

——. 1969. *The Raw and the Cooked*. New York: Harper and Row.

Lorien, Gail Skinner. 1984. "The Transformation of Energy and Consciousness Through Dance." M. A. thesis, University of California, Los Angeles.

Lysloff, René T. A. 1993. "A Wrinkle in Time: The Shadow Puppet Theatre of Banyumas (West Central Java)." *Asian Theatre Journal* 10/1, 49–80.

McAllester, David. 1954. *Enemy Way Music*. Papers of the Peabody Museum, Harvard University, vol. 41, no. 3.

McClary, Susan. 1995. "Music, the Pythagoreans and the Body." In *Choreographing History*, edited by Susan Leigh Foster, pp. 82–104. Bloomington and Indianapolis: Indiana University Press.

McKean, Philip F. 1979. "From Purity to Pollution? The Balinese Ketchak (Monkey Dance) as Symbolic Form in Transition." In *The Imagination of Reality: Essays in Southeast Asian Coherence Systems*, edited by A. Yengoyan and A. L. Becker. Norwood, N.J.: Ablex Publishing Company.

McPhee, Colin. 1936. "The 'Absolute' Music of Bali." In *Modern Music* 12, 163–69.

——. 1946. *A House in Bali*. New York: The John Day Co.

——. 1948. *A Club of Small Men*. New York: The John Day Co.

——. 1955. "Children and Music in Bali." In *Childhood in Contemporary Cultures*, edited by Margaret Mead and Martha Wolfenstein. Chicago: University of Chicago Press.

———. 1966. *Music in Bali*. New Haven and London: Yale University Press.

———. 1970."The Balinese Wayang Kulit and Its Music." In *Traditional Balinese Culture*, edited by Jane Belo, pp. 146–211. New York: Columbia University Press.

Marcus, George, E., and Michael M. J. Fischer. 1986. *Anthropology as Cultural Critique*. Chicago: University of Chicago Press.

Mead, Margaret. 1970. "The Arts in Bali." In *Traditional Balinese Culture*, edited by Jane Belo, pp. 331–40. New York: Columbia University Press.

Murchie, Guy. 1967. *Music of the Spheres: The Material Universe—From Atom to Quasar, Simply Explained*. Vol. 2. New York: Dover.

Murgiyanto, Sal. 1990. *Four Indonesian Choreographers: Dance in a Changing Perspective*. Ph.D. dissertation, New York University.

Napier, A. David. 1986. *Masks, Transformation, and Paradox*. Berkeley: University of California Press.

Nettl, Bruno, and Philip V. Bohlman. 1991. *Comparative Musicology and Anthropology of Music: Essays in the History of Ethnomusicology*. Chicago: University of Chicago Press.

Ornstein, Ruby. 1971. "*Gamelan Gong Kebyar*: The Development of a Balinese Musical Tradition." Ph.D. dissertation, UCLA.

Panitia Penyusun Kamus Bali-Indonesia. 1979. *Kamus Bali-Indonesia*. Denpasar: Dinas Pengarajan Propinsi Daerah Tingkat I Bali.

Peacock, J. L. 1968. *Rites of Modernization: Symbolic and Social Aspects of Indonesian Proletarian Drama*. Chicago: University of Chicago Press.

Pucci, Idanna. 1992. *Bhima Swarga: The Balinese Journey of the Soul*. Boston, Toronto, and London: Little, Brown and Company.

Ramseyer, Urs. 1977. *The Art and Culture of Bali*. Oxford: Oxford University Press.

Rassers, W. H. 1959. *Panji, the Culture Hero: A Structural Study of Religion in Java*. The Hague: Nijhoff.

Rembang, I Nyoman. 1975. "Gambelan Gambuh dan Gambelan Lainya di Bali." In *Panitithalaning Pagambuhan*, edited by I Madé Bandem. Denpasar: Listibiya Daerah Bali.

Robson, S. O. 1971. *Wangbang Wideya, A Javanese Panji Romance*. The Hague: Nijhoff.

———. 1972. "The Kawi Classics in Bali." Bijdragen tot de Taal-, Land-en Volkenkunde 128.

Roseman, Marina. 1991. *Healing Sounds from the Malaysian Rainforest*. Berkeley: University of California Press.

Said, Edward. 1978. *Orientalism*. New York: Pantheon Books.

Sakurai, Chuichi, et al. 1968. *Kadensho*. Kyoto: Sumiya-Shinobe Publishing Institute.

Schafer, R. Murray. 1977. *The Tuning of the World*. New York: Alfred A. Knopf. Republished as *The Soundscape: Our Sonic Environment and the Tuning of the World*. Rochester, Vermont: Destiny Books, 1994.

Schechner, Richard. 1985. *Between Theater and Anthropology*. Philadelphia: University of Pennsylvania Press.

Schumann, Peter. 1970. "Bread and Puppets." *The Drama Review* 14/3 (T47), 35.

Seeger, Anthony. 1987. *Why Suya Sing: A Musical Anthropology of an Amazonian People*. Cambridge: Cambridge University Press.

Shadeg, N. 1977. *A Basic Balinese Vocabulary*. Denpasar: Dharma Bakti.

Snyder, Gary. 1957. *Earth House Hold*. New York: New Directions Books.

———. 1980. *The Real Work*. New York: New Directions Books.

Sontag, Susan. 1961. *Against Interpretation*. New York: Dell.

Sugriwa, I Gusti Bagus. 1963. *Ilmu Pedalangan/Pewayangan*. Denpasar: KOKAR-Bali, Denpasar.

———. 1978. *Penuntun Pelajaran Kakawin*. Denpasar: Proyek Sasana Budaya Bali.

Sumandhi, I Nyoman. 1978. "Gending Iringan Wayang Kulit Bali." In *Pakem Wayang Kulit Bali*, pp. 3–10. Denpasar: Yayasan Pewayangan daerah Bali.

Sumarsam. 1976. "Inner Melody in Javanese Gamelan Music." *Asian Music* 7/1.

———. 1995. *Gamelan: Cultural Interaction and Musical Development in Central Java*. Chicago: University of Chicago Press.

Tedlock, Barbara. 1982. *Time and the Highland Maya*. Albuquerque: University of New Mexico Press.

Tenzer, Michael. 1992. *Balinese Music*. Singapore: Periplus Editions.

Trungpa, Chogyam. 1973. *Cutting Through Spritual Materialism*. Berkeley: Shambhala.

Turner, Victor. 1969. *The Ritual Process*. Ithaca: Cornell University Press.

Vickers, Adrian. 1987. "Hinduism and Islam in Indonesia: Bali and the Pasisir World." *Indonesia* 44, 31–58.

———. 1989. *Bali: A Paradise Created*. Singapore: Periplus Editions.

Vickers, Adrian, ed. 1996. *Being Modern in Bali*. Monograph 43/Yale Southeast Asia Studies.

Wallis, Richard. 1980. "The Voice as a Mode of Cultural Expression in Bali." Ph.D. dissertation, University of Michigan.

Walton, Susan Pratt. 1978. *Mode in Javanese Music*. Athens, Ohio: Ohio University Center for International Studies.

Wasisto Suryodiningrat, et al. 1968. "Tone Measurement of Outstanding Javanese Gamelans in Jogjakarta and Surakarta." *Padalangan Ringgit Purwa* seminar, Universitas Gaja Mada.

Wikan, Unni. 1990. *Managing Turbulent Hearts: A Balinese Formula for Living*. Chicago and London: University of Chicago Press.

Wilson, Peter J. 1974. *Oscar: An Inquiry into the Nature of Sanity*. New York: Random House.

Wolters, O. W. 1970. *The Fall of Sriwijaya in Malay History*. Ithaca: Cornell University Press.

Yayasan Pewayangan daerah Bali. 1978. *Pakem Wayang Kulit Bali*. Denpasar.

Young, Elizabeth Florence. 1980. "Topeng in Bali: Change and Continuity in a Traditional Drama Genre." Ph.D. dissertation, University of California, San Diego.

Zemp, Hugo. 1978. "'Are 'Are Classification of Musical Types and Instruments." *Ethnomusicology* 22, 37–68.

———. 1979. "Aspects of 'Are 'Are Musical Theory." *Ethnomusicology* 23, 5–48.

Zoete, Beryl de, and Walter Spies. 1938. *Dance and Drama in Bali*. London: Faber and Faber, Ltd. New edition, Kuala Lumpur: Oxford University Press, 1973.

Zoetmulder, P. J. 1974. *Kalangwan: A Survey of Old Javanese Literature*. The Hague: Nijhoff.

———. 1982. *Old Javanese-English Dictionary*. The Hague: Nijhoff.

Zurbuchen, Mary S. 1987. *The Language of Balinese Shadow Theater*. Princeton: Princeton University Press.

———. 1989. "Internal Translation in Balinese Poetry." In *Writing on the Tongue*, edited by A. L. Becker, pp. 215–79. University of Michigan: Center for South and Southeast Asia.

Index

✿

acoustics: at ceremonial events, 136; in the environment, 7, 15; and spatial characteristics of amplified sound, 137; and vocal technique, 30–31

Adri, tembang: lyrics, 172; shaping the sound, 29–31; thematic use, 41; tuning, 34, 45

aesthetics: Balinese and Japanese, 159–61; and place, time, and context, 121–33

Agama Tirtha 'religion of holy water', 6

ambiguity: within *angklung* tuning, 45–46; between dancer and *gambelan*, 10; playful, between *sléndro* and *pélog* tunings, 37, 42; in *Sinom Cecantungan*, 48; vague melodic movement, 31; vague shaping of vowels, 29

amerta 'water of eternal life', 19, 108, 109

amplification: and characterization, 61; and new contextual meanings, 135–36; *kawi suara*, 136

angklung: five-tone *gambelan* of Sawan, 173; with high *ndéng*, 34; and playful ambiguity, 45–46; tuning, 37

angsel: and interdependency, 112; in *panasar*'s dance, 80; as signal from dancer to *arja* musicians, 101

Anoman, 107, 135

arja: and Basur, 38; *Bon Bali* professional ensemble, 98n, 114; historical development, 90, 91n; modern context, 114; *panasar*s and voice stylization, 63; performative elements, 101; and shaping sound, 30; singing style, 51; *tembang* lyrics, 172–75

Arjuna, 62; Wiwaha, 157

Art Centre, 114

Artaud, Antonin, 113

bali-balihan 'entertainment genres', 129–31

Balinese Arts Council (Listibiya): commissioning new works, 62; legislating, 127–29

Bandem, Madé, 33, 34, 37, 107, 131

bantén 'offerings'; and efficacy, 124; as microcosmic entity, 133; preceding performance, 131; and *wali*, 128

bapang 'ostinato', 26n; 80

baris gedé, 129

barong: and *Calonarang*, 66; and ceremonial time, 103; *landung*, 3, 83; origin and mystical significance, 107–110

Basur, 38

Bates, Marston, 116

Batuan, village of: and and classical *gambuh*, 101; and ceremonial *rejang*, 124; and modern *godogan*, 151; Pak Kakul, 17n

Bawa, Anak Agung, 13

bayu sabda idep: and aesthetics, 121–33; *bayun kalangan* 'energy of the performance space', 124; "three ways of knowing," 122

beats, acoustical: and amplification, 138; and *gambelan* tuning, 36n, 41

beauty: and efficacy, 121; and ceremonial dance, 125; subjective and objective experience, 122

bebali: performance genres and sacred/secular categorization, 128–31

Bebes, Déwa Putu, 151

Becker, Alton, 88

Becker, Judith, 109n, 121, 142n
Bedaulu, village of, 6
Bertong, Wayan, 99, 101
Beyer, Stephan, 142n
Bharata natyam, South Indian dance, 146
Blahbatu, village of, 13–14
bondrés, comic antics and plot deviations, 72n; and *désa kala patra*, 89; joke, 83
Boon, James, 115
Brahma, betara 'deity', 70
Bread and Puppet Theatre, 95
breath: and expressing emotion, 54; and learning, 10; and shaping the sound, 27
buana agung, buana alit: and demons, 125n; as ways, 8; and world music, xvii; and worship, 132–33. *See also* macrocosmos-microcosmos
Buddhism: in Balinese thought, 125, 131; and Ch'an story, 24; and Sardono's choreography, 23n. *See also* Tantric Buddhism
buta 'demons' or 'elements', 125n; and offerings for troublesome spirits, 131; and place, 2

Cage, John: and ceremony, 139; on structure, method, and material, 147–50
cak, 130, 151
Calonarang: creative and historical origins, 66n; and pick-up ensemble, 98; and temple festivals, 103; tourist and sacred perspectives, 129
Candri, Ni Nyoman, 8–10, 24, 28, 30, 32, 42, 45, 47, 50, 51, 53, 54, 55, 67, 77, 95, 98, 101, 102; *tembang* and lyrics, 172–75
carangan 'branching out': in *arja* performance, 55; with numbers, 91; as subplots in narrative, 98
Catra, Nyoman, 89n
Cebaang, Anak Agung Rai, 36, 68–69
cecantungan 'branching out': as poetic quotations, 63 ; and translation, 73
characterization: and proscenium staging, 138; as unified aesthetic, 9, 64–65. *See also masolah*
children: and artistic growth, 16; as audience, 115; and collective learning, 155–56; in community, 14–15; and learning in context, 11
choreography: fixed and spontaneous, 112; in form versus practice, 101; and mask characterization, 65; and proscenium staging, 138; resources, 101n. *See also* dance

colotomic structure, 79, 85
condong, maidservant: lyrics, 173; singing *Pangkur*, 44; and voice placement, 28
Coomaraswamy, Ananda K., 142n
Cupak: as entertainment, 129; by Pak Gerindem, 70; in spiritual light, 130–31

dalang 'shadow puppet master': characterization, 57–62; and esoteric teachings, 20; as Kama, 'god of love', 109; as medium, 135; and microphones, 134–37; and vocal qualities, 25–26; waking puppets, 87. *See also wayang*
Dalem: and *panasar's tembang*, 40; dance characterization, 65; *tandak*, 175–77; vocals and dance, 83–86
Dalem Bedaulu 'He Who Changed Heads', 7
dance: *agem, tandang, tangkis* and place, time, and context, 98; *arja* and *topéng* with music, 77, 79; cadence phrasing for *panasar*, 80; of *Dalem*, 85–86; Javanese learning process, 154–55; and *masolah*, 9, 65–66; *ngigel*, 69
Délem: and characterization, 57–60; and *dedéleman* masks, 71–73
désa kala patra: and characterization, 88; and dance, 98; and lyrics, 90–91; and masks, 63; orientation, 1–4; and themes, 89; and variation, 118; as what, where, and how, 149–50
Déwa Putu Dani, 105–106
déwa 'deities': and ceremony 8; and masks, 63; and shadow puppetry, 59
déwasa: and interpretation, 23; and kinds of time, 103–106; in scheduling sessions, 19
dharma: and human activity, 133; *Prawretti* text, 17; and Tantric thread, 29n
Dharma Pawayangan: and secret teachings, 20n; and stimulating audience, 109; on vocal characterization, 60
Dibia, Wayan, 37, 90, 91, 99, 114, 124
Diya, Wayan, 8, 22–23, 103, 157n
drum: and acoustics, 139; interlocking rhythms, 112; syllables, 78–79
Durma, tembang: and dance, 68; and developing a melody, 50; form and melodics, 39–40; *manis* 'sweet' lyrics, 171; *manis* and *marah* 'angry' melodics, 51–52; *manis*, and tuning, 34, 45; and *panasar's* vocal style, 27, 31, 34, 43, 50, 80; and Punta's dance characterization, 64; Punta's lyrics, 76, 91; Punta's song, 172; Punta's song with *gambelan*, 174–75; and transcendence, 17

ecology: and amplification, 134, 136; dynamics, 116; relating to culture, 115
Eiseman, Fred B., 133n
Ellingson, Ter, 109, 149
Ellis, A. J., 33
Emigh, John, 107n
ethnographic present, xix
Euro-American: aesthetics, 121; ideals, 112; performance, 87
experience: of audience, 23; and community, 15; and data, 22; of entering the music, 155; and inner-outer flow, 162; and knowledge, 116; and learning, 16, 19, 21; and performance skills, 115; and theory, xx; and vibrations, 7

female styles, 30, 63
form: and basics, 21; and classifications, xx; and dance, 79; and esoteric teachings, 20; and invisible energies, 66; and macro-micro-cosmos, 133; and morphology, 148; *pokok* and melodic development, 50; sacred/secular, 130; as space-time patterns in learning, 154; and spatial perception, 153–54; structural, in learning, 152–56; as structure and temporal dynamics, 102; and technique, 11; as vibrations, 142–44; as "where," 156

Gableran, Pandé Madé, 92
gaguntangan ensemble, 37, 48, 172; recordings, 172, 174
Gaja Mada: *patih* of Majapahit kingdom, 7; University, 117
galuh 'princess': and *Adri* lyrics, 172; and intonation, 45; and melodic phrasing, 53; and *tembang* themes, 41; and vocal quality, 29–31; and voice placement, 28
Galungan: and *Kala tiga*, 107; and performance genres, 103
gambelan: and amplification, 137–38; *bebarongan*, 172; and collective ownership, 155; definition, 151–56; *gong*, 36; *gong*, accompanying vocalists, 48; *gong kebiar*, 36; *gong*, recording, 177; *luang*, 28, 37; qualities, 18; sacred, 129; and singer-dancer, 10, 102; spatial relationship with *dalang*, 61; spelling, xxiii; tunings, 33–34, 41
gambelan mulut 'mouth gambelan': recordings, 172, 175; and teaching dance, 77–79
gambuh: and ceremony, 103; competing for attention, 135; and *lebeng* tuning, 28; and

Malat literature, 91; in Singapadu and Batuan, 101; and tunings, 36, 37, 41
gedong céngkok: as comic style, 54, 73; and vocal technique, 28, 30
Geertz, Clifford, 83n, 106n, 113n, 115, 123, 126n, 128
Geertz, Hildred, 93n
geguritan: development of, 90; and didactic content, 16; and form, 38, 39; in performance, 55
gendér wayang: and learning, 153; and tunings, 33, 34, 37, 45–46; varieties, 115
Gennep, Arnold van, 146, 150
Gerana, Pak, 32
Geria, Wayan, 13
Gerindem, Madé, 63, 70, 119–20, 154
gesture: as form, and leaning point, 157–59; in hermeneutic context, 142; language, 54; in learning to sing, 10
Ginada, tembang: Éman Éman, 47; and form, 39; and mood, 41; *lumbrah*, 46–47; recording, 173; and variations, 54
Ginanti, tembang, 41, 82
godogan dance drama, 151
government: and culture policy, 130, 134
Granyam, Pak, *dalang*, 25
guntang 'bamboo zither', 78
Gunung Agung mountain, 2, 6, 131, 133

hearing: compared with listening, 15; loss of, 139
Heisenberg's Principle, 148
Hendrix, Jimi, 139
Hindu-Balinese culture, 131
Holt, Claire, 105, 107n, 142n, 151
Hood, Mantle, 33
Hooykaas, C., 20n, 60, 109
humor, 3, 14, 29, 57, 97

ilegan: 'melodic flow', 28; *gending* 'melodic contours', 77; *ilegan nyutra*, 30, 54; *ucapan* 'melodic speech', 84; *kembangan* 'flowering' ilegan, 54
Illich, Ivan, 141
imagination, 157–58; of audience, 23, 146
improvisation, 77, 98; and choreography, 73; and extemporaneous composing, 55–56
India, 142n
Indra, *betara* 'deity', 6
interpretation: of time, *wariga*, 103; by *panasars*, 74; in performance, 82
intervals, xxvi, 33, 46; intervallic relationships, 44, 45

intonation, 42; and *laras*, 32; and *suara ngilik*, 30

jangér dance drama, 130
Japanese *Nō* theater, 146, 158, 159
jauk dance, 67, 87, 108, 172
Javanese: discourse, 23n; music, 28; physicists and acousticians, 117; *wayang kulit*, 59, 88, 97, 110n
Jelaika village, *gambelan gong*, 177
jiwa, of mask, 63; *menjiwai* 'transmitting spirit', 61, 63
juru tandak, 62, 86

kaja-kelod 'north-south axis', 2, 132
kakawin: and poetry, 32; as source of lyrics, 55. See also Kawi
Kakul, Nyoman, 8n, 17, 66, 70, 74, 93, 94, 120, 126; *sendon* and lyrics, 177
kala, 2, 103–110; as Balinese and Tibetan Buddhist deity, 109; as era, 105; in lyrics, 91; kinds of time, 103; and transcendence, 97. See also *désa kala patra*
kalangan 'performance area', 131–32
kalangén 'rapture', 88, 150
Kantor, Ketut, 151
kartala, 13n; and humorous singing, 29, 82; and parody of refined prince, 73. See also *panasar*
Kawi, 26n; and *dalang*'s voice amplified, 136; interpretation, 74; and *kakawin* poetry, 38; language, and poet, 58; and manifestation of *kawi suara*, 109; peculiar and funny, 73; prose, 61, 84; paraphrasing, 55
Kenyir, Pandé Madé, 30, 66, 172
keras: strong, forceful character, 66, 67; coarse, 72; mask style, 71; 'strong' voice, 26
kidung poetry, 8, 32, 38, 82, 85
kinesthetics: and characterization, 57; and memory, in learning *gambelan*, 154; realities, 134; and transmission, 22
kinetics: and amplification, 137; in Tantric Buddhist ritual, 24
kirta basa 'etymology', 5, 13, 63, 92, 109
Kirttimukha, 107
knowledge: from experience, 21; and garlic, 5; levels, 19; pedagogy, 22; and sharing, 16–17
Kodi, Ketut, 74
kotékan 'interlocking melodic ornamentation': and learning, 153–54; social and spatial dynamics, 112

Kredek, Madé, 10, 13, 34, 45, 73, 81–82, 172
Kunst, Jaap, 33

lagu 'melody', 50
langö, and aesthetic experience, 122
langsé 'curtain': and *mungkah lawang* 'opening the curtain', 13, 65; and orientation entering and exiting, 87–88
language: and aesthetics, 122; intermediating realms, 88–89; and metaphysics, 29
Lansing, J. Stephen, 122, 125n
laras 'tone series', 36, 41; *pélog selisir gong*, 33, 34
laugh: in everyday life, 14; in learning, 12; of Merdah, 61; of Punta, 64, 81
Leach, Edmund, 145–46, 150
learning process, xviii, xxvii, 16–18; aural, 152; and ceremony, 124; in context, 9; in ensemble, 112; forcing the voice, 20, 21, 22, 27, 63–64; in getting to know *tembang*, 11; with *macapat*, 51; through recordings, 140–41; and teaching, 12; and vocal training, 24
Lebah, Madé, 37
lebeng 'well-cooked': in aesthetic taste, 27, 65; in intonation, 32, 34, 42, 45
légong: and *Calonarang*, 117; and formal structure, 102; *tandak* for, 85
Lévi-Strauss, Claude, 147
limbur 'queen mother': language, 63; and male performers, 13; phrasing, 53; and pronunciation, 28; song choice, 40
listening, 3, 7
Los Angeles Times, 151
Lucier, Alvin, 36n
Lysloff, René, T. A., 110n

mabasan 'poetry readings', 52
macapat: and poetic form, 39, 40; phrasing, 51, 52; poetic meter, 10. See also *tembang*
macrocosmos-microcosmos: as inside and outside experience of time, 103; and penetration, 158; between performer and audience, 89; in relation to puppets, masks, 25, 57, 158; and social science, 147. See also *buana agung*
maha buta, panca 'five great elements', 132–33; in performance, 23n. See also *buta*
Mahabharata, 58, 89, 108n
Malat literature, and *gambuh*, 91
Mandera, Anak Agung Gedé, 13
manifestation, 20, 67; of Kala, 107
mantra: amplified, 137; and cosmic manifes-

tation, 133; as esoteric teachings, 20; and Pak Kakul, 126; for *topéng* masks, 87; and voice preparation, 25

mantri buduh 'crazy prince', 28; phrasing, 54

mantri manis 'refined prince' 28n; and composing, 55; improvised dialogue in song, 56; interacting with comic Wijil, 73; lyrics, 171, 173, 174; in nature and tonality, 50; and phrasing, 52–53; and signals to musicians, 102; and themes, 40–41

mask: and characterization, 57, 68, 69; and etymology, 62–63; half-mask, 71; *keras* strong style, 71; making, 70; mediation, and puppets, 136; and puppet stylization, 157–59; use of, 92; and sacredness, 3, 129–30

masolah, 57–70; contrasted with social context, 93; as multidisciplinary approach, 9; and tunings, 36

Maya Danawa, demon-king, 6

McLuhan, Marshall, 135

McPhee, Colin, 21, 33, 37, 45n

Mecaling, Jero Gedé, 124

media institutions, 117

meditation: in caves, 2, 6; and dimension, 133; disciplines, 158; and esoteric practices, 20; and fears, 24, and *rejang* dance, 125; and state, 155

Merdah, and Sangut, 57–61

Mijil, tembang, 42

Moerdowo, Dr., 24

mouth, and voice, 29–30

Murgiyanto, Sal, 23n

Naba, Pak, 32, 36

narrative: with *bondrés* comics, 72; construction, 97. *See also* plot construction

Nartha, Wayan, 25, 62, 66

naturalistic art forms, 157

nature, 16, 19, 123, 132–33, 161

Ndembu, terminology, 146

ngigel, 9. *See also* dance

ngilik 'water passing through a small hole', 32

ngisep 'sucker', 36. *See also* beats, acoustical

ngumbang 'hummer', 36. *See also* beats, acoustical

noise, 16

notation: for *Voices in Bali*, xxv–xxvii; and aural learning, 152, 155

nyutra suara, 28–30

objectification: and ethnographic studies,

xix, xx ; and learning by tape, 21, 22; and media, 134; in teaching performance, 9

odalan 'temple festival': and amplified *kakawin*, 134–35; and *barong landung*, 3; and feedback, 139; and "traveling around the world," 8

ombak 'soundwaves'. *See* beats, acoustical

Orang Tua 'Old Man' mask, 70, 92

pacapeiring, syllabic reading of songs, 39, 43, 54

padalingsa, rules of *tembang* form, 38–39

palawakya, prose Kawi, 61, 63, 84

paméro pitches, 32, 41, 44, 49, 75

panakawan, 57–60. See also *panasar*, Punta

panasar, 71–86; characterization, 69; and intonation, 34; and multidisciplinary skills, 81; *sendon* style, 74; study, 13; *tandak*, 83–86; and translation, 5; transmitting spirit, 61, 63; and vocal quality, 25; and vowels, 28, 31; word origin, 59

pandangan, focus of eyes and energy, 67–68; and mask, 92

Pangkur: lyrics and recording, 173; song of *condong*, 44–45; standard form, 39

Panitia Penyusun Kamus Bali, 59

Panji, 55. See also *gambuh*

Panyacah Parwa: and amplification, 137; and vocal qualities, 25

papeson 'coming out': and music-dance structure, 80; and *panasar*'s lyrics, 76; and *panasar*'s melodic style, 77; and song composition, 50, 55

Partini, Cokorde Rai, 99

patra: 2; and ceremony, 123; and dramatic characters, 89. See also *désa kala patra*

Pedungan, village of, 101

Péjéng, village of, 6

pélog, and *sléndro*: and notation in *Voices in Bali*, xxv–xxvi; as tuning systems, 33–37, 41, 42, 44

penetration, 13, 24; hearts of audience, 89; and spirit entering a mask, 69

Pengejukan, ritual *topéng* character, 94; enacting ritual, 126

perception: of hearing, 15; with intellect or heart, 23; in learning *gambelan*, 154; and mediation, 134; through stylized forms, 157–58

perkembangan 'flowering', xvii, 97–102; and Japanese aesthetics, 160–61; and learning, 8, 18, 21

physiological process, 25, 30

pleasure: as aspect of art, 19; puppet master's vehicle for subduing Kala 'Time', 109; versus work, 113–14

plot construction, 94, 99, 101. *See also* narrative

pragina 'dancer/actor/singer', 9

prémbon dance drama, 36, 38

proscenium staging: as spatial mediation, 138

psychic: dynamics, 20; experience, 126

Pucung, tembang: didactic content, 16; lyrics and levels of meaning, 5; and melodics in *lebeng* tuning, 34–35, 47–48; and mood, 54; and poetic form, 39; recording of *sléndro* and *pélog*, 171

Pugra, Pak, 8n

Punta, 13n; *Dening kecatri* lyrics, 76; *Durma* recordings, 172, 174–75; intonation, 43, 45, 77; "mouth gambelan" recording, 175; skills, 65; *Tuwuh jatma* lyrics, 91, 174–75; and Wijil characterization, 68, 73. *See also panasar*

puppets: and characterization, 57, 62, 66; and stylization, 157–58. See also *dalang, wayang*

pupuh poetic form, 38–39

Purna, Wayan, *tembang* and lyrics, 174

Radio Républik Indonesia (RRI), 8, 32, 36, 117

Rajeg, Nyoman, 59, 95

Rama, 107

Ramayana, 17, 58, 74, 107, 108

Rangda: and *barong*, 66; and *Basur*, 38; and *légong*, 117; and masks, 13n, 63

Rangkus, Wayan, 67, 82, 91, 99, 101

rasa 'feeling': and fitting song to *gambelan*, 28; and tunings, 36; 'subjective' and 'objective' aspects, 122

Rawa, Pak, 25

Rawana, 58, 107

Reagan, President and Mrs., 151

Regep, Pak, 99

Regug, Madé, 70

rejang dance, 124

Rembang, Nyoman, 32, 34, 36, 37, 77

resonance: and acoustics of social environment, 14–15; in *gambelan* aesthetics, 18; with new environment, 136; and singer's body, 25–32, 59–60, 86; sympathetic, 10

Retug, Wayan, 70, 71, 99

ricefields, 2, 6; as auditory environment, 15; farming and performance schedules,

116n; and sense of place, 119–20; and swaying plants as dance movement, 108

Rinda, Ketut, 5, 13, 34, 65, 69, 71, 73, 75, 91, 107, 108–109; *sendon* and lyrics, 177

Rindi, Wayan, 8n

ritual: and beauty, 122; blessing for costumes and gambelan, 124; and Bread and Puppet Theatre, 96; dramaturgy, 93; event as a moment in time, 143; formulas, 60; frog dance, 151; offerings, 126; phenomena, 159; and water, 6

rivers: and spirituality, 2; for training, 24

Rouget, Gilbert, 154

sacred and secular, 127–31

saih pitu, seven-tone tuning system, 28, 37, 42. See also *gambuh*

sajén ritual offerings, 93

Sakurai, Chuichi, 159

Sang Hyang, trance dance, 128, 130; trance song, 148, 158; *Widi Wasa*, one divinity, 91, 132

sanggah family shrine, 132, 133

Sangut, 59, 60

Saplug, Wayan, 8n

Sardono, 17, 23

Sardru, Wayan, 72

Schafer, R. Murray, 139

schools: 21, 28; SMKI (KOKAR), Indonesian High School for Traditional Performing Arts, 32, 37, 59; STSI (ASTI), Indonesian College of the Arts, 8, 37, 45, 108n, 111n, 114, 118

Schumann, Peter, 95

Seeger, Charles, 152

seka village organizations, 112–13; *super seka*, 118

sekar alit, 38. See also *tembang*

selisir, 77, 92. See also *pélog*

selonding, gambelan, 36n, 130

Semar Pagulingan, gambelan, 18, 37

Semarandana, tembang, 45

sendon: defining the term, 26n, 77; lyrics, 26, 73–74; recording, 172, 177–78; themes, 55, 76; and tunings, 49; and vocal qualities, 26–27

séndratari dance drama: and amplification, 136–38; and *dalang* transmitting spirit, 61, 69; and propitious times, 104

sense of place, 1, 97, 141

serodan 'swirls of melody', 29–30

Sidha Karya, ritual *topéng* character: 93–94, 126

Sija, Madé, 12, 13, 26, 52, 59, 62, 65, 67, 71, 74, 77, 89, 92–95, 132–33

Singapadu, village of, 3, 13, 34, 83, 101; *gambelan gaguntangan* recording, 174; music for *jauk*, 172

singing: in everyday life, 10–12, 14–15; learning kinesthetically, 10

Sinom, tembang, form, 39

Sinom Cecantungan, tembang: composing lyrics, 55; and modal ambiguity, 48, 49; and phrasing, 51; and Punta's vocal intonation, 77

Sinom lumbrah, tembang: and kinesthetic learning, 9; and themes, 40; and tunings, 42

Sinom Wug Payangan, tembang: lyrics, 172; and themes, 41; tunings, 43–44

Skinner, Beth, 17n

sleep, stylization, and imagination, 22–23, 146

sléndro: and *pélog* notation in *Voices in Bali,* xxv–xxvi; as tuning system, 33–34, 37, 39, 43, 45–46

Snyder, Gary, 102

Sontag, Susan, 113n

spatial: characteristics of language, 143; characteristics of melody, 112; criteria for sacredness, 129; effects of amplification, 137

spontaneity: Cage's, 148; and story in *arja* and *topéng,* 81–82; and *tandak,* 86; and vocal intonation, 50. *See also* improvisation

Sriwijaya, kingdom, 141n

standardization: and aesthetics, xix; and media, 134

stillness, within motion, 15, 156–59

structure: and John Cage, 147–50; in mythology, 145; "where," 161

Stutterheim, Willem F., 105

stylization: and aesthetic unity, 113, 143; in *arja* and *topéng,* 68; in character, 65; and distance, 63; in forms, 22; as nexus for penetration and receptivity, 159; and perceptual process, 146–47

Suanda, Endo, 83n

suara ncah 'coarse voice', 25–26

Sugriwa, I Gusti Bagus, 38, 59, 129

Sukawati, village of, 66

suling 'bamboo flute': and intonation, 48; in relation to *gambelan,* 43; and subtle vocals, 37

Sumandhi, Nyoman, 37

Sumarsam, 149, 152

Suryodiningrat, Wasisto, 117

synchronization: facial expression with music, 101; in notating *Voices in Bali,* xxvii; of student and teacher, 10; of voice with dance and *gambelan,* 79

systematization: avoiding artificial, xviii–xix; characterization, 57; contrasted with aesthetic in practice, 42; and pedagogy, 41; of tunings, 34

T'ai-chi, 146, 158

tabuh: in *arja* musical structure, 79; *suara* 'stylized speech', 63

taksu 'spiritual energy': and blessing, 124, 131; and concentration, 20 ; and *dalang*'s prayer, 26; and *masolah,* 57; and puppets, 61

Tampaksiring, village of, 6, 7

tandak: composing for *Dalem,* 83–86; one definition, 77; and intonation, 32, 36–37, 49–50; and literary sources, 82; lyrics, 84–85, 175–77

Tantri dance drama, 66

Tantric Buddhism: and discourse, 142n; and language, 29; and vanquishing Time, 109

tape recording: and ambient sounds, 15; benefits of, 139; and collecting songs, 9; for comparing *gambelans,* 18; and transcription, xxvii; and objectified pedagogy, 21; and musical analysis, 36

taste: and aesthetics, 27–28; transcending, 17

tebek 'piercing focus', 67

technique: and children, 11; and the seed, 160; and training, 112

technology, 102; and power, 135

tekep 'modal configuration', 36, 37, 42, 45, 48, 49, 50, 75, 77

television and radio, 117

tembang: composing, 31; in dialogue, 56; and dramatic context, 8, 9, 40; form in relation to flowering, 55–56; intent, 10; *macapat,* 32, 38–39; and *nembang,* verb form, 50; tunings, 32–37

temples: Besakih, mother temple, 2, 133; and ceremonial dance, 124; and membership, 99n; *pura dalem* 'temple of the dead', 63, 66, 103; and sense of locale, 2

Tempo, Madé Pasek, 7, 16–18, 26, 28, 32, 45, 50, 52, 68, 69, 71, 73, 76, 77, 80, 81, 97, 100, 104, 105; *tembang, tandak* and lyrics, 172, 175–77

Tenganan, village of, 130n

tenget 'magically charged', masks, 38, 63, 129

throat, and voice, 25–26, 28, 60

Tibetan: '*Brong* 'wild yak', 109; chants, 149
Tihingan, village of, 7
Tirtha Mpul, 105
tone, "how," 156
topéng: didactic element, 89; and interpretation, 5; *pajegan*, 92–94, 126; regional styles, 65; theme and context, 90; varieties, 115. *See also* mask
tourism, 117, 108n, 129, 134; and sacred performance, 127
trance, 70, 128, 129, 130; as indigenous feature, 131
Trungpa, Chogyam, 29n
Tublen, Cokorde Oka, 13
tunings, xxv, xxvii. See also *pélog, sléndro, tekep*
Turner, Victor, 110n, 146, 147, 150
Twalén, 19, 57, 59

ucapan 'melodic speech': in *topéng*, 84; "spoken text" of Punta, 174
useran, whirlpool, 31

variety: in arts and culture, 115; in creative process, 160–61; and genetic diversity, 116
vibrations, 142–44; *getaran*, 27, 32, 41
Vickers, Adrian, 90–91

wali, sacred genres, 128–31; *wali-bebali, bali-balihan*, 147
Wallis, Richard, 32, 38, 85, 133n
wanara: army, 58; semidivine animals, 107–110
wariga, calendrical accounting of time, 22–23
water: holy spring, 6; and vocal training, 24, 25. See also *amerta*
waves: in melody, *ngengkuk*, 31; in acoustical space, *ombak*: see beats, acoustical
wayang: and amplification, 137; *arja*, 62; *Cupak*, 131; and esoteric teachings, 20n; *gambuh*, 62; *lemah*, 92, 95; and microphones, 136; and shadow puppets, 25, 61; *Tantri*, 61; and vocal characterization, 25–26, 57–61. See also *dalang*
wayang wong: and ceremony, 103, 108; characters, 57, 71
Wija, Wayan, 62
Windia, Gusti, 34
wirama kakawin, Old Javanese poetry, 32. *See also* Kawi
Wolters, O. W., 142n

Ze-ami, *Kadensho* treatise, 159–61
Zoetmulder, P. J., 74n, 122, 133n, 157n
Zurbuchen, Mary, 29, 97, 122n

UNIVERSITY PRESS OF NEW ENGLAND publishes books under its own imprint and is the publisher for Brandeis University Press, Dartmouth College, Middlebury College Press, University of New Hampshire, Tufts University, and Wesleyan University Press.

ABOUT THE AUTHOR

Edward Herbst teaches at Middlebury College and is a composer, musician, and Assistant Editor of *Ethnomusicology*.

Library of Congress Cataloging-in-Publication Data

Herbst, Edward.

Voices in Bali : energies and perceptions in vocal music and dance theater / Edward Herbst ; foreword by Judith Becker ; afterword by René T. A. Lysloff.

p.   cm.

Includes bibliographical references (p.   ) and index.

ISBN 0–8195–6316–1 (cl: alk. paper). — ISBN 0–8195–6319–6 (pa: alk. paper)

1. Folk music—Indonesia—Bali Island—History and criticism. 2. Dance—Indonesia—Bali Island. 3. Theater—Indonesia—Bali Island. I. Title.

ML3758.I53H47   1997

781.62'9922—dc21   97–19855